MW01006094

A WAY TO PRAY

A WAY TO PRAY

*A Biblical Method for Enriching
Your Prayer Life and Language by
Shaping Your Words with Scripture*

by
Matthew Henry

Edited & Revised by
O. Palmer Robertson

THE BANNER OF TRUTH TRUST

THE BANNER OF TRUTH TRUST
3 Murrayfield Road, Edinburgh EH12 6EL, UK
P O Box 621, Carlisle, PA 17013, USA

© O. Palmer Robertson 2010

First published in 1710 under the title,

A Method for Prayer, with Scripture Expressions
Proper to be Used under Each Head

ISBN-13: 978 1 84871 087 0

Typeset in 12/14 pt Adobe Caslon Pro
at the Banner of Truth Trust,
Edinburgh

Appreciation

*W*ith grateful appreciation to the following students of African Bible University of Uganda who made this work possible by patiently typing out the full original manuscript of Matthew Henry's *A Method for Prayer* so the text could be revised and edited:

Banda Thom Jack
Chiwale Maxwell Tisaiwale
Gondwe Kennedy Mchinanguwo
Hahirwabatuma Kamanzi Innocent
Jamu Joseph Elias
Jere Margaret
Katani Lydia
Manda Steven
Matandika Joseph R. A.
Mtimaunenenji Alinafe
Musinguzi Justus
Mwanza Charles Jabulani
Nkhoma MacDuff Kutha
Odongo Bernard

*A*nd with deepest love and appreciation for my wife Joanna and her constant encouragement, which enabled me to press on through many temptations to 'grow weary in well doing'.

O. Palmer Robertson
African Bible University
Kampala,
Uganda
July 2010

Contents

Introduction

to this 300th Anniversary Edition of
Matthew Henry's A Method for Prayer

*V*irtually everyone in the evangelical community of Christians knows of Matthew Henry's
Commentary on the Bible. These six volumes, packed
with devotional insight, sound theology and prac-
tical wisdom, have blessed the whole world of
Christians over the past 300 years.

It is not generally realized that no less than 14
different individuals contributed to the completion
of Matthew Henry's *Commentary*, beginning with
the Epistles of the New Testament. According to his
own notations, Matthew Henry considered another
work of his to be so important that he interrupted
the writing of his *Commentary* and as a consequence
never completed it. That other work was his laying
out a method for prayer altogether based on the
expressions of Scripture.

Distinctive is Matthew Henry's model for Christians to make exclusive use of the language of Scripture to express their prayers. What could be more obvious as a proper method of praying? What could be more encouraging to Christians desiring to enrich their prayer experience, and to make their prayers more likely to be heard and answered by the Lord? What could be more threatening to the devil than to hear believers in Christ approaching the throne of grace with expressions in prayer that will be honoured by the Lord?

Prayer in this form is nothing more and nothing less than what the old Puritans called 'pleading the promises'. God has made promises to his people. His people respond by redirecting those promises to the Lord in the form of prayer. How could a God who is faithful to his word fail to answer prayers of this kind? He has promised. He will honour that promise. If Christians would join together and form their prayers with the maturity and insight provided by Scripture itself, the impact on the world could not be measured.

Not only would prayer be answered that would give great glory to God. Christians would be transformed as they reshaped their souls daily by praying in the language of Scripture itself. These could be some of the dramatic results if God's people prayed regularly in the richness of the language of Scripture.

Matthew Henry is distinctive in who he was as well as what he has provided in this book on praying according to Scripture. He was an exegete of the highest quality. He was a biblical theologian, naturally connecting the shadows of the old covenant to their fulfilment in the new. He was a systematic theologian, joining scripture with scripture to display the wonders of God's order in creation, redemption and consummation. He was first and foremost a pastor with a heart filled with love for God's people and a passion to minister to their needs and necessities.

This year marks the 300th anniversary of the publication of Matthew Henry's *A Method for Prayer with Scripture Expressions Proper to Be Used under Each Head*. For the past fifty years this book has been my constant companion. My copy was passed down to me by my mother. It had been in use in the family for several previous generations. Almost daily I have been blessed by its use in my times of personally seeking the face of God. Next to the Bible it has been the most read and the most influential book in my life. For many years I have wanted to update the language of the book so it could be accessible to future generations of believers in Christ. I wanted to pass it on to my own children and grandchildren. By now the pages of my old copy have begun to disintegrate. Every time I open it, a few pieces of page flake off. So I am grateful to God that I finally have had the opportunity to offer this revised, edited and updated version of the book. Considering the state of my personal copy, this edition comes 'just in the nick of time'.

This fully revised, edited and updated version has been given a new title: *A Way to Pray*. Of course there are many ways to pray, as Matthew Henry himself acknowledges in his introduction. But in a distinctive sense, praying in the language of Scripture may be regarded as a very special way to pray. The subtitle of this current edition is: *A Biblical Method for Enriching Your Prayer Life and Language by Shaping Your Words with Scripture*. This subtitle underscores the distinctiveness of this book on prayer, and points to the possible benefits of making use of this method in your praying.

A few notes about the substance of the original edition. A British copy preceded the American printing. In that original edition, prayers were offered for 'our Lord the king' that God would give him 'long life and length of days for ever and ever' in the language of Psalm 72, which is quite clearly a messianic psalm describing the rule of our Lord Jesus Christ over all the nations of the world. That section was omitted in the American version. The original printing also offered prayers for the extinguishing of the hopes of 'our popish adversaries' that they not be allowed to seize the throne of England once more.

That section was also omitted from the American printing.

Matthew Henry naturally wrote according to the mode of expression common to his day. All his biblical phrases are taken from the King James translation of the Bible, which continued to be the standard English version for 250 years after he wrote his book on prayer. His sentences extend into paragraph length. Phrase is joined to phrase by the constant use of colon and semi-colon. The wording simply does not match the language of the heart for Christians of the 21st century. In other areas of Christian life and worship, ancient expressions may function with some effectiveness, as found in the wording of the classic creeds of the church. But when it comes to prayer, the soul seeking intimate connection with the living God cries out for a wording that engages the heart. The present revised and edited work has made an attempt to speak the language of prayer in today's mode of expression. While always attempting to stay true to Scripture, the intent has been to communicate biblical truth in prayer language that would suit the soul of God's people today.

An extensive effort has also been made to reorganize the material in a way that would be more 'user-friendly' to the modern reader. Instead of having twenty-one points under a single heading, with almost as many sub-points under various topics, the material has been broken down into smaller units. At some points, new or additional material has been introduced where it seemed useful or appropriate. For instance, Matthew Henry had a special prayer for the baptism of children. But he had no prayer for the baptism of adults. Presumably this omission may be explained in terms of the day in which he lived, a time when the poet John Milton could speak of 'God's England'. The prayer for the baptism of children has been retained, while a prayer for the baptism of adults has been introduced. May the Lord be pleased to continue to add to his church daily those who are being saved, so that the church may be constantly called upon to offer prayers at the baptism of converted adults!

At some points, Matthew Henry knowingly makes application of Scripture in prayer-form that is not true to the original meaning of the text. He attempts to justify this procedure in his introductory notes, but his arguments are based more on traditional use of Scripture than on supporting sound biblical praying. In the current revised edition, a serious effort has been made to see that every prayer rises out of the significance of Scripture in its original context. In the process, the original languages of the Bible have been regularly consulted, along with several modern English versions. Literally hundreds of exegetical decisions have been made in the process. This current edition does not represent simply an effort to modernize the language of Matthew Henry's original. Instead it is an effort to provide a respectful but thorough reworking of the text of Matthew Henry in light of careful exegetical considerations. A major reason for this procedure is based in the conviction that lies behind Matthew Henry's original design. The more closely a prayer is framed according to the wording of the Lord himself, the more certain will be God's answer to that prayer. He has proven himself faithful to his word across the centuries. Not one word he has spoken has ever fallen to the ground. He delights in his own truth as it is 're-presented' to him in the form of the prayers of his people. He will hear and he will answer according to his Word.

Because almost the entirety of this work is Scripture, any recasting of the language requires a large concentration of effort at Bible translation. The reader of this revised edition will find that it falls more in the category of 'dynamic' rather than 'literal' renderings of Scripture. This approach is justified in large part by the fact that the effort is being made to make the reading as natural as possible in the language of today so that the reader will be able to express himself naturally before God in his mother tongue. Prayer is always best framed in the language of the heart. At the same time, a sincere effort has been made to render the biblical text in terms of the root meaning of the Scriptures.

Matthew Henry concluded the introduction of his work with a request that the person benefiting from his material offer a prayer for the author himself. In the same spirit I would request that the reader who might benefit from this current edition offer a prayer for the current editor. Pray, if you will, that God who has begun a good work in me will continue to perform it until the Day of Jesus Christ.

O. Palmer Robertson
2010

How to Read This Book

*Y*ou may read this book as any other ordinary publication you might pick up. But this is not an ordinary book. To gain the fullest benefit, you must read this book in a different way.

Indeed, you may want to begin by reading this book from cover to cover. In this way you will experience something of the full impact of the work. You will be introduced to a new and richer way of praying to God. You will begin to sense the breadth of matters properly belonging to prayer. But then to get the fullest benefit, you will have to read the book again, and in a different way.

This book is packed with the riches of God's own words shaped in the form of prayers. Their fullness cannot be comprehended by one reading. A great deal of meditation on these compacted expressions is the only way to get the full benefit of these words.

The best way to read this book is while you are on you knees, not while sitting in an easy chair. Then you may proceed to read in the following way:

Read a brief section of the work – a phrase, a sentence, a paragraph. Then close your eyes or lift them to heaven. Rephrase what you read in your own words. If you can't remember what you read, look at the section again. Make the words applicable to your own situation.

If the words offer praise to God for his amazing work in shaping a human being in the womb of the mother, personalize the thought. Praise God for the time and circumstances of your own birth. Glorify him for the special abilities of body, mind, disposition and soul he has placed in you.

If the words confess the sin of misuse of the tongue, recall the ways during the past twenty-four hours you have spoken in haste or anger. Admit that you were ashamed to speak boldly for Christ and his gospel when you had the opportunity. Ask the Lord to be gracious, to forgive you, and to deliver you from your sins of the tongue.

Then go to the next short section of the work. As you move through the book, let your own soul be purified by the sword of the Spirit, which is the Word of God.

You may move consecutively through all the pages of the book in this manner. But it may take you quite a while – perhaps even as much as a year. But persist until your thoughts and your words are being shaped more and more by the very words of God.

Or you may place markers in the various segments of the book that arrange Scripture under the different elements of prayer. Then you may begin with a section of praise to God, followed by a section of confession of sin, then thanksgiving for mercies, then intercession for others and finally petitions for yourself. In this manner, you may maintain a balance in your approach to God in prayer. Spending several weeks or months exclusively on confession of sin may become rather discouraging to your spirit. But if you proceed from confession to thanksgiving for the full forgiveness found in Christ, you will maintain a more balanced perspective on your life before God, man and yourself.

Finally, make this book your constant life-companion. By continuing to shape your prayers in conformity with God's own words, you will find few disappointments in your fellowship with your heavenly Father. For he is more ready to give than you are to ask, if only your heart continues to conform to his.

I

Praise

Praise

✣

Approach God with a Heart Full of Praise for the Glories of His Person and Work

Turn your attention totally to this special moment of drawing near to Almighty God. Gather in all your wandering thoughts. Present yourself to him as a living sacrifice with a lively faith. Then bind the sacrifice of your heart and mind with cords to the horns of the altar by the very words of Scripture. Rom. *12:1;* Psa. *118:27*

Let us now lift up our hearts along with our eyes and hands to God in the heavens. Let us stir ourselves up to take hold of God as we seek his face. Let us give him the glory due his Name. Let us now worship God, who is a spirit, in spirit and truth, for the Father is seeking these kinds of people to worship him. *Lam.* 3:41; *John* 17:1; *Isa.* 64:7; *Psa.* 27:8; 29:2; *John* 4:23, 24.

We lift up our souls to you, O Lord. Help us to direct our full attention to you with undistracted devotion. Keep our hearts from being far from you as we draw near to you with our mouths and honour you with our lips. With humble boldness we enter the most holy of all places through the blood of Jesus, by the new and living way which he has consecrated for us through the veil, which is his torn flesh. *Psa.* 25:1; *1 Cor.* 7:35; *Matt.* 15:8; *Heb.* 10:19, 20.

Now focus your attention on this glorious God you dare to approach. Present yourself to him as someone who fully believes in his uniqueness and is filled with awe at his greatness. Distinguish yourself from people who worship all kinds of false gods.

Holy, holy, holy Lord God Almighty, the one who is, and was, and is to come. You alone are the great I AM, and you alone are the Most High over all the earth. *Rev.* 4:8; *Exod.* 3:14; *Psa.* 83:18.

O Lord, you are our God. We seek you in all earnestness. Our souls thirst for you, our bodies long for you in a dry and weary land where there is no water. You are our God, and we will praise you, our father's God, and we will exalt you. You are the true God, the living God, the one only living and true God, the everlasting King, the Covenant Lord our God who is one Lord. *Psa.* 63:1; *Exod.* 15:2; *Jer.* 10:10; *Deut.* 6:4.

The idols worshipped among the nations are silver and gold. They are vanity and a lie, the work of men's hands. They that make them are like them, and so is everyone that trusts in them. But the God that we have inherited as your adopted sons is nothing like these other gods. For you are the one who has formed all things, and we are the people you have claimed for your inheritance. The Lord of hosts is your name, God over all, blessed for evermore. *Psa.* 115:2, 4, 8; *Jer.* 10:15, 16; *Rom.* 9:5.

Their rock is not like our Rock, even as they themselves must admit. For our God is the Rock of Ages, the unchanging LORD of the Covenant. Your name shall endure forever, and your fame across the generations. But the gods that have not made the heavens and the earth will perish from the earth and from under the heavens. *Deut.* 32:31; *Isa.* 26:4; *Psa.* 135:13; *Jer.* 10:11.

Express your wonder at this one true and living God who is altogether self-existent and self-sufficient. Acknowledge him to be an infinite and eternal spirit that has all perfections in himself. Give him the glory reflected in his names, titles, attributes and works.

O Lord our God, you are so great. You are clothed with honour and majesty. You cover yourself with light as with a garment. Yet to us you make darkness your pavilion. We do not know how to approach you because of the darkness that veils your essence. *Psa.* 104:1, 2; 18:11; *Job* 37:19.

We have heard this message concerning you, and we affirm that it is true. You are light, and in you is no darkness at all. You are the Father of lights. In you there is no inconsistency. You do not change like shifting shadows. You are love, and those who dwell in love dwell in you, and you in them. Every good and perfect gift comes from you. You are the blessed and only potentate, King of the kings and Lord of the lords. You alone are immortal. You live in the light which no man can approach. No man has ever seen you, or can see you. *1 John* 1:5; *James* 1:17; *1 John* 4:16; *1 Tim.* 6:15, 16.

Acknowledge God's Existence to Be beyond Dispute

*T*he heavens declare your glory, and the skies display the work of your hands. Your eternal power and divine essence can be clearly seen and understood through your creation. They are fools without excuse who say there is no God. Clearly there is a God that judges in the earth as well as in heaven. There is a reward for the righteous. We therefore come to you believing that you are, and that you bountifully reward those who diligently seek you. *Psa.* 19:1; *Rom.* 1:20; *Psa.* 14:1; 58:11; *Heb.* 11:6.

Admit That You Can Never Fully Grasp the Greatness of God

Great are you, O Lord and greatly to be praised. Your greatness is unsearchable. We can never by our searching uncover your greatness as our God. We cannot fully understand you, the Almighty One. Who can adequately proclaim your wondrous works? Who can declare all the praise you deserve? *Psa.* 145:3; *Job* 11:7; *Psa.* 106:2.

Who is a God like you, majestic in holiness, awesome in glory, working wonders? Who on the earth can compare to you, O Lord? Who among the creatures in heaven is equal to you? O Lord God Almighty, who is a mighty God like you? Who can be compared to you in your faithfulness that encompasses all you do? Among the so-called 'gods' there is none like you. No one can do any works like your works. For you are great, and you do wondrous things. You alone are God. There is no creature that has an arm like yours, or can thunder with a voice like yours. *Exod.* 15:11; *Psa.* 89:6, 8; 86:8, 10; *Job* 40:9.

You are God and not man. You do not have eyes of flesh, and you do not see things as man sees. Your days are not as the days of man, and your years are not as man's years. As heaven is high above the earth, so are your thoughts above our thoughts and your ways above our ways. All nations before you are like a drop in a bucket, or as small as dust on a scale. You weigh continents as though they were the tiniest of particles. To you their massive substance is as nothing. They are judged by you to be less than nothing, and altogether vanity. *Hos.* 11:9; *Job* 10:4, 5; *Isa.* 55:9; 40:15, 17.

Bring before Your Mind Some of the Glorious Aspects of This Great God

1. He is an eternal God who has no beginning of days, end of life, or change caused by the passing of time.

You are the King eternal, immortal, invisible. Before the mountains were brought forth or you had formed the earth and the world, from everlasting to everlasting you are God. You are the same yesterday, today and forever. At the beginning of time you laid the foundation of the earth, and the heavens are the work of your hands. They shall perish, but you endure. All of them shall age as though they were articles of clothing. You shall treat them as a change of garments, and they shall be discarded. But you are the same, and your years shall never end. *1 Tim.* 1:17; *Psa.* 90:2; *Heb.* 13:8; *Psa.* 102:25-27.

You are God. You never change, and for that reason alone we are not consumed. Are you not from eternity, O Lord our God, our holy one? You are the everlasting God, the Lord and Creator of the farthest reaches of the earth. You never faint with exhaustion. You never grow weary. There is no way that your understanding can ever be comprehended. *Mal.* 3:6; *Hab.* 1:12; *Isa.* 40:28.

2. He is present in all places and at all times with all his glory.

You are a God at hand, never a far-away God. None can hide himself in some secret place where you cannot see him, for you fill heaven and earth. You are not far from any one of us. We will never escape your presence or elude your Spirit. If we ascend to heaven, you are there. If we make our bed in the earth's depths, Look! there you are! If we fly away on the outstretched wings of the morning's rays or sail to the uttermost parts of the sea's expanse, even there your hand shall lead us and your right hand shall sustain us. We can never outrun you. *Jer.* 23:23, 24; *Acts* 17:27; *Psa.* 139:7-10.

3. He knows all persons and things perfectly, and sees clearly their most hidden secrets.

All things are naked and exposed before the eyes of you, the one with whom we have to do. Even the secret thoughts and intents of every human heart are fully known by you. Your eyes are in every place scrutinizing the evil and the good. They run back and forth throughout the earth that you may show yourself strong in support of those whose hearts are right with you. *Heb.* 4:12, 13; *Prov.* 15:3; *2 Chron.* 16:9.

You search the heart and examine the mind, so that you may give to every man a reward according to his ways and fruit according to his doings. You have searched us out and known us. You know when we sit down and when we rise up. You understand our thoughts while they are still far off. You carefully analyse the path we travel and wherever we come to rest. You are intimately aware of all our ways. Before a word is formed on our tongue you know it completely. This kind of knowledge astounds us. It is impossible for us to comprehend. Even the darkness is not dark to you, for darkness is as light to you. *Jer.* 17:10; *Psa.* 139:1-4, 6, 12.

4. His wisdom is unsearchable, and its ultimate purposes past human comprehension.

O Lord, your understanding is infinite. You know the exact number of the stars. You even have a name for each one of them. You are fantastic in your designs, and excel all others in your achievements. Your wisdom is profound and your strength enormous. *Psa.* 147:4, 5; *Isa.* 28:29; *Job* 9:4.

How infinitely diverse are your works! In wisdom you have made them all. All things occur according to the perfect design of your will. O the depth of the wisdom and knowledge of God! How unsearchable are your judgments, and your ways past finding out. *Psa.* 104:24; *Eph.* 1:11; *Rom.* 11:33.

5. His sovereignty is incontestable, for he is the absolute Lord of all.

The highest heavens are yours, including the countless multitude of stars. The earth is yours and everything in it, the world and everyone who lives in it. You hold in your hand the depths of the seas and the peaks of the mountains. The oceans are yours, for you made them, and your hands formed the continents. Every beast in forest and jungle is yours, and the cattle on a thousand hills. You are a great God and a great King above all the gods. In your hand is the life of every living thing, and the breath of all mankind. *Psa.* 115:16; 24:1; 95:3-5; 50:10; *Job* 12:10.

May the King of heaven be praised, exalted and glorified. For everything you do is right, and all your ways are just. You know how to humble the proud. Your dominion is an everlasting dominion, and your kingdom endures from generation to generation. You do according to your will in the armies of heaven and among the inhabitants of the earth. No one can hold back your hand or say to you, 'What are you doing?' *Dan.* 4:34, 35, 37.

6. His power is irresistible, and his exercise of it cannot be limited by anyone in heaven or on earth.

O God, we know that you have the power to do everything according to your perfect will. Not one of your thoughts can ever be frustrated. Power is your unique possession. Indeed, all power in heaven and earth is yours. You wound and you heal. You kill and you make alive. Nobody can deliver anyone out of your hand. What you have promised you are able to perform, for with you nothing is impossible. *Dan. 4:35; Psa. 62:11; Matt. 28:18; Deut. 32:39; Rom. 4:21; Luke 1:37.*

7. He is a God of unspotted holiness and perfect uprightness.

You are holy. The worshipful praises of your people confess your holy and righteous rule. Holy and awesome is your name. You are holy in all your works, and holiness adorns the place where you dwell. We give thanks whenever we remember your holiness. *Psa. 22:3; 111:9; 145:17; 93:5.*

Evil can never exist alongside you, for you are of purer eyes than to look on iniquity. You are the Rock, your work is perfect. All your ways are truth and uprightness. You are a God of absolute integrity. No corruption may be found in you. You are our Rock, and there is no unrighteousness in you. *Hab. 1:13; Deut. 32:4; Psa. 92:15.*

8. He is just in the administration of his government, for he has never done wrong to any of his creatures, and never will.

The perfections of your righteousness may be compared to the highest heights, your justice to the deepest depths. Though clouds and thick darkness surround you, righteousness and justice remain the foundation of your throne. *Psa.* 36:6; 97:2.

O God, you openly exhibit your righteousness whenever we plead our case before you. You are proved right whenever you speak, and justified whenever you declare your judgment. Far be it from God that he would do wickedness, and from the Almighty that he would do anything wrong, for you repay every man exactly according to what he deserves. *Jer.* 12:1; *Psa.* 51:4; *Job* 34:10, 11.

9. His truth is unchangeable, and the treasures of his goodness inexhaustible.

You are good, and your mercy endures forever. Your lovingkindness is great toward us, and your truth endures to all generations. You have proclaimed your name to be the Covenant LORD, merciful and gracious, slow to anger, abundant in goodness and truth. You constantly manifest mercy toward thousands, forgiving iniquity, transgression and sin. This name of yours stands forever as our strong tower. *Psa.* 100:5; 117:2; *Exod.* 34:6, 7; *Prov.* 18:10.

You are good and do good. You are good to all, and your tender mercy permeates all your works. But in a special manner you are good to your chosen people, to those that are of a clean heart. Lord, please cause your goodness to pass before us, that we may taste and see that the Lord is good. Let your loving-kindness be always manifest to us. *Psa.* 119:68; 145:9; 73:1; *Exod.* 33:19; *Psa.* 34:8; 26:3.

10. Praise God for what you have heard about the glory he manifests in heaven above.

You have established your throne in heaven. It is a throne of glory, high and lifted up. Before you the seraphim cover their faces. In your compassion toward us, you veil the glories of your throne, spreading a cloud over it. *Psa.* 103:19; *Isa.* 6:1, 2; *Job* 26:9.

You make your angels like the winds, and your ministers like a flame of fire. A thousand thousand of them constantly minister before you. Ten thousand times ten thousand stand before you, ready to do whatever you please. They excel in strength, they listen to your voice.

Now we have come by faith, hope, and purified love into communion through the Spirit with that vast company of angels, and the spirits of just men made perfect. In our worship we have entered the church of the firstborn assembled in the heavenly Jerusalem. *Psa.* 104:4; *Dan.* 7:10; *Psa.* 130:20, 21; *Heb.* 12:22, 23

11. After having said everything you can about the glorious perfections of the Lord, admit that you fall infinitely short of adequately proclaiming his greatness.

We are capable of describing only a tiny portion of your wondrous ways. We have been privileged to hear only a barely audible whisper of your grandeurs as God. Who can comprehend your thunderous power? Touching the subject of the Almighty, no one is capable of finding you out. You exceed all others in power, justice, and righteous judgment. You are exalted far above all praise that a mere man could ever bring. *Job* 26:14; 37:23; *Neh.* 9:5.

Give Glory to God as the Creator of All Things, the Ruler and Benefactor of the World

*Y*ou are worthy O Lord, to receive blessing, and honour, and glory and power. For you have created all things, and for your pleasure and praise they are and were created. We worship you, the one who made heaven and earth, the sea and everything in them. You spoke, and that was it. You commanded, and it stood firm. You said, Let there be light, and there was light. You declared, Let the expanse of the skies come into being, and so it was. You made all things very good, and they are maintained up to this day by your sovereign appointment. For everything in creation exists to serve you. *Rev.* 4:11; 14:7; *Psa.* 33:9; *Gen.* 1:3, 6, 7, 31; *Psa.* 119:91.

The day is yours, the night is also yours. You established the sun and the moon. You are the one who determined all the boundaries of the earth. You made the seasons of summer and winter. Lord Christ, you sustain all things by your powerful word. In you all things hold together in harmony. *Psa.* 74:16, 17; *Heb.* 1:3; *Col.* 1:17.

The earth is full of rich diversity that all comes from you. The same is true of oceans wide. The eyes of all creatures look to you, and you give them their food at the right season. You open your hand and satisfy the desires of every living thing. You preserve man and beast, providing food for all. *Psa.* 104:24, 25; 145:15, 16; 36:6; 104:27, 28.

You alone are Lord of all. You made heaven, and the heaven above the heavens. You made the heavenly host as well as the earth, the sea, and all that is in them. You preserve them all. The angelic host of heaven worships you. Your domain embraces all things. Not even a sparrow falls to the ground apart from your sovereign, superintending will. *Neh.* 9:6; *Psa.* 103:19; *Matt.* 10:29

In the beginning you made man from the dust of the ground and breathed into him the breath of life. So then and there he became a living being. From that one bloodline you made all the nations of men that are now scattered across the face of the whole earth. Long millennia ago you determined the times for the rise and fall of nations. You sovereignly set the bounds of their habitation. *Gen.* 2:7; *Acts* 17:26.

You are the Most High who rules over the kingdoms of men. You give authority to whoever you wish. Men seek favour at the hands of their ruler, but true justice comes only from you. Hallelujah! For the Lord God omnipotent reigns, and does according to the determinations of his sovereign will. May his own glory be praised. *Dan.* 4:25; *Prov.* 29:26; *Rev.* 19:6; *Eph.* 1:11, 12.

O God, you made us and so we are yours. We are not our own. We are your people, the sheep of your pasture. Let us therefore worship and fall down, kneeling before the Lord our Maker. *Psa.* 100:3; 95:6.

You are the one who formed our bodies. They are fearfully and wonderfully made. Your eye saw our substance while it was not yet perfectly shaped in our mother's womb. All our days were written in your book before a one of them had happened. You clothed us with skin and flesh. You knit us together with bones and sinews. You gave us life and favour, and your watchful care preserves our spirit. *Psa.* 139:13-16; *Job* 10:11, 12.

You are the Father of our spirits, for you formed the spirit of man within him, and made these immortal souls for us. The Spirit of God has made us, and the breath of the Almighty has given us life. You put wisdom in our inward part, and gave understanding to our mind. You are God our Maker. You teach mankind more than the beasts of the earth, and make us wiser than the birds of heaven. We are the clay and you our potter. We are the work of your hands. *Heb.* 12:9; *Zech.* 12:1; *Job* 33:4; *Jer.* 38:16; *Job* 38:36; 35:10, 11; *Isa.* 64:8.

You are the one who took us out of the womb and kept us safe when we were helpless babes at our mother's breasts. We have been cast on you from the womb, and are continually sustained by you. You were our God before our mother gave birth to us. Therefore our praise will continually be all about you. In you we live and move and have our being. For we are your offspring. *Psa.* 22:9, 10; 71:6; *Acts* 17:28.

You hold our lives in your hand. You are present in all our ways, for determining the way of a man is not in himself. No person has the capacity to direct his own steps. Instead, our times are in your hand. Who can speak something and make it happen if you have not determined it? O Most High God, out of your mouth the decree goes forth for both good things and bad. If you take away our breath, we die. Then we return to the dust out of which we were taken. You are the God that has shepherded us all our life up to this day. You have redeemed us from all evil. Because of your covenant love we are not consumed, for your compassions never fail. They are new every morning. Great is your faithfulness. *Dan.* 5:23; *Jer.* 10:23; *Psa.* 31:15; *Lam.* 3:37, 38; *Psa.* 104:29; *Gen.* 48:15; *Lam.* 3:22, 23.

Give Distinctive Honour to Each of the Three Persons in the Godhead

Father, we adore you as Lord of heaven and earth. You are the father of our spirits, the one to whom we should be in subjection and live. You are the father of lights, the father of mercies, and the God of all consolation. You are the eternal Father from whom, through whom, and for whom are all things. *Heb.* 12:9; *James* 1:17; *2 Cor.* 1:3; *Isa.* 9:6; *Rom.* 11:36.

We worship you, the eternal Word, who was in the beginning with God, and is God. For all things were made by you, and without you nothing was made that has been made. In the fullness of time you were made flesh and tabernacled among us. You manifested your glory, the glory of the unique Son who abides face to face before the Father, full of grace and truth. *1 John* 5:7; *Matt.* 11:25; *John* 1:1-3, 14.

Since it is the will of God that all men honour the Son as they honour the Father, we adore you, O Christ, as the brightness of your Father's glory and the exact replica of his person. We join with the angels of God who were all commanded to worship you. We give all honour to you, the eternal Son of God, as the exalted Redeemer, the faithful witness, the first to rise from the dead, the Prince of the kings of the earth. We confess that Jesus Christ is Lord, to the glory of God the Father. *John* 5:23; *Heb.* 1:3, 6; *Rev.* 1:5; *Phil.* 2:11.

We also worship you, O Holy Spirit, the Comforter whom the Son has sent from the Father, even the Spirit of truth. You are the one who inspired the Scriptures, so that holy men of God wrote as they were moved by you. You are the one who proceeds from the Father and the Son. As the Spirit of truth, you teach us all things and preserve in our memory everything the Son has said. *2 Pet.* 1:21; *John* 15:26; 14:26; *2 Pet.* 1:21.

Gratefully Acknowledge the Privilege of Approaching God in Prayer

1. Affirm this God to be your God, and acknowledge his ownership of you and his dominion over you.

Our hearts declare to you, O Lord: You are our God. Apart from you we have nothing good. Even if we were righteous, we would have nothing to give back to you. You are our sovereign King. Other lords besides you have exercised their dominion over us. But from now on we will mention only your name. *Psa.* 16:2; *Job* 35:7; *Psa.* 44:4; *Isa.* 26:14.

We attest this day that you, the Covenant Lord, are our God. We commit ourselves to walk in your ways, to keep your laws, your commandments and your judgments. We are prepared to listen to your voice and give ourselves wholly to you. We recognize ourselves to be your unique people, a people holy to the Lord our God, whose calling is to make your name renowned, praised and glorified. *Deut.* 26:17-19; *Jer.* 13:11.

O Lord, we are your servants, born in your house. You have loosed our bonds. We were bought with a price, and are not our own. We yield ourselves to you, and join ourselves to you in an everlasting covenant that shall never be forgotten. Save us, for we seek to understand all your commandments. Whatever we give you is already yours, and comes from your hand. *Psa.* 116:16; *1 Cor.* 6:19, 20; *2 Chron.* 30:8; *Psa.* 119:94; *1 Chron.* 29:16.

2. Accept with deepest gratitude the enormous privilege you have of being not only allowed but even encouraged to draw near to God in prayer.

You have commanded us to pray always with all prayer and supplication with thanksgiving. You have admonished us to watch with constant intercession and great perseverance for all the saints. You have told us to keep on praying, and in everything to make our desires known to you with prayer and supplication. You have directed us to ask, seek, and knock. You have promised that we shall receive, we shall find, and the door shall be opened to us. *Eph.* 6:18; *Col.* 4:2; *Phil.* 4:6; *Matt.* 7:7, 8.

You have appointed for us a great high priest in whose name we may come boldly to the throne of grace. Through our mediator we shall find mercy, and grace to help in time of need. You have assured us that while the sacrifice of the wicked is an abomination to the Lord, the prayer of the upright is his delight. You have said that he who offers praise glorifies you, and the sacrifice of thanksgiving will please you more than the offering of an ox or bull that has horns and hoofs. *Heb.* 4:14-16; *Prov.* 15:8; *Psa.* 50:23; 69:30, 31.

You are the one that hears prayer. Therefore people from all nations shall come to you. You say, Seek my face, and our hearts answer, Your face, Lord, we will seek. For should not a people seek after their God? Where shall we go but to you? You alone have the words of eternal life. *Psa.* 65:2; 27:8; *Isa.* 8:19; *John* 6:68.

3. Express your own unworthiness to draw near to God and speak to him.

But will God actually dwell with man on the earth? Can God whom the heaven of heavens cannot contain dwell with man that is a worm, and the son of man that is less than a worm? Who are we, O Lord God, and what is our father's house, that you have brought us to this point? Do we dare present ourselves before the Lord? Yet we have found through Christ an entrance by one Spirit to the Father. And as though this was just a little thing for you to do, you have made promises concerning your servants for a long time stretching into the future. But what is man that you are mindful of him, and the son of man that you care for him? You magnify him by making him ruler over all creation. *2 Chron.* 6:18; *Job* 25:6; *2 Sam.* 7:18, 19; *Eph.* 2:18; *Psa.* 8:4, 6.

Please, O Lord. Do not be angry if we who are nothing but dust and ashes dare to speak to you, the Lord of glory. We are not worthy to receive the least of all your mercies, and all the faithfulness you have shown your servants. It would never be right to take the children's bread and throw it to people like us. Yet dogs eat crumbs that fall from their master's table, and you are rich in mercy to all that call on you. *Gen.* 18:27, 30; 32:10; *Matt.* 15:26, 27; *Rom.* 10:12.

4. Make known to God the longing of your heart toward him, for he alone is the source of true happiness. Recognize him to be the only thing worth possessing in this life, and the fountain of every other blessing.

Who do we have in heaven but you? We desire none on earth besides you. Nothing can compare to you. When our flesh and our heart fail, you are the strength of our life. You are our portion forever. You are our cup of blessing in this world, and our inheritance in the world to come. When we possess you, then we must say that the markings of our boundaries have fallen to us in pleasant places, and we have the choicest inheritance. *Psa.* 73:25, 26; 89:6; 16:5, 6.

The chief desire of our souls is for you. We delight in every remembrance of you. During the night our whole being yearns for you, and in the morning our spirits long only for you. As the deer pants for brooks of water, so our soul pants for you, O God. Our inner being thirsts for God, for the living God. Display your covenant love in the daytime. In the night let our song ascend as a prayer to you, the God of our life. *Isa.* 26:8, 9; *Psa.* 42:1, 2, 8.

We come hungering and thirsting after righteousness, for you fill the hungry with good things but the rich you send away empty. Our souls thirst for you, and our flesh longs for you in a dry and thirsty land where there is no water to quench our thirst. We long to see your power and your glory as you have manifested them in your holy place. Your covenant love is better than life. Our souls shall be satisfied with you as with marrow and fatness, and our mouths shall praise you with joyful lips. *Matt.* 5:6; *Luke* 1:53; *Psa.* 63:1-3, 5.

5. Make clear profession of your believing hope and confidence in God, and in his all-sufficiency, his power, providence, and promise.

In you, O God, we put our trust. Let us never be ashamed. Let no one ever be embarrassed for trusting you. Our souls wait on you, for our salvation comes from you. You only are our Rock and our salvation. In you is our glory, our strength and our refuge. Our every expectation in life rests in you. *Psa.* 31:1; 25:3; 62:1, 5-7.

When every other refuge fails and no one cares for our lives, we cry to you, O Covenant LORD. You are our refuge and our portion in the land of the living. Some trust in chariots and some in horses, but we always remember the name of the Lord our God. We trust in your covenant love forever and ever. We put our hope in your name. For your name is rich in all the promises it brings to your saints. We have hoped in your word. Remember the word you have spoken to your servants, for you have encouraged us to trust your promises. *Psa.* 142:4, 5; 20:7; 52:8, 9; 119:49.

6. Ask the Lord to accept you despite the pitifulness of your prayers.

Hear our prayers and our supplications, O Lord. Answer us in your faithfulness. Be near us when we call on you, however weak our prayers may be. Never let the children you love so much be frustrated when they seek you. You hear the young ravens when they cry, so do not be silent to us. For if you remain silent, we will be like those who fall into their grave. Let our prayer rise to you as incense, and the lifting up of our hands be acceptable as the evening sacrifice. *Psa.* 143:1; *Deut.* 4:7; *Isa.* 45:19; *Psa.* 147:9; 28:1; 141:2.

Many people say, Who will show us anything good in life? But we respond, Lord, let the light of your face shine favourably on us. Then our hearts will be filled with greater joy than people whose prosperity abounds with the abundant increase of their corn and wine. We beg for your favour with our whole heart. Let us be accepted by you whether we continue to be present in this body or absent from the body. *Psa.* 4:6, 7; 119:58; *2 Cor.* 5:9.

7. Openly profess your entire reliance on the Lord Jesus Christ alone for acceptance with God, and come in his name.

We could never present our requests to you because of our own righteousness. We are exposed in our sin before you. We cannot stand in your presence because of our guilt. But we make our plea on the basis of Christ's righteousness alone. For he is The Lord Our Righteousness. *Dan.* 9:18; *Ezra* 9:15; *Psa.* 71:16; *1 Cor.* 1:30; *Jer.* 23:6.

We know that even our spiritual sacrifices are acceptable to you only through Christ Jesus. We cannot hope to receive anything unless we ask in his name. So we appear before you as those who have been accepted by you in your beloved Son. We understand that much incense from his sacrifice of himself must be joined with the prayers of the saints as they are offered on the golden altar before your throne. *1 Pet.* 2:5; *John* 16:23; *Eph.* 1:6; *Rev.* 8:3.

We come in the name of the great High Priest who has passed into the heavens, even Jesus the Son of God. Lord Jesus, you can fully sympathize with our weaknesses, since you also lived with the limitations of human flesh and blood. So you are able to save with consummate completeness everyone who comes to God by you. For you live forever to make intercession for us. *Heb.* 4:14, 15; 7:25.

O Father, let your full attention be focused on the one who is our shield. Look intently on the face of your anointed. For by a voice from heaven you declared yourself to be altogether pleased with him. Lord, be altogether pleased with us since we are one with him. *Psa.* 84:9; *Matt.* 3:17.

8. Plead with the Lord for the powerful assistance of his Spirit in your prayers.

Lord, we do not know what to pray for as we ought. But let your Spirit help our infirmities, and make intercession for us. Pour on us an abundance of the Spirit of grace and supplication that teaches us to cry, Abba, Father. Inspire our hearts to pray this prayer by the Spirit of our adoption. *Rom.* 8:26; *Zech.* 12:10; *Rom.* 8:15; *2 Sam.* 7:27.

Direct your light and your truth to come to us. Let them lead us to your holy hill and to the place where you dwell. Let them guide us to God who is our greatest joy. Open our lips, and our mouth will declare your praise. *Psa.* 43:3; 51:15.

9. Make the glory of God your highest goal in all your prayers.

You have declared that you will be sanctified and glorified before all the world's people by those who draw near to you. We therefore worship you, so that we may glorify your name. We call on you, that you may deliver us and we may glorify you. For from you, and through you, and for you are all things. *Lev.* 10:3; *Psa.* 86:9; 50:15; *Rom.* 11:36.

2

Confession

Confession

CONFESS YOUR SINS BEFORE A HOLY GOD,
AND HUMBLY REPENT FOR THEM ALL

First we praise the Lord in prayer for his great glory, which is precisely what he deserves. Now we must confess with great shame all our sins, for shame is exactly what we deserve. We must humble ourselves before him, being painfully aware of our defilement, our corruption and our guilt. We must also give full respect to him as our righteous judge, for we deserve to be condemned by him. At the same time, we must express our hope to be forgiven and declared innocent despite our proven guilt through the grace that is found in Jesus Christ.

Confess the Many Ways You Have Rebelled against Him and Violated His Laws

Acknowledge that you deserve his just punishment for all the ways you have broken his law. Be ashamed when you come into his presence, since you have abused his holiness and stand condemned as a lawbreaker before his justice.

O our God, we are ashamed. We want to hide our faces from you. For our iniquities exceed the height of our head, and our trespasses reach up to the heavens. To us belong shame and confusion of face, because we have sinned against you. *Ezra* 9:6; *Dan.* 9:8.

How can we give a proper account to you? We lay our hand on our mouth and put our mouth in the dust. You put no trust in your holy ones, and the heavens are not clean in your sight. How much more abominable and filthy is man, who drinks iniquity like water. If there is any hope for us, we must cover our lips and cry out with the leper under the law, 'Unclean, unclean.' When our eyes catch a glimpse of the King, the Lord of hosts, we have every reason to cry out, 'Woe to us, for we are ruined.' *Job* 40:4; *Lam.* 3:29; *Job* 15:15, 16; *Lev.* 13:45; *Isa.* 6:5.

Dominion and dread are always with you. You maintain a just order in your heavenly heights. Can your agents who enforce your just judgments be counted? Is there anyone on whom your light does not arise? Even the stars are not pure in your eyes. How then can man be justified with God, or how can he be pure that is born of a woman? If we justify ourselves, our own mouth condemns us. If we say we are perfect, that very statement proves us perverse. If you contend with us, we are not able to answer one of your accusations out of a thousand. *Job* 25:2-4; 9:3, 20.

You must be feared, for who can stand in your sight once your wrath is aroused? Who knows the power of your anger? For you, our God, are a consuming fire. If we were aware of none of our own faults, that would not justify us. For the one who judges us is the Lord who is greater than our hearts and knows all things. But within ourselves we know that we have sinned. Father, against heaven and before you we have sinned. We are not worthy to be called your children. Treat us as one of your hired servants. *Psa.* 76:7; 90:11; *Heb.* 12:29; *1 Cor.* 4:4; *1 John* 3:20; *Luke* 15:21.

Acknowledge the Corruption of Your Origins

Confess that you are the offspring of a long line of rebellious parents, which has produced in you a nature that is depraved and degenerated from its primitive purity and uprightness.

Lord, you made man upright, but we have invented many perverse schemes. By one man sin entered into the world, and death by sin. So death passed over to all men, for all sinned. By that one man's disobedience many were made sinners, including ourselves and everyone else. *Eccles.* 7:29; *Rom.* 5:12, 19.

We are a seed of evil doers. Our father was no better than an alien Amorite, and our mother no better than a pagan Hittite. We ourselves were rightly called rebels from the womb. You knew how treacherously we would deal with you. You planted the nature of man as a choice and noble vine, altogether an upright seed. But it has become the degenerate plant of a corrupted vine, producing the grapes of Sodom and the clusters of Gomorrah. How has the gold lost its lustre, and the most fine gold become tarnished! *Isa.* 1:4; *Ezek.* 16:3; *Isa.* 48:8; *Jer.* 2:21; *Deut.* 32:32; *Lam.* 4:1.

We were shaped in sin while still in the womb. We have been sinful since the time our mother conceived us. For who can bring a clean thing out of an unclean? We are by nature children under your wrath. We are sons of disobedience along with everyone else. All flesh has become corrupt in its total lifestyle. We have all turned aside from your original purpose for us. We are altogether filthy. No one does anything good, no, not one. *Psa.* 51:5; *Job* 14:4; *Eph.* 2:2, 3; *Gen.* 6:12; *Psa.* 14:3.

Grieve Over Your Controlling Inclination toward Thinking and Doing Evil, and Your Inherent Alienation from Everything Good

1. Note the blindness of your mind toward the things of God, and its inability to receive rays of divine enlightenment.

By nature our mind is darkened, being alienated from the life of God through the ignorance that is in us. Our hearts are blinded. The things of the Spirit of God are foolishness to our nature. We cannot know them, because they are spiritually discerned. We are clever about doing evil, but have no clue how to do good. We know nothing correctly. We have lost all capability of understanding. We walk on in darkness. God speaks once, twice, but we are incapable of comprehending what he says. We keep on hearing, but do not understand. We see men as trees walking. *Eph.* 4:18; *1 Cor.* 2:14; *Jer.* 4:22; *Psa.* 82:5; *Job* 33:14; *Matt.* 13:14; *Mark* 8:24.

2. Lament the stubbornness of your will, and its con-stant resistance to every suggestion that it should live in submission to God's law.

We have a carnal mind that stands at enmity against God. It will not and cannot live in subjection to the law of God. You have written for us the great things of your law, but they have been regarded by us as a strange thing. Our corrupt hearts have been constantly saying, 'Who is the Almighty that we should serve him?' We ignore God's law. Yet we are ready and eager to do whatever we formulate in our own heart and proclaim with our own mouth. We have walked in the way of our own heart, and done what was pleasing in the sight of our own eyes, constantly fulfilling the desires of the flesh and the self-pleasing mind. *Rom.* 8:7; *Hos.* 8:12; *Job* 21:15; *Jer.* 44:17; *Eccles.* 11:9; *Eph.* 2:3.

Our neck has been as rigid as though it were made of iron sinews. We have made our hearts as hard as stone. We have refused to listen, and turned away from you with the shrug of a stubborn shoulder. We have stopped our ears like the deaf adder that will not listen to the voice of the charmer, though he charm with the greatest skill. How we have hated instruction! Our heart has despised reproof. We have not obeyed the voice of our teachers, and refused to offer a listening ear to those that would instruct us. *Isa.* 48:4; *Zech.* 7:11, 12; *Psa.* 58:4, 5; *Prov.* 5:12, 13.

3. Ask God's forgiveness for your absorption with things that deserve little or no consideration, and your failure to concentrate on subjects that nourish the soul.

The first impulse of every imagination of our heart has been evil, only evil, all day long. These fruitless contemplations have occupied our thinking from our youth. How long have these vain thoughts taken up lodging within us! Our foolish thoughts are riddled with sin. From the inner self, out of the heart proceed these evil thoughts. As we lie in bed during the meditative hours of the night, we constantly plot how we can manipulate everything to our own advantage. Our eyes, like the eyes of a fool, carry the imaginings of our vain hearts to the ends of the earth. *Gen.* 6:5; 8:21; *Jer.* 4:14; *Prov.* 24:9; *Matt.* 15:19; *Mic.* 2:1; *Prov.* 17:24.

O God, you are not the centre of all our thoughts as you should be. We are doing well if you have a place in any of them. You are the Rock that brought us into existence, yet we have forgotten you, the God that formed us. Days without number we have forgotten you. Our hearts have focused on things utterly hollow and useless. Our deepest inward thought has been that our achievements in life — our houses, our families, what we have produced with our lives — would last indefinitely. Like the rich fool, we have forgotten that you could bring death to our door tonight and we would be required to give you a full accounting. How foolish we have been! *Psa.* 10:4; *Deut.* 32:18; *Jer.* 2:32, 5; *Psa.* 49:11, 13; *Luke* 12:20.

4. Be ashamed for the lust of your flesh, and the disorder of your desires.

We have set our affection on things below, when they should have been set on things above. We should have been storing up treasures in heaven where they will last forever, where Christ sits at your right hand. But we have concentrated on collecting earthly treasures that will inevitably prove worthless. The things we should be seeking have not controlled our desire. We have been consumed with the pursuit of vanities that lie to us. We have even forsaken your mercies that you have so graciously offered to us. We have exchanged the gushing fountain of living waters for putrid cisterns, broken cisterns that can hold no water. *Col.* 3:1, 2; *Matt.* 6:21; *Jon.* 2:8; *Jer.* 2:13.

We have panted after the dust of the earth, and have been full of care about what we will eat, what we will drink, and how we will be clothed. Instead of seeking first the kingdom of God and his right-eousness, we have focused our whole life on things central to godless unbelievers. We have stretched out the desire of our spirits toward empty vanities, and have focused our eyes on things that are not even

real. We have set our affection on things t_
seen, which last only for a little while. But the t_
that will continue throughout eternity we have c
believed, postponed, or forgotten. *Amos* 2:7; *Mat*
6:31-33; *Psa.* 24:4; *Prov.* 23:5; *2 Cor.* 4:18.

*5. Express your deepest heartfelt sorrow over the
corruption of your whole person, which has fostered
inordinate passions while alienating your mind from the
life of the Spirit.*

We are born with a fallen, sinful nature, and we
are quite content to continue in that same condition.
Nothing good is inherent in our flesh. If to will the
good is sometimes present with us, we cannot find
the wherewithal to carry it out. The good which we
would do, we do not do. But the evil we would not
do, that is what we do. We have a prevailing principle in all the different members of our body that
wars against what we know to be right. We are constantly being brought into captivity to this prevailing
principle of sin that controls the various members of
our body. When we would do good, our evil inclination is too strong to overcome. *John* 3:6; *Rom.* 7:18,
19, 21, 23.

The whole head is sick, and the whole heart is
faint. From the sole of the foot to the crown of the
head there is no soundness in us. Instead, we have

only the consequences of our sin which brings nothing but wounds, bruises and putrefying sores. There is in us a bent to turn aside from the living God. Our hearts are deceitful above all things and desperately wicked. Who can know what they will come up with next? They shoot crookedly like a faulty bow. *Isa.* 1:6; *Hos.* 11:7; *Jer.* 17:9; *Hos.* 7:16.

Make Full Confession of Your Failure To Do Your Duty

Acknowledge the way you have trifled in your duty. Feel ashamed that you have done so little since you came into this world of the great work God sent you to do. Express your sincere regret that you have profited so little from your baptism into Christ and from all the other means of grace God has provided for you.

We have been as fig trees planted in the vineyard. You have come many years seeking fruit from us, but have found nothing. We might justly be cut down and cast into the fire for uselessly taking up space in the ground. You came looking for plump, sweet grapes but you found only sour grapes instead. We have been unprofitable vines bringing forth fruit only to satisfy ourselves. *Luke* 13:6, 7; *Matt.* 3:10; *Isa.* 5:4.

We have known to do good, but have not done it. We have hid our Lord's money, and deserve the doom of a wicked, slothful servant. We have been unfaithful stewards that have wasted our Lord's wealth. Though we are only one sinner among many, as one sinner we have destroyed a lot of good. *James* 4:17; *Matt.* 25:18, 26; *Luke* 16:1; *Eccles.* 9:18.

Abundant resources have been put into our hands to get wisdom. But we have had no desire to live in the fear of God. When on occasion we have sought some godly wisdom, our divided heart has remained at our left hand. Our childhood and youth were spent in vanity, all our days fade away under your wrath, and our years come to their end with nothing more than a sigh. *Prov.* 17:16; *Eccles.* 10:2; 11:10; *Psa.* 90:9.

We have not recognized or improved the day of our opportunity. We have not provided meat in summer, or gathered food in harvest. Yet we have had guides, overseers and rulers to direct us. We are slow of heart to understand and believe. Considering the time and the opportunities we have had, we should have been teaching others. But instead, we have failed to learn the first principles of the oracles of God. Even until today, we need milk and cannot bear strong meat. *Luke* 19:44; *Prov.* 6:7, 8; *Luke* 24:25; *Heb.* 5:12.

We have put the fear of the Lord far away from us. We have suppressed inclinations to pray. We have not called on your name, and have not stirred up ourselves to take hold on you. We have come before you as your people come, and have sat before you as your people sit. We have heard your words, while all the time our hearts have been filled with distracting thoughts about the pleasures of this world. So we have brought the torn, the lame and the sick for our sacrifice. We have offered you, our God, the kinds of sacrifices we would never present to our governor. We have taken a solemn vow, and then sacrificed to you a corrupt thing, while all the time we had an unblemished male in our flock. *Job* 15:4; *Isa.* 64:7; *Ezek.* 33:31; *Mal.* 1:8, 14.

Repent for Your Many Specific Transgressions in Thought, Word and Deed

We have sinned, Father, against heaven and before you. We have all sinned and fallen short of your glory. We have failed to honour you, the God who gives us every breath and sustains our every step. Against you, you only, have we sinned, and have done much evil in your sight. We have not obeyed your voice to walk in your laws which you have plainly set before us, though they are holy, just, and good. *Luke* 15:18; *Rom.* 3:23; *Dan.* 5:23; *Psa.* 51:4; *Dan.* 9:10; *Rom.* 7:12.

Who would want to make a complete list of all his errors? Cleanse us from our secret faults. In many different ways we all offend, and our iniquities are more numerous than the hairs of our head. As a spring spews out its waters, so our hearts spew out wickedness. This has been our manner of life from our youth, for we have never really wanted to obey your voice. Out of the evil treasury of our hearts we have brought forth many evil things. *Psa.* 19:12; *James* 3:2; *Psa.* 40:12; *Jer.* 6:7; 22:21; *Matt.* 12:35.

1. Humble yourself by confessing the pride of your life.

We have every reason to be humbled for the pride of our hearts, which has deceived us. We have thought of ourselves more highly than we ought to think. We have not made an honest, sober evaluation of ourselves. We have not walked humbly with you our gracious God. *2 Chron.* 32:26; *Obad.* 3; *Rom.* 12:3; *Mic.* 6:8.

We have leaned on our own understanding and trusted in our own hearts. We have sacrificed to our own net. We have sought our own glory more than the glory of him that sent us. We have been puffed up in pride about the very things for which we should have mourned. *Prov.* 3:5; 28:26; *Hab.* 1:16; *John* 7:18; *1 Cor.* 5:2.

2. Be ashamed for the times you have broken out in passion and rash anger.

We have not maintained the rule over our own spirits. We have been like a city whose protecting walls have been broken down. We have been short-tempered and have allowed our anger to simmer. When our spirits have been provoked, we have spoken rashly with our lips just as Moses did. We have been guilty of an angry and bitter spirit which we should have gotten rid of long ago. *Prov.* 25:28; 14:17; *Eccles.* 7:9; *Psa.* 106:33; *Eph.* 4:31.

3. Repent for your covetousness and love of the world.

Our lifestyle has never been without covetousness. After all this time, we still have not learned to be content with the things we have. Who can say he is free from the love of money, which is the root of all kinds of evil? We have been controlled in thought and action by a covetousness which is nothing less than idolatry. We have sought great things for ourselves, though you have plainly said, 'Seek them not.' *Heb.* 13:5; *Phil.* 4:11; *1 Tim.* 6:10; *Col.* 3:5; *Jer.* 45:5.

4. Repudiate your sensuality and flesh-pleasing.

We have been more concerned about the things of the flesh than the things of the spirit. We have lived on this earth in luxury and self-gratification. We have indulged our hearts as though we were fattening ourselves for the slaughter. *Rom.* 8:5; *James* 5:5.

We have been careful to make provision for the flesh to fulfil its unending desires. We have encouraged the very lusts that war against the soul. We have been lovers of pleasure more than lovers of God. When we ate and drank, did we not eat and drink to gratify ourselves rather than to glorify God? *Rom.* 13:14; *1 Pet.* 2:11; *2 Tim.* 3:4; *Zech.* 7:6.

5. Renounce your self-security and disregard for the changes that inevitably come in the course of this life.

We have put out of our minds every prospect of a future evil day. In our prosperity we have said, 'We will never suffer setback.' We have assumed that tomorrow will be just as prosperous as today, or even better. *Amos* 6:3; *Psa.* 30:6; *Isa.* 56:12.

We have encouraged our souls to relax, to eat, drink and be merry. We have lived as though we had resources stored up for many years, never recognizing that this very night our souls could be required of us. We have trusted in uncertain riches more than in you, the living God. We have addressed gold, saying, 'You are our hope.' We have spoken to the finest gold, declaring, 'All our confidence is in you.' *Luke* 12:19, 20; *1 Tim.* 6:17; *Job* 31:24.

6. Express genuine sorrow for your fretfulness and impatience, your murmuring under affliction, your inordinate dejection, and your distrust of God and his providence.

When you chastened us, we have been as a bull unaccustomed and resistant to the yoke. Our heart has resented you, though it was our own foolishness that led us astray and got us into trouble. In our times of stress, we have multiplied our offences. We have either despised your chastening, or fainted when we you corrected us. Yet we know from your word that if we faint in a day of adversity our strength is small. *Prov.* 19:3; *2 Chron.* 28:22; *Prov.* 2:11; 24:10.

In haste we have concluded, 'We are hidden from your sight! The Lord has forsaken us! Our God has forgotten us!' We have acted as though you would never be favourable to us again. In our dejection we have assumed that you have forgotten how to be gracious to us, and have shut up all your tender mercies in your wrath. Our weak faith has led us astray. *Psa.* 31:22; *Isa.* 49:14; *Psa.* 77:7.

7. Repent for the lack of love you have displayed toward your brothers and sisters. Confess with sorrow the times you have not lived in peace with your relatives, neighbours, and friends. Seek God's pardon for the times you have treated them unjustly.

We have been very guilty in our relationships toward our brothers and sisters. We have not studied carefully the things that make for peace. We have failed to maximize our use of the ways we might build them up and encourage them. *Gen.* 42:21; *Rom.* 14:19.

We have been ready to judge our brother, and to regard him as though he were of no value to us. We have forgotten that we will all soon stand before the judgment seat of Christ. Contrary to the royal law of love, we have been puffed up and proud. We have been rude and sought our own advantage above the wellbeing of others. We have been easily provoked. We have rejoiced when others have fallen into sin, and been secretly glad at their calamities. *Rom.* 14:10; *1 Cor.* 13:4, 5; *Prov.* 17:5.

We have had an insatiable desire for recognition among men. We have provoked one another, spurring others on to sin. We have envied the gifts or positions of others when we should have been considering ways in which we could promote our brother. We have failed to encourage one another in love and good works. *Gal.* 5:26; *Heb.* 10:24.

Our heart of compassion has been shut up so that we have shown no sensitivity toward people in real need. We have insulated ourselves from any awareness of the needs of our own flesh and blood. At times we have looked with an evil, resentful eye toward our poverty-stricken brother. We have even despised the poor. *1 John* 3:17; *Isa.* 57:7; *Deut.* 15:9; *James* 2:7.

Wherever we have wronged our brother or taken advantage of him, show it to us that we may correct our faults. If we have trod on our brother because of our pride, or if our feet have walked in deceitful ways, lead us into a path of humility, truth, and true servanthood. If any sin has left a blot on our dealings with others, uncover it so we may make amends and do it no more. *1 Thess.* 4:6; *Job* 31:5, 7; 34:32.

8. *Confess that your tongue leads you into sin.*

In the multitude of our words there never has been a lack of sin, for man full of talk will never be justified. While the lips of the righteous feed many, our lips have poured out foolishness and spoken perversity. Much corrupt communication has come out of our mouths. We are guilty of foolish talk and jesting, which are always out of place in your presence. We have spoken little of things useful for building up others in the faith. We have failed to speak words that could minister grace to our hearers. *Prov.* 10:19; *Job* 11:2; *Prov.* 10:21, 32; 4:2; *Eph.* 4:25; 5:4.

If we must give account for every idle word that we have spoken, we stand condemned. If by our words we shall be justified and by our words we shall be condemned, then woe to us. We are ruined, for we all have unclean lips, and live among people with unclean lips. What would happen to us if you should turn our own tongue against us? *Matt.* 12:36, 37; *Isa.* 6:5; *Psa.* 64:8.

9. Confess your slothfulness and spiritual decay.

We have been slothful in seeking the face of God, and have not been fervent in spirit while serving the Lord. The few things of our spiritual life which still remain are on the verge of dying, and our works have been judged to be deficient in your sight. *Rom.* 12:11; *Rev.* 3:2.

We have been too concerned about unfavourable winds and decided not to sow. We have observed the threatening clouds and decided not to reap. With the sluggard we have frightened ourselves with the figment of a lion in the highway, a lion in the city streets. We have turned on our bed as a door turns on its hinges. We keep pleading, 'Let us have a little more sleep, a little more slumber, a little more folding of the hands in rest.' *Eccles.* 11:4; *Prov.* 29:13, 14; 6:10.

We have lost our first love. Where is now the joy of our salvation which we first experienced? Our goodness has been as the morning clouds and the early dew which quickly pass away. At the root of all this coolness toward the things of God is our evil, unbelieving heart that inclines us to turn away from you, the living God. *Rev.* 2:4; *Gal.* 4:15; *Hos.* 6:4; *Heb.* 3:12.

Ask God To Show You the Great Evil in Sin

Plead with God's Holy Spirit to convict you of sin's cancerous nature, and the constant havoc it works in your life.

1. Consider the sinfulness of sin.

O that sin may appear to us as for what it really is, which is sin! Let us see it in its true colours. Through the perfections of God's commandments let us see sin to be exceedingly sinful. Let us understand sin to be rebellious lawlessness. *Rom.* 7:13; *1 John* 3:4.

By every wilful sin we defiantly declare, 'We will not have this man [that is, God] to reign over us! Who is the Lord, that we should obey his voice?' By sin we have shown that we despise you, disregard your laws, and cast them behind our back. *Luke* 19:14; *Exod.* 5:2; *Num.* 15:30; *Neh.* 9:26.

2. Recognize the foolishness of sin.

O God, you know our utter foolishness. The folly of our sins cannot be hid from you. We have openly displayed our foolishness by our disobedience. How foolish and hurtful are our lusts, plunging us into ruin and destruction. *Psa.* 69:5; *Titus* 3:3; *1 Tim.* 6:9.

Foolishness was bound up in our hearts even when we were children. Though we might vainly pretend to be wise, a witless person can no more become wise than a wild donkey's colt can be born a man. We have sinned greatly in what we have done, and have done a very foolish thing. How foolish and ignorant have we been! In your presence we have acted no better than the brute beasts. *Prov.* 22:15; *Job* 11:12; *2 Sam.* 24:10; *Psa.* 73:22.

3. Admit the unprofitableness of sin.

What have we profited if we should gain the whole world by our sinful ways and lose our own souls? We have sinned and perverted what was right, and it has profited us absolutely nothing. What fruit do we get from those actions that have shamed us? Their final end is nothing less than death. *Matt.* 16:26; *Job* 33:27; *Rom.* 6:21.

4. Beware of the deceitfulness of sin.

The pride of our heart has deceived us. Sin has deceived us and by your just decree has put us to death. Our hearts have been hardened through the deceitfulness of sin, so that we have been dragged down by our own lust and enticed to more and more sin. *Obad.* 3; *Rom.* 7:11; *Heb.* 3:13; *James* 1:14.

Sin has promised freedom from restraint, but has made us slaves to corruption. Sin has promised that we shall not die, directly contradicting your word. It has promised that if we sin, we shall become as gods, free to determine for ourselves what is good and what is evil. But even as sin has flattered us, it has spread a net for our feet. *2 Pet.* 2:19; *Gen.* 3:5; *Prov.* 29:5.

5. Recognize the offence sin has committed against a Holy God.

By breaking the law we have dishonoured you, and have provoked you, the Holy One of Israel, to anger. We have done many things that have greatly displeased you. You must be grieved by our whorish hearts, for our eyes have continually lusted after our idols. *Rom.* 2:23; *Isa.* 1:4; *Hos.* 12:14; *2 Sam.* 11:27; *Ezek.* 6:9.

We have tempted you, tested you, and grieved you as we have wandered through the wilderness of this life. We have rebelled against you so that you have turned against us and become our enemy. We have grieved the Holy Spirit of God, by whom we are sealed to the day of redemption. *Psa.* 95:9, 10; *Isa.* 63:10; *Eph.* 4:30.

6. Become fully aware of the damage sin has done to your own soul.

By our iniquities we have sold ourselves into slavery. In sinning against you we have wronged our own souls. By hating you we have loved death. Our sins have separated us from you so that you will not hear us. By our sins our minds and consciences have been defiled. *Isa.* 50:1; *Prov.* 8:36; *Isa.* 59:2; *Titus* 1:15.

Our own sin has become our punishment, for one of your greatest judgments on sin is to give up the sinner to further degeneration in the pit of sin. Our backsliding administers its own rebuke to us. What a bitter thing it is to forsake you, the Lord our God, and to live without the protective wisdom that comes from fearing you. What fools we are who make mockery of sin. *Jer.* 2:19; *Rom.* 1:24, 26, 28; *Prov.* 14:9.

Be Aware of the Things that Make Sin More Abhorrent in the Sight of God

1. The clearer your understanding of what is good and what is evil in God's eyes, the greater your sin.

We have known our master's will, but have not done it. So we deserve to be beaten with many stripes. Both as leaders and as people we have known your way and your requirements. Yet we have broken off your yoke and repudiated your bonds. *Luke* 11:47; *Jer.* 5:4, 5.

We have known your righteous judgments, that they which live in sin's depravity are worthy of death. Yet we have gone ahead with our rebellious ways. We have even found pleasure in encouraging others to practise the same things. We have taught others many things about you, but have not taught our-selves. We profess to know you as our God, but have denied you by our actions. Though pretending to be your devoted servants, we are defiled, self-willed, and disqualified from doing anything good. *Rom.* 1:32; 2:21; *Titus* 1:16.

2. The greater profession you have made of devotion to Christ, the greater your sin.

We identify ourselves as loyal citizens of your holy city. We profess our trust in you, the God of Israel. We have made solemn commitments in your name. But we do not lend credibility to these professions by practising truth and righteousness. By our inconsistencies we have dishonoured your worthy name by which we are called, and have given great opportunity for the Lord's enemies to mock you and your people. We have named the name of Christ and yet we have not departed from iniquity. *Isa.* 48:1, 2; *James* 2:17; *2 Sam.* 12:13; *2 Tim.* 2:19.

3. The more mercies you have received from God, the greater your sin.

Is this the way we should have repaid you, O Lord? You have nourished and brought us up as your own children, but we have rebelled against you. We have been a foolish and unwise people. You are our Father, our Creator. You claimed us as your people even though you found us wandering and lost in a barren wasteland. You cared for us and guarded us as the apple of your eye. Yet we have proven to be a warped and crooked generation. We have not shown proper gratitude in response to the benefits you have heaped on us, so your wrath has rested on us. *Deut.* 32:5, 6, 9, 10; *Isa.* 1:2; *2 Chron.* 32:25.

4. The fuller the warning you have received from the Word of God as well as from your own conscience about the danger of sin, the greater the sin when you have gone on in it.

We have been regularly reproved. Yet we have hardened our neck and gone on stubbornly in the way of our heart. Again and again you have spoken to us, saying, Do not do this abominable thing which I hate. But we have refused to listen. We have paid no attention to you. *Prov.* 29:1; *Isa.* 57:17; *Jer.* 44:4, 5.

Your word has come to us precept on precept, line by line, a little at a time, as we have been able to understand. So we are without excuse. We have seen our true nature in the mirror of your word. Yet we have walked away and completely forgotten the kind of people we are. *Isa.* 28:13; *Mark* 4:33; *Rom.* 1:20; *James* 1:23, 24.

5. The greater the chastenings you have received for your sin, the greater the sin if you go on in it.

You have struck us for our sin, but we have shown no grief in repentance. We have refused to receive correction. We have made our faces harder than a rock. Your rod of correction has not been able to drive the foolishness out of our hearts. You have chastened us with the rod you use for correcting men, and with the stripes intended to reform men. Yet we have not returned to you, the one who has struck us. We have not sought you, the Covenant LORD, the Lord of hosts. *Jer.* 5:3; *Prov.* 22:15; *2 Sam.* 7:14; *Isa.* 9:13.

We have seen some people overthrown with a violence like that which destroyed Sodom and Gomorrah. As brands plucked out of the fire, we have been spared these severest of your judgments. Yet we have not returned to you, our Lord. When your hand has been lifted up over us, poised to descend in judgment, we have had no consciousness of our impending doom. *Amos* 4:11; *Zech.* 3:2; *Isa.* 26:11.

6. The more vows and promises you have made of better obedience, the greater your sin.

We have not fulfilled the covenantal vows which pledged us to death if we disobeyed. Instead, as traitors we have acted in treachery. *Jer.* 34:18; *Isa.* 24:16.

Did we not say, 'I admit my guilt, but I pledge that I will not commit these same offences again? I have done wrong, but I will never do it again?' We did! Yet we have reverted to our same filthy sins just as the dog who licks up his own vomit and the pig who goes back and wallows in the muck after he has been washed. You have promised peace to your people despite all their offences. Yet we have gone back to the folly of our same sins. *Job* 34:31, 32; *2 Pet.* 2:22; *Psa.* 85:8.

7. The more aware you are that you are violating God's law, the more liable you are to his just punishments.

We know that your law curses everyone that does not obey every commandment written in the book of the law. We understand that the wages of every sin is death. We acknowledge that for immorality, impurity, greed, obscenity, idolatry, foolish talk, coarse joking, and any other transgression of the commandments, your wrath falls on the disobedient. *Gal.* 3:10; *Rom.* 6:23; *Eph.* 5:3-6.

What can we say after all the mercies you have shown us despite our continuing rebellion? Once again we have forsaken your commandments. We have repeated our same sins. What can we possibly do to make amends, you Watcher of mankind? *Ezra* 9:10; *Job* 7:20.

We are guilty, for the Scriptures have included each one of us under the condemnation of sin. Therefore you might justly be angry to the point of consuming us all, so that there would not be any surviving remnant, not a single person who might escape your wrath. If you should use perfect righteousness as the measuring line and absolute justice as the plumb, you might justly set us all apart to every imaginable evil according to all the curses of the covenant. You could blot out our names forever from any remembrance under heaven. *Rom.* 3:19; *Gal.* 3:22; *Ezra* 9:14; *Isa.* 28:17; *Deut.* 29:20, 21.

You could justly swear in your wrath that we should never enter your rest. You could set us out in a wilderness naked and bare. You could take away our corn even when it is in season. In perfect righteousness you could put your cup of judgment that makes men tremble into our hands, and make us drain it to the dregs. You are just in whatever punishment you are pleased to lay on us. For you do only what is right, but we do only wickedness. Whatever our calamity, you have graciously punished us less than what our iniquities deserve. *Psa.* 95:11; *Hos.* 2:3, 9; *Isa.* 51:17, 22; *Ezra* 9:13; *Neh.* 9:33.

You are totally transparent in your righteousness whenever you judge, and completely justified in whatever sentence you pronounce. So we accept the punishment of our iniquity. We humble ourselves under your mighty hand, declaring that the Lord is righteous. Why should a man who is still alive complain for the punishment of his sins? No! We will bear your indignation, since we have sinned against you. *Psa.* 51:4; *Lev.* 26:43; *1 Pet.* 5:6; *2 Chron.* 12:6; *Lam.* 3:39; *Mic.* 7:9.

Earnestly Pray for the Full and Free Forgiveness of All Your Sins

Sin's wounds have been opened, and you have sensed its guilt, its power, and its remnants still remaining in you. Now ask God for the healing and help that he alone can give to deliver you from sin's guilt, condemnation and power. Feel in your heart a deep sense of your need for God's mercies. Accept the fact that you are totally ruined apart from his gracious forgiveness. Understand that you will experience true blessing both in this life and the life to come only if you receive these mercies of forgiveness and restoration from the Lord. Be fully aware of your own misery and danger because of sin, and the desperate need you have for full and free forgiveness.

For your name's sake, O Lord, pardon my iniquity, for it is great. Countless evils have surrounded me. My iniquities have taken me captive so that I am unable to see my way clearly. They are more than the hairs of my head, and my soul despairs. Lord, please! Deliver me! Hurry to help me. *Psa.* 25:11; 40:12, 13.

Do not remember our former sins against us. Let your tender mercy come quickly, for we are in desperate need. O God of our salvation, help us for the glory of your name. Deliver us as you purge

away our sins. Remember not the sins or the rebel-
lions of our youth. Instead, remember us according
to your mercy, for your goodness is great. *Psa.* 79:8,
9; 25:7.

Lord, I come to you like the self-convicted tax
collector that stood far off from your presence, and
would not even lift his eyes toward heaven. Instead,
he beat his breast as he prayed. So I pray as he
prayed, God be merciful to me, the sinner. For I,
like him, see myself as the worst man in the world.
Wash me thoroughly from my iniquity, and cleanse
me from my sin. For I admit my transgression, and
my sin is painfully obvious to me. Purge me with
the sprinkled blood of Christ's Passover sacrifice so
I can be clean. Wash me and I shall be whiter than
snow. Hide your face from looking on my sins, and
blot out my iniquities. *Luke* 18:13; *Psa.* 51:2, 3, 7.

So now, Lord, what am I looking for? My hope is
altogether in you. Deliver me from all my transgressions. Do not let me be ridiculed by fools when they
see my guilt. Be merciful despite my unrighteousness. Never remember my sins and wrongdoings
again. Graciously forgive the great debt I owe you.
Justify me freely by your grace through the redemption that is in Christ Jesus from all those sins from
which I could never be justified by keeping the law
of Moses. *Psa.* 39:7, 8; *Heb.* 8:12; *Matt.* 18:32; *Rom.*
3:24; *Acts* 13:39.

Brush aside our offences like a passing cloud, and let our sins quickly fade away from your sight like the morning mist. We return to you because you are the one who has redeemed us. Keep our sin from ruining us. Take away our iniquity so we do not die. Deliver us so we will not be hurt by that second death that lasts forever. Do not let us who are your servants stand condemned before your judgment seat, for no mortal man can be justified in your sight. Do not condemn us though we deserve it. Deliver us from sinking down into the pit, for you have found a ransom for our souls. *Isa.* 44:22; *Ezek.* 18:30; *1 Sam.* 12:13; *Rev.* 2:11; *Psa.* 143:2; *Job* 10:2; 33:24.

Take away all our iniquity, and receive us graciously. Heal our apostasy, and love us freely. Turn your anger away from us. Though our sins be red as scarlet, let them be as pure as snow. Though they be a brilliant red, let them be as wool. As we show ourselves willing and submissive rather than rebellious and resistant, allow us to eat the good of the land. *Hos.* 14:3, 4; *Isa.* 1:18.

1. Give God the glory for his patience and longsuffering toward you, and his willingness to be reconciled to you.

O the riches of the kindness, patience, and longsuffering of God! In all your dealings with us you have intended to bless us by leading us to repentance. How tolerant you are toward us, not wishing that any should perish but that all should come to repentance. You have not dealt with us according to our sin. You have not rewarded us according to our iniquities. Instead, you have shown continual patience in your graciousness toward us. *Rom.* 2:4; *2 Pet.* 3:9; *Psa.* 103:10; *Isa.* 30:18.

A sentence of condemnation against our evil works has not been executed speedily. You have given us space to repent and make our peace with you. You call even backsliding children to return to you, and have promised to heal their backslidings. Therefore we come to you, for we are still in covenant with you, the LORD our God. *Eccles.* 8:11; *Rev.* 2:21; *Jer.* 22:23.

Clearly your longsuffering opens the door to salvation. For if you had intended to kill us, you would not have shown us the wondrous things you have done and continue to do. O that your goodness might lead us to repentance! For though we have trespassed against you, yet still there is hope despite our sin. *Rom.* 2:4; *Ezra* 10:2; *2 Pet.* 3:15; *Judg.* 13:23.

You have declared it, and then confirmed it with an oath, that you have no pleasure in the death of the wicked. You are delighted when they turn back to you so they can live. Therefore we will tear our hearts in true repentance rather than merely ripping up our clothing in an outward show of piety. We will return to you, the Lord our God, for you are gracious and merciful, slow to anger and of great kindness. Who knows? You may turn and have mercy, and leave a blessing behind you. *Ezek.* 33:11; *Joel* 2:13, 14.

2. Claim for yourself the great encouragement God has given sinners to humble themselves before him, and confess your sins with sorrow and shame.

O Lord, if you should keep a record of our iniquities, who could stand! But there is forgiveness with you, so that you may be feared. With you there is mercy. Indeed, with our God there is the hope of total restoration. For you are able to redeem your people from all their sin and all its consequences. *Psa.* 130:3, 4, 7, 8.

O God, the sacrifice you will accept is a broken spirit. You will never reject the broken heart that is truly sorry for its sin. You are the high and exalted one that inhabits eternity. Your name is holy. Heaven is your throne and earth your footstool. Yet you look with favour on the person that is poor and humble, having a broken and sorrowful spirit who trembles at your word. You refresh the spirit of the contrite, and revive the heart of the humble. *Psa.* 51:17; *Isa.* 57:15; 66:2.

You have graciously assured us that though people who try to cover up their sins will never prosper, yet those who confess and forsake them will always find mercy with you. When a poor repentant sinner declared, 'I will confess my transgression to the Lord', you forgave all the guilt of his sin. In the same way, everyone who wants to walk with God should pray to you at the time when you may be found. We are only fooling ourselves and denying the obvious if we say we have no sin. But you have promised that if we confess our sins you are faithful and just to forgive us our sins, and to cleanse us from all unrighteousness. *Prov.* 28:13; *Psa.* 32:5, 6; *1 John* 1:8, 9.

3. Humbly express your sense of shame for your sin. Seek an abundant supply of God's grace, so that you can live a life more honouring to him from this day forward.

Lord, we repent, for the kingdom of heaven is at hand. In proof of the arrival of this kingdom, you have exalted King Jesus the Christ, empowering him to give repentance and remission of sins to the nations of the world. Our iniquities have overwhelmed us as a burden too heavy to bear. But weary and heavy laden under this burden we come to you, O Christ, for you have promised that in you we shall find rest for our souls. *Matt.* 3:2; *Acts* 5:31; *Psa.* 38:4; *Matt.* 11:28.

Almighty God, our ears have heard of you, but now the eyes of our hearts see you through the revelation of your Son. Therefore we despise ourselves and repent in dust and ashes. We have become like doves of the valley, every one mourning for his own iniquities. If only our heads were pools of water, and our eyes fountains of tears. Then we could weep day and night for our transgressions. Let us sow in tears that we might reap in joy. Let us go forth weeping, bearing precious seed, that in due time we may return with rejoicing, bringing our sheaves with us. *Job* 42:5, 6; *Ezek.* 7:16; *Jer.* 9:1; *Psa.* 126:5, 6.

Help each one of us to know the plague of his own heart, so that we may look in faith to the one we have pierced. Let us mourn and be in bitterness for him as one that is in bitterest mourning for the loss of a firstborn son. Let us sorrow in a godly manner with the kind of sorrow that works repentance leading to salvation, for this sorrow never ends with regret. When we see the price you have paid to make atonement for us, let us remember our sin and be ashamed. Let us never presume to open our mouth again because of our humiliation. *1 Kings* 8:38; *Zech.* 12:10; *2 Cor.* 7:10; *Ezek.* 16:63.

We have gone astray like lost sheep. Seek your servants, for we do not forget your commandments. Empower us to bring forth fruit worthy of repentance. Sustain us so that we never return again to the folly of sin. For why should we have anything more to do with useless idols made by men's hands? Sin shall no longer have dominion over us, for we are not under the condemning strictures of the law but under freeing grace of your forgiveness and restoration. *Psa.* 119:176; *Matt.* 3:8; *Psa.* 85:8; *Hos.* 14:8; *Rom.* 6:14.

Base Your Plea for the Pardon of Your Sin on God's Self-revelation about His Nature as the True and Living God

1. Remind yourself of the Lord's infinite goodness, his readiness to forgive, and his delight in displaying his mercy.

O our Covenant Lord, you are good and always ready to forgive. You are rich in mercy to all that call on you. You are a God full of compassion. You are gracious, patient, and plenteous in mercy and truth. You are a God who pardons sin. You are merciful, slow to anger, and of great kindness. You do not always reprimand, and you do not harbour resentment against sin forever. You blot out our transgressions for your own sake, and never remember our sins again. *Psa.* 86:5, 15; *Neh.* 9:17; *Psa.* 103:9; *Isa.* 43:25.

Lord, let your great power bring about the full salvation of your people. Show yourself to be slow to anger and of great mercy, forgiving sin and rebellion. Pardon the iniquity of your people once more according to the greatness of your covenant love, even as you have done from the first day of our salvation until now. For who is a God like you, pardoning iniquity and overlooking the transgression of the remnant of your people. You do not retain your anger forever, for you delight in showing mercy. Have compassion on us, tread our sins under foot, and hurl all our iniquities into the depths of the sea. *Num.* 14:16-19; *Mic.* 7:18, 19.

2. Be greatly encouraged as you consider the merit and righteousness of the Lord Jesus Christ. Rely completely on the virtues of his life and death as the basis of your right-standing before God despite your sinfulness.

We know that you are gracious and merciful. But you are also a righteous God who will by no means clear anyone who remains with his guilt. It would be utterly foolish for us to say, Have patience with us and we will repay you all we owe for the damage we have done by our sin. For we are all as an unclean thing, and all our righteousnesses are as filthy rags in your sight. *Psa.* 11:7; *Exod.* 34:7; *Matt.* 18:26; *Isa.* 64:6.

But let Jesus Christ be our righteousness, holiness, and redemption according to your own provision for sinners. Let us be the objects of your redeeming love. Let us become the righteousness of God in him. For though he never sinned, he has been made sin for us. Despite our sin, let Jesus Christ the righteous one be our advocate with you. Let his atoning sacrifice for our sins remove your wrath against us. Let his death in the place of sinners serve as the atoning sacrifice not only for our sins, but for the sins of people from all across the whole world. *1 Cor.* 1:30; *2 Cor.* 5:21; *1 John* 2:1, 2.

You are the only one who can declare us righteous despite our sin. For the atoning blood of Christ perpetually speaks better things than the condemning blood of Abel. Who then is left to condemn us? Christ Jesus has died for us, and has been confirmed as God's Holy One by his resurrection from the dead, for he could not experience corruption. He is now seated at God's right hand where he makes continual intercession for us. *Rom.* 8:33, 34; *Acts* 2:27, 31, 32; *Heb.* 12:24.

We count every bit of merit that some people might reckon as righteousness to be loss, that we might gain Christ. We regard any goodness in us as dung. So let us possess Christ, and be found in him not having any righteousness of our own, but only the righteousness that comes through faith in him. This is the name by which he will be identified: 'The Lord Our Righteousness.' Let the Lord Christ be our righteousness. Lord, we believe in him. Free us from any unbelief that remains. *Phil.* 3:7-9; *Jer.* 23:6; *Mark* 9:24.

Lord, remember David and all his troubles. Remember David's greater Son and the offering he made of himself for our sins. Accept his burnt sacrifice, and do not turn not away the face of your anointed, for by his own blood he has entered into heaven itself and now appears in your presence for us. Did not you yourself set forth your son Jesus Christ to be an offering to appease your wrath against sin through faith in his blood? Has not his sacrifice served to declare at this time your right-eousness for the remission of sins, so that you may be just as well as the justifier of the one who be-lieves in Jesus? By faith in him we now receive his atonement for our sins. *Psa.* 132:19; 20:3; *Heb.* 9:24; *Rom.* 3:25, 26; 5:11.

3. Plead before the Lord the promises he himself has made to pardon all those who truly repent and believe his gospel.

Is not this the word which you have spoken, that if the wicked forsakes his way and the unrighteous man his thoughts, you will have mercy on him? Have you not promised that if the covenant-breaker returns to the Lord his God, you will abundantly pardon? Is it not true that mercy and forgiveness belong to you our Covenant LORD, even though we have rebelled against you? *Isa.* 55:7; *Dan.* 9:8.

Is not this the covenant which you made with all those who belong to your chosen people, that you will take away their sins, forgive their iniquity, and remember their transgression no more? Have you not declared that a thorough search shall be made for the sin of God's Israel, and none shall be found? Have you not stated that Judah's iniquity shall be sought for, and none shall be found? *Rom.* 11:27; *Jer.* 50:20.

Have you not promised that if the wicked turns from his sins and keeps your commandments, he shall live and not die? Have you not declared that none of his transgressions will ever be remembered against him? Have you not stated that you take no pleasure in the death of the wicked? Have you not commanded that repentance and remission of sins should be preached in Christ's name to all the nations? *Ezek.* 18:21, 22; *Luke* 24:47.

Did you not promise that when all the wickedness and rebellion of Israel had been transferred to the head of the scapegoat, the sin along with the goat would be banished into the wilderness, into a land with no inhabitant to testify against their sin? Have you not declared that as far as the east is from the west, so far will you remove our transgressions from us? *Lev.* 16:22, 33; *Psa.* 103:12.

Graciously recall these words you have spoken to your servants, for on these promises you have caused us to have great hope. *Psa.* 119:49.

4. Rejoice in the blessedness of those whose sins are forgiven.

How blessed we are that our transgression is forgiven and our sin is covered. What a joy it is to know that the Lord no longer reckons us to be guilty. What a relief that we never need to conceal our sin. How happy we are because of the immeasurable blessing of redemption through Christ's blood, which includes the full forgiveness of all our sins according to the riches of your grace. We stand amazed at the abundance of your wisdom in the way you have provided salvation for us. We revel in the peace we have with you, our God, and the freedom from all condemnation since we are in Christ Jesus. *Psa.* 32:1, 2; *Eph.* 1:7, 8; *Rom.* 5:1; 8:1.

How wonderful it is for us to have the blessing of assurance that our sins, which are many, have been forgiven, so that we may go from your presence in peace. As inhabitants of the heavenly Mt Zion, we rejoice in our freedom from many ills, since our sins have been forgiven. *Luke* 7:47, 50; *Heb.* 12:22; *Isa.* 33:24.

MAY GOD BE FULLY RECONCILED TO YOU SO THAT YOU CAN RECEIVE HIS FAVOUR, HIS BLESSING, AND HIS GRACIOUS ACCEPTANCE

1. May God be at peace with you so that his anger is totally turned away from you.

Since we have been declared righteous by faith, let us rejoice that we have peace with you through our Lord Jesus Christ. Through him let us enjoy constant access into that grace by which believers stand. Let us rejoice in the hope of enjoying your great glory. Let us who previously were far off from you be made near by the blood of Christ. Let him be our peace, who has broken down the dividing wall of hostility that existed between your ancient people the Jews and people from other nations. Let us both be reconciled to you by the cross of Christ, so that all animosity can be abolished and permanent peace established. Through him let us who have been strangers and foreigners become fellow citizens with the saints and members of your household. *Rom.* 5:1, 2; *Eph.* 2:13-16, 19.

Do not terrorize us, for you are our only hope in the evil day. Who would set up briars and thorns as a defence against you in battle? You would consume them with fire. You have encouraged us to take refuge in you, that we may be at peace. You have offered to make peace. Let us therefore submit ourselves to you and be at peace, that we may experience your blessing. Heal us, and we shall be healed. Save us, and we shall be saved. You are the one we praise. Do not be angry with us forever, but revive us again that your people may rejoice in you. Show us your mercy, O Lord, and grant us your salvation. *Jer.* 17:17; *Isa.* 27:4, 5; *Job* 22:21; *Jer.* 17:14; *Psa.* 85:5, 6.

2. May you be sealed in covenant with God, so that you will have a permanently binding relationship to him.

Lord, cause us to pass under the rod, and bring us into the bond of covenant. Give us your solemn covenantal oath, that we may become your people. Make an everlasting covenant with us, even the sure mercies of David. We bind ourselves to you in an everlasting covenant, and hold fast that covenant. Be to us as God, and take us as your people. Make us a people willing to serve you in the day of your power. *Ezek.* 20:37; 16:8; *Isa.* 55:3; *Jer.* 50:5; *Isa.* 56:4; *Heb.* 8:10; *Psa.* 110:3.

3. May you continue to have God's favour as the object of his special love.

O our Lord, we plead for your ongoing favour with our whole hearts. Be merciful to us according to your word, for in your favour is life. O God, it's true! Your covenant love is better than life itself! Let your face radiate acceptance toward us and be gracious to us. Let your smiling face bless us and give us peace. Remember us with the constant favour you show those who are your people. Enrich every part of our lives that we may witness for ourselves the good that comes to your chosen ones. Let us rejoice in the blessings of your nation, and enjoy the prosperity of your inheritance. *Psa.* 119:58; 30:5; 63:3; *Num.* 6:25, 26; *Psa.* 106:4, 5.

4. May you always have God's blessing on your life.

O God, be merciful to us, bless us, and cause your face to shine on us. Pronounce your blessing over us. May the Lord who made heaven and earth bless us from his throne in the heavenly Mount Zion. May he bless us with all spiritual blessings as heavenly realities come to earth through Christ Jesus. *Psa.* 67:1, 6; 134:3; *Eph.* 1:3.

What is life if you do not bless us! Command the ultimate blessing for us, which is life for evermore.

For whatever you bless will surely be blessed. Let us receive that special blessing from the Lord which is righteousness from you, the God of our salvation. Let the blessing of Abraham descend on us, which through faith comes on people from all nations. Let us also have the blessing of Jacob, for we will not let you go until you bless us. *1 Chron.* 4:10; *Psa.* 133:3; *1 Chron.* 17:27; *Psa.* 27:5; *Gal.* 3:14; *Gen.* 32:26.

5. May the presence of God always be with you.

If your presence will not go with us, do not move us one step from where we are. Never, never, never, never, never leave us or forsake us. Do not expel us from your presence. Never take your Holy Spirit from us. Let us live out our whole lives in your presence along with all those who are upright. *Exod.* 33:15; *Heb.* 13:5; *Psa.* 51:11; 140:13.

6. May you have a comforting sense of your reconciliation to God and your acceptance by him.

(i) May he graciously allow you to have some clear evidence that all your sins are pardoned and you have been adopted as his son.

Allow us to experience joy and gladness so that the bones you have crushed because of our sin may rejoice. Say to each one of us, Son, daughter, celebrate! Your sins are all forgiven! *Psa.* 51:8; *Matt.* 9:2.

Let the blood of Christ, who through the eternal Spirit offered himself without spot to God, cleanse our conscience from deeds of death, so we can offer acceptable service to you, the living God. Let your Spirit bear constant witness to our spirit that we are your children. Assure us that we are your heirs, heirs of God and co-heirs with Christ. Speak reassuringly to our spirits, affirming that you are our salvation. *Heb.* 9:14; *Rom.* 8: 16, 17; *Psa.* 35:3.

(ii) May God bless you with a well-grounded peace of conscience. May he give you a peace of mind arising from your justification, and a sense of the good work he has done in you.

May the Lord of peace himself give us peace, all peace, all the time, by all means. May he give us the peace which Jesus has left us, which he himself gives to us. Put in us the peace that the world can neither give nor take away, the peace of Christ that calms our hearts so that they are neither troubled nor afraid. *2 Thess.* 3:16; *John* 14:27.

Let the work of righteousness in our souls produce peace, and the effect of righteousness be quietness and assurance forever. Speak peace to your people, to all those who are your holy ones. Let us never turn back to the folly of sin that shatters all peace. *Isa.* 32:17; *Psa.* 85:8.

Bless our lips with the fruit that brings peace, peace to those that are far off and to those that are near. Provide comfort to those who mourn. Where the sons of peace are, let our peace find them out and rest on them. Let us hear of your covenant love in the morning. Let us taste that you are gracious, for we trust in you. *Isa.* 57:18, 19; *Luke* 10:6; *Psa.* 143:8; *1 Pet.* 2:3.

Let the peace of God, which passes all understanding, guard our hearts and minds in Christ Jesus. Let the peace of Christ rule in our hearts, since as one body we have been called to peace. May the God of hope fill us with all joy and peace in believing, that we may abound in hope through the power of the Holy Spirit. *Phil.* 4:7; *Col.* 3:15; *Rom.* 15:13.

3

Petition

Petition

PRAY EARNESTLY FOR THE MANY THINGS YOU CONSTANTLY NEED FROM GOD'S GRACIOUS HAND

In all our prayers for the good things we need from God, we must come boldly to his throne that we may obtain a rich supply of grace to help us in every time of need. Gracious God, let us receive the full measure of the grace that is in Jesus Christ, the one in whom you were pleased that all fullness should dwell. From his abundance let us receive grace on top of grace that will prove to be more than enough for every situation we face in life. Heb. 4:16; Col. 1:19; John 1:16

Plead the Promises of God as the Supporting Foundation of All Your Petitions

Lay open the Lord's own promises before him, and put your entire trust in the faithfulness of the God who has given them.

Lord, you have given us many exceedingly great and precious promises. They are all confirmed as 'Yes' and 'Amen' in Jesus Christ. Now let it happen to your servants exactly according to the word you have spoken. *2 Pet.* 1:4; *2 Cor.* 1:20; *Luke* 1:38.

Let us draw water with joy from your wells of salvation. Let us suck and be satisfied from the breasts of your consolation. Let us drink deeply with delight from your overflowing abundance. Let the word you have spoken regarding your servants be established forever. Do exactly as you have promised. Deal with us according to the terms of the everlasting covenant, which is orderly in all its provisions and fully confirmed. In the bonds of this covenant let us find everything we need for our salvation, and all we could ever desire in life. *Isa.* 12:3; 66:11; *2 Sam.* 7:25; 23:5.

Look graciously on us and be merciful to us as you always do to those who love your name. Supply all our needs according to your riches in glory by Christ Jesus. Do all you have promised in redeeming us, which will prove to be exceeding abundantly above all we can ask or think. *Psa.* 119:132; *Phil.* 4:19; *Eph.* 3:20.

Ask the Lord to Give You Grace to Resist Every Evil Thought, Word and Deed

Lord, you have removed sin's guilt from us so that we will not die for it as a crime. Now break sin's power in us so we do not die from it as a disease. Help us put sin to death. *Rom.* 8:13.

By your abundant grace, keep us from allowing sin to dominate us. For we are not restricted to our own resources as dictated by the strictures of the law in our struggle against sin. Instead, let us live every moment of the day with the full resources of your grace. Help us crucify the flesh with its insatiable desires and lusts. Empower us to walk in the Spirit, so we will no longer live under the compulsion to fulfil the lusts of the flesh. *Rom.* 6:14; *Gal.* 5:16, 24.

Let our old self be crucified with Christ, that the body of sin may be destroyed. Let us no longer be enslaved to sin. Let not sin reign in our dying bodies that we should obey its lusts. As we are being made free from sin, let us become the servants of righteousness. Give us grace to put off the old man which is corrupted by its many deceitful lusts. Enable us to put on the new man which is being re-created after your image in righteousness and true holiness. *Rom.* 6:6, 12, 13; *Eph.* 4:22, 24.

Let the law of the Spirit of life in Christ Jesus set us free from the law of sin and death. Let us boast only about the cross of Christ, by which the world is crucified to us, and we are crucified to the world. Considering our weakness in the flesh, do not lead us into temptation, but deliver us from the evil one. Keep us from supposing that our temptation is something extraordinary which makes it impossible for us to overcome. Reassure us that however severe our testing may seem to us, you will allow only the kind of testing that is the common experience of mankind. Never allow us to be tempted or tried beyond what we are able to endure. As our faithful God, always provide a way of escape for us. *Rom.* 8:2; *Gal.* 6:14; *Matt.* 6:13; 26:41; *1 Cor.* 10:13.

Help us put on the whole armour of God so we can stand against the schemes of the devil. Enable us to stand firm in the day when evil manifests its greatest power. After we have done everything we can to be prepared for the conflict with sin and evil in this world, help us to keep standing strong. Let our waists be girded firmly with the belt of truth. Help us put on the breastplate of righteousness. As shoes for our feet, let us have the readiness to move forward with the gospel news that brings peace. Enable us to take up the shield of faith, by which we can extinguish all the flaming arrows unleashed against us by the wicked one. Let our heads be guarded by the helmet of salvation, and let the sword of the Spirit, which is the word of God, be always ready for combat. Help us resist the devil, so he will flee from us. Let us stand against him with firmness of faith. May you, the God of peace, crush Satan under our feet, and do it soon. *Eph.* 6:11-17; *James* 4:7; *1 Pet.* 5:9; *Rom.* 16:20.

Pray That the Work of Grace Will Be Perfected in You
Pray for Grace to Equip You for Every Good Thought, Word, and Work

Do not ask only that you be kept from sinning. Ask as well that you become all that you ought to be, and do all that you ought to do. Let Christ be in you as your wisdom, sanctification, righteousness and redemption. Ask him to empower you to die to sin and be buried with Christ in his death, so you may walk in newness of life just as he was raised from death by the glory of the Father. 1 Cor. 1:30; Rom. 6:2, 4.

Fulfil in us all your good pleasure. Carry forward the work of faith by your divine power. Since you have begun a good work in us, perform it until the day of Jesus Christ. Gracious Lord, perfect everything that concerns our salvation. Your mercy endures forever. Do not forsake the work of your own hands. *2 Thess. 1:11; Phil. 1:6; Psa. 138:8.*

Let your grace prove to be altogether sufficient for us. Let your strength be made perfect in our weakness. Where we are weak, may we be strong in the Lord and in his mighty power. *2 Cor. 12:9, 10; Eph. 6:10.*

Pray for the <u>Particular Grace</u> That You Need in All the Different Areas of Your Life

1. Let your grace <u>make us intelligent in the things of</u> God.

O Lord, make our hearts cry out to know you, the one true living God. Give us a proper understanding of your ways. Let us seek your divine wisdom as for silver, and search for it as though it were hid treasure. Let us come to a full understanding of what it means to fear you, and discover the depths of knowing you. Let us all know you, from the least to the greatest. Let us know you personally, the only true God, and Jesus Christ whom you have sent, for this knowledge alone can give us eternal life. *Prov.* 2:3-5; *Heb.* 8:11; *Hos.* 6:3; *John* 17:3.

Give us a spirit of wisdom and revelation through the knowledge of Christ. Let the eyes of our understanding be enlightened. May we know the hope of our calling, and the riches of our glorious inheritance among the saints. May we experience the superabounding greatness of your power in us who believe, according to the working of your overpowering strength. *Eph.* 1:17-19.

INDIGNATION

Open our eyes that we may see the wonderful things of your law as well as your gospel. Let us know the certainty of the things we have been taught. Let our knowledge increase so that we possess all the richness of a full assurance of understanding. Enable us to have a full knowledge of the mystery of your will which you have purposed in Christ your Son. *Psa.* 119:18; *Luke* 1:4; *Eph.* 1:9.

Deal with your servants according to your mercy, and teach us your commandments. We are your servants. Give us understanding that we may grasp the full meaning of your statutes. Hear our cry as it comes before you, O Lord. Give us understanding in accordance with your word. Let us have the good understanding which is reserved only for those who do what you command. May your praise endure forever. *Psa.* 119:124, 125, 169; 111:10.

2. Let your grace lead us into all truth.

Let the Spirit of truth guide us into all truth. Show us where we are in error. Make plain to us what we do not understand. Enable us to test every word and work, and to hold to our commitment to everything good. *John* 16:13; *Job* 6:24; 34:32; *1 Thess.* 5:21.

Instruct us so we will not be like children who are tossed back and forth, blown about by every wind of doctrine propounded by clever men. Let us mature in Christ in all things as we learn to speak the truth in love. Let Christ be as the head of the body to us. *Eph.* 4:14, 15.

Give us everything we need to understand your will so we can know whether a teaching is really from you. Make us free by your truth. Strengthen us so we can uphold the standard of wholesome words that we have heard. Let us maintain the truth with the faith and love that is in Christ Jesus. Help us to keep on holding firmly to the things we have learned and confidently believed, knowing the person from whom we have learned them. *John* 7:17; 8:32, 36; *2 Tim.* 1:13; 3:14.

3. Help our memories, so the truth of God will be immediately accessible to us.

Let your Spirit teach us all things, and bring everything you have said to our remembrance. Let the word of Christ dwell richly in us in all wisdom and spiritual understanding. *John* 14:26; *Col.* 3:16.

In view of the constant danger of gradually slipping away from the truth, help us focus our attention on the things we have heard from the Lord and from those who heard him. Keep us from letting go of what has been preached to us. Let us retain these truths utmost in our memory, so that we will not prove to have believed in vain. *Heb.* 2:1; *1 Cor.* 15:1, 2.

Make us mighty in the Scriptures so that we may be complete, thoroughly equipped for every good work. After being well instructed in the kingdom of heaven, let us bring out new and old treasures from the riches of our storeroom as the wise manager of an estate. *Acts* 18:24; *2 Tim.* 3:17; *Matt.* 13:52.

4. Educate our consciences, show us our duty, and make us wise and judicious Christians.

Above all other blessings in this life, give us a wise and understanding heart that we may know how to discharge our duties as your servants. Endow us with wisdom that is profitable to direct our way in all the varying circumstances of life. Give us discernment that will enable us to clearly understand the way we should go. *1 Kings* 3:9; *Prov.* 14:8.

Let our love abound more and more in knowledge and good judgment. Enable us to make wise decisions when we have difficult choices to make. Let us give our approval only to the best of options. Help us to be pure and blameless until the day of Christ. Let us abound with the fruits of righteousness which come through Jesus Christ, to the glory and praise of God. *Phil.* 1:9-11.

Fill us with the knowledge of your will in all wisdom and spiritual understanding, that we may walk worthy of you, our God, and please you in every way. Let us be fruitful in every good work, constantly increasing in the knowledge of God. Teach us your way, O God, and lead us in a straight path because of people who are constantly watching us with a critical eye. *Col.* 1:9, 10; *Psa.* 27:11.

Covenant LORD, the perplexities of life are so great that we do not know what to do. But our eyes are on you. Let us hear your voice behind us saying, 'This is the way, walk in it.' May we not turn away from your path either to the right hand or to the left. Order our steps by your word, and let no iniquity have dominion over us. *2 Chron.* 20:12; *Isa.* 30:21; *Psa.* 119:133.

5. Sanctify our nature, and implant in our inmost being all the principles and graces necessary for living a God-glorifying life.

May God himself, the God of peace, sanctify us in every part of our life. May he preserve our whole spirit, soul, and body as blameless until the coming of our Lord Jesus Christ. For he who calls us is faithful, and he will do it. *1 Thess.* 5:23, 24.

Create in us a clean heart, O God, and renew a right spirit within us. Cast us not away from your presence, and do not take your Holy Spirit from us. Restore the joy of your salvation to us, and put in us a generous spirit. *Psa.* 51:10-12.

Write your law on our hearts. Inscribe it in our inward being, that we may appear to everyone as letters sent from Christ, written by the Spirit of the living God. Let our hearts be tender, fleshly tablets rather than hardened tablets of stone, that your law may be engraved on them. Do not let our steps slide. Let our chief happiness come from doing your will. Let us delight in your law in our inmost being. *Heb.* 8:10; *2 Cor.* 3:3; *Psa.* 37:31; 40:8; *Rom.* 7:22.

Help us practise from the heart the principles you have taught us. Let our whole soul be moulded by your law, our whole being permeated by it. Let us never be conformed to this world, but transformed by the renewing of our mind. Let us no longer fashion ourselves after our former lusts in our ignorance, but as obedient children let us be consecrated to you in our entire lifestyle, just as you, the one who has called us, are set apart as holy. *Rom.* 6:17; *Matt.* 13:33; *Rom.* 12:2; *1 Pet.* 1:14, 15.

(i) Pray for faith.

Give us the grace to believe, for the faith that saves does not come from ourselves, but only as your gift. Lord, increase our faith. Perfect what is lacking in it, that we may be strong in faith, giving you the glory. *Phil.* 1:29; *Eph.* 2:8; *Luke* 17:5; *1 Thess.* 3:10; *Rom.* 4:20.

Let us be daily crucified with Christ, so that the life we live in the flesh will be by faith in the Son of

God who loved us and gave himself up to be crucified for us. As we continually bear in our bodies the
dying of the Lord Jesus, let his life also be manifested in us. *Gal.* 2:20; *2 Cor.* 4:10.

As we have received Christ Jesus the Lord by
faith, let us walk in him with the same faith. Let
us be rooted and built up in him, established in
the faith as we have been taught, abounding with
thanksgiving. Let every word of yours profit us as
it is mixed with faith. By our faith let us receive the
testimony of Jesus, and then offer our own testimony
that you, our God, are always true. Work in us that
faith which makes substance out of things hoped for,
and provides confirmation for things not seen. Let
us look beyond visible things that are temporal and
focus on invisible things that are eternal. *Col.* 2:6, 7;
Heb. 4:2; *John* 3:33; *Heb.* 11:1; *2 Cor.* 4:18.

Enable us by our faith to always perceive you
as being immediately in our presence. Let us have
our eyes directed toward you, that in everything we
may act as though we see you, the one who forever
remains invisible to the human eye. Instead of focusing on the dangers of this life, let us set our attention
on your reward for those who continue to trust in
you. *Psa.* 16:8; 25:15; *Heb.* 11:26, 27.

Let our hearts be purified by faith. Let our faith
be the victory that overcomes the world. Keep us
from fainting as we continue to believe that we

shall see the goodness of the Lord in the land of the living. *Acts* 15:9; *1 John* 5:4; *Psa.* 27:13.

(ii) Pray for the fear of God.

Lord, work in us that fear of you which is the beginning of wisdom. Let us be instructed by this wisdom, which is the fountain of life even as it teaches us to depart from the snares of death. *Prov.* 1:7; 15:33; 14:27.

Give us an undivided heart that we may fear your name and keep your commandments, which is the whole duty of man. Put your fear in our hearts, that we may never depart from you. Let us be zealous for your fear. Let us live in the fear of the Lord every day, and all day long. *Psa.* 86:11; *Eccles.* 12:13; *Jer.* 32:40; *Psa.* 119:38; *Prov.* 23:17.

(iii) Pray that love for God may be rooted in you and love for the world rooted out of you.

Give us grace to love you, the Lord our God, with all our heart and soul and mind and strength, which is the first and greatest commandment. Let us set our love on you, and delight ourselves always in you. For you have promised that then we shall have the desire of our hearts. *Matt.* 22:37, 38; *Psa.* 91:14; 37:4.

Circumcise our hearts to love you, the Lord our God, with all our heart and soul, that we may live.

Let your love be poured out into our hearts by the Holy Spirit. Let Jesus Christ be precious to us, as he is to all that believe. Though we have never seen him, yet let us love him. Though we do not now see him, yet believing let us rejoice with an inexpress-ible and glory-filled joy. *Deut.* 30:6; *Rom.* 5:5; *1 Pet.* 2:7; 1:8.

Let Christ's love constrain us to live no longer for ourselves, but for him who died for us and rose again. Help us not to love the world, or the things in the world, for if any man love the world, the love of the Father cannot be in him. Let our desire focus on things above, where Christ is seated at the right hand of the Father, and not on earthly things. *2 Cor.* 5:14, 15; *1 John* 2:15; *Col.* 3:1, 2.

(iv) Pray that your conscience may be always tender, and that you may live a life of repentance.

Lord, take the stony heart out of us, and give us a sensitive heart of flesh. Help us stay away from all different kinds of evil. Let us beware of being outwitted by Satan, for we are not ignorant of his schemes. Give us the happiness of those who always revere you rather than hardening our hearts. When we think we stand, let us be fully aware of the danger of falling. *Ezek.* 11:19; *1 Thess.* 5:22; *2 Cor.* 2:11; *Prov.* 28:14; *1 Cor.* 10:12.

(v) Pray that God will work compassion and broth-erly love in you.

Lord, put in us the love toward one another that perfects our unity. Enable us to keep the oneness of the Spirit in the bond of peace. Let us live in love and peace, that you, the God of love and peace, may be with us. Give us the grace to love our neigh-bour as ourselves, with that love which fulfils all the requirements of the law. Let us love one another with a pure heart fervently, that all men may know that we are Christ's disciples. *Col.* 3:14; *Eph.* 4:3; *2 Cor.* 13:11; *Rom.* 13:9, 10; *1 Pet.* 1:22; *John* 13:35.

As you have taught us to love one another, let us abound in love more and more. As we have opportunity, let us do good to all men. As much as it is possible for us, let us live in peace with every-one. Help us to follow after the things that make for peace, and that edify one another. *1 Thess.* 4:9, 10; *Gal.* 6:10; *Rom.* 12:18; 14:19.

Make us able to love our enemies, to bless those that curse us, and to pray for those that persecute us. Help us do good to those that hate us. Let us bear patiently with one another and forgive one another in love, even as Christ forgave us. *Luke* 6:27, 28; *Matt.* 5:44; *Col.* 3:13.

(vi) Pray for the grace of self-denial.

Give us grace to deny ourselves, to take up our cross daily and to follow Christ. Let us maintain constant restraint over the desires of the body, and bring it into subjection. Keep us from being lovers of our own selves, from being wise in our own eyes, and from leaning on our own understanding. *Luke* 9:23; *1 Cor.* 9:27; *2 Tim.* 3:2; *Prov.* 3:5, 7.

Keep us from always seeking our own advantage. Instead, let each of us focus on his brother's welfare. Let none of us live for ourselves, or even die for ourselves. Whether we live or die, let us be the Lord's, so that we live and die for him. *1 Cor.* 10:24; *Rom.* 14:7, 8.

(vii) Pray for humility and meekness.

Enable us to learn from Christ how to be meek and lowly in heart, that we may find rest for our souls. Let the same attitude be in us that was in Christ Jesus, who humbled himself even though he was in his very essence God. Eliminate our pride, and enable us to clothe ourselves with humility. Put on us the unfading adornment of a gentle and quiet spirit, which is priceless in your sight. Give us grace to walk in a manner that is worthy of the calling to which we have been called, with all humility and meekness. Let us manifest patience and consideration toward one another in love. *Matt.* 11:29; *Phil.* 2:5, 6; *Job* 33:17; *1 Pet.* 5:5; 3:4; *Eph.* 4:1, 2.

Let anger never simmer in our hearts. Keep us from allowing the sun to go down while we still have a wrathful spirit toward anyone. Enable us to show complete humility toward all men, since we ourselves have been foolish and disobedient many, many times. *Eccles.* 7:9; *Eph.* 4:26; *Titus* 3:2, 3.

As the undeserving elect of God, consecrated and loved by you, let us be endowed with hearts overflowing with compassion, kindness, humility of mind, gentleness, and patience. Let us be merciful as you, our heavenly Father, are merciful, that we may be perfect as you are perfect. *Col.* 3:12; *Luke* 6:36; *Matt.* 5:48.

(viii) Pray for the graces of contentment, patience, and a selfless indifference to all the things of sense and time.

Teach us to be content whatever may be our outward condition in life. Let us know how to handle being in need and in abundance. In any and all circumstances, teach us the secret of how to be full and to be hungry, how to have plenty and to have serious need. Let a God-centred life with contentment be great gain to us. Let a little with the fear of the Lord, quietness with contentment mean more to us than possessing great treasure which normally brings trouble with it. By patient endurance in trials, let us retain control of our own souls. Let patience do its perfecting work, that we may be mature and complete, lacking nothing. *Phil.* 4:11, 12; *1 Tim.* 6:6; *Prov.* 15:16-18; *Luke* 21:19; *James* 1:4.

Let our whole way of life be unmarred by a constant desire for more than we have. Show us how to be content with the things we have, since we always possess you, the one who has promised, 'I will never, ever leave you or forsake you.' Whatever may be ahead of us in life, let us say, 'The will of the Lord be done.' *Heb.* 13:5; *Acts* 21:14.

In view of the shortness of time, give us grace to weep as though we were not even weeping, and to rejoice as though we were not rejoicing. If we buy anything, let us not think of it as our personal possession. Let us make good use of this world though not abusing our privileges, for the time is short, and the current world order is passing away. *1 Cor.* 7:29-31.

(ix) Pray for the grace of a hope focused on God and Christ that anticipates eternal life.

Let us know the reality of being born again into a living hope by the resurrection of Jesus Christ from the dead. Let that hope be secured and firmly settled for us. Let it be anchored in the Holy of Holies on the other side of the curtain, where Christ our forerunner has entered for us. *1 Pet.* 1:3; *Heb.* 6:19, 20.

Let patient endurance produce character in us, and let character produce hope, a hope that will never disappoint us. Through perseverance and the encouragement that comes from the Scriptures, let us have hope. In this hope let us be saved. *Rom.* 5:4, 5; 15:4; 8:24.

Let the God of Jacob be our help, and let our hope always be in the Covenant Lord our God. Let Christ in us be our hope of glory. Let us never be distracted from our hope in the gospel. Enable us to be diligent so we can enjoy the full assurance of hope until the consummation of all things. *Psa.* 146:5; *Col.* 1:23, 27; *Heb.* 6:11.

(x) Pray for grace to preserve you from sin, and from all approaches you may be tempted to make toward it.

Restrain us from doing anything wrong. Let us never give a basis for accusation against us by others. Enable us to live without fault, as the children of God in the midst of a crooked and perverse generation, so that we may appear as lights shining in a dark world. *2 Cor.* 13:7; *Phil.* 2:15.

Turn away our eyes from contemplating any vain thought. Enliven us as we walk in your way. Remove from us every impulse to lie, and give us grace to live according to your law. Keep our hearts from being inclined to anything evil. Help us to avoid works of wickedness with those that make a practice of doing wrong. Let us not be tempted to taste their delicacies. *Psa.* 119:37, 29; 141:4.

Cleanse us from our secret sins. Restrain your servant from presumptuous pride. Keep sin from ruling over us. Let us live upright lives so we can be free from sins of great magnitude. Let us prove that we have moral integrity by restraining ourselves from potential evildoing. *Psa.* 19:12, 13; 18:23.

Help us to hide your word in our hearts, so that we will not sin against you. Let your grace be always sufficient for us, constantly with us, and mighty in us. Never give us up to our own heart's lust, that we should walk according to our own devisings. *Psa.* 119:11; *2 Cor.* 12:9; *Psa.* 81:12.

Keep us from walking without cautious analysis of what we are doing. Let us not live as naïve fools, but as people of wisdom, having sharp discernment. Let us minimize occasions for people who are looking for opportunities to blaspheme the worthy name of the Christ. By constantly doing good, let us put to silence the ignorant talk of foolish men. Let us make the doctrine of God our Saviour as attractive as possible in all things. *Eph.* 5:15; *2 Cor.* 11:12; *James* 3:10; *1 Pet.* 2:15; *Titus* 2:10.

(xi) Pray for grace that will enable you to govern your tongue, and to use it well.

Lord, enable us to be very careful about everything we say, so that we do not offend either you or men with our tongue. Help us to restrain our mouth as with a horse's bridle, that we may not be too quick to utter whatever comes into our head. Set a watchman right in front of our mouth, guard the door of our lips, so that we do not sin with our words. *Psa.* 39:1; *Eccles* 5:2; *James* 3:2, 3; *Psa.* 141:3; *James* 3:2; *Eccles.* 5:6.

Enable us to always open our mouth with wisdom. Let the law of kindness be under our tongue. Let us know what is acceptable in your hearing for us to say, that our tongue may be as choice silver, and our lips may feed many. *Prov.* 31:26; 10:32; 10:20, 21.

Let our speech be always full of grace, seasoned with salt, that we may always bring forth good things out of the good treasure of our heart. Let our mouth speak wisdom, and our tongue declare sound judgment. Let the truth of your words never depart out of our mouth, or out of the mouth of our children, or our children's children, from this point on and forever after. *Col.* 4:6; *Matt.* 12:35; *Psa.* 37:30; *Isa.* 59:21.

Pray That in All Your Duties God Will Direct You, Enliven You, Strengthen and Assist You

Let your saving grace which has appeared to all men keep training us to renounce all godless living and the lusts of this present world-order. Let your grace instruct us how to live self-controlled, upright, and godlike lives in this present world. May this same grace teach us to eagerly wait for the blessed hope and the glorious manifestation of the great God and our Saviour Jesus Christ. Let this grace transform us, for Christ gave himself up for us that he might redeem us from all iniquity. Let your grace purify us as a people for your own possession, and make us zealous in our performance of good works. *Titus* 2:11-14.

1. May God make you wise so you can fulfil all your duties.

You have promised that if any man lacks adequate wisdom for the task before him, he must ask God who gives generously to all people, and wisdom shall be given him. Lord, we freely admit that we lack wisdom. Make us wise as serpents and harmless as doves. Let your wisdom make our face shine. Let your wisdom be better to us than weapons of war. *James* 1:5; *Matt.* 10:16; *Eccles.* 8:1; 9:18.

Enable us to walk in wisdom toward those that live outside the realm of faith. Show us how to make the most of every opportunity, seeing that we live in an evil age. Help us to order all our affairs with discretion, and to behave wisely in every realm of life with complete integrity of heart. *Col.* 4:5; *Psa.* 112:5; 101:2.

2. May you be honest and straightforward in your duty.

Let the wisdom that guides us never originate from the realm below, which is earthly, sensual, and from the devil. Instead, let our wisdom be from the realm above, which is first pure, then peace-loving, gentle, willing to be persuaded by the opinions of others, full of mercy and good fruits, without partiality, and without hypocrisy. Let our way of life in this world be characterized by openness and constant readiness to be exposed to the revealing rays of divine sunlight. Let us not be directed by conniving, worldly wisdom, but by the saving grace of God. *James* 3:15, 17; *2 Cor.* 1:12.

Uphold us in our integrity, and let us live with an awareness that you are always looking on. Let integrity and uprightness preserve us, for we put our trust in you. Let our hearts be found constantly meditating on your commandments, so that we never will be ashamed. Let our eye be healthy, so that our whole body may be full of light. *Psa.* 41:12; 25:21; 119:78, 80; *Matt.* 6:22.

3. May you be diligent in your duty.

Inspire us to work the works of him that sent us while it is day, since the night comes when no man will be able to work. Whatever good our hands find to do, let us do it with all our might. For there is no work in the grave where we are going. Let us never be slothful in any good business of yours. Enable us to be fervent in spirit as we serve you, our Lord. Train us to be fixed in purpose, undeterred, always abounding in the work of the Lord, since we can be confident that our labour will never be in vain in the Lord. *John* 9:4; *Eccles.* 9:10; *Rom.* 12:11; *1 Cor.* 15:58.

Lord, let us be zealous for every good work. Whatever we do, let us do it wholeheartedly, for we are not serving men, but the Lord Christ. Enable us to do the work of every day in its day, just as the duty of the day requires. Help us make full use of every opportunity, since we live in an evil age. When our Lord returns, let him find us busily doing the work he has commissioned us to do. *Gal.* 4:18; *Col.* 3:23; *Ezra* 3:4; *Eph.* 5:16; *Luke* 12:43.

4. May you be courageous in your duty, knowing that though you may be temporarily losers for Christ, you will not be losers by him in the end.

Teach us to endure hardship as good soldiers of Jesus Christ. Keep us from ever cringing at the ridicule of men. Let us never be in the least ashamed of Christ or his words, knowing with certainty the one to whom we have entrusted our future. For he is the very one who is able to keep what we have committed to him in anticipation of that great consummation-day. *2 Tim.* 2:3; *Isa.* 51:7; *Mark* 8:38; *2 Tim.* 1:12

Even if prisons and persecutions should be our constant lot in life, let none of these things detract us from our unswerving commitment to you. Let us not count even life itself a precious possession to be preserved at any cost. Instead, let us focus on finishing our life's course with joy. *Acts* 20:23, 24.

Enable us in all things to seek your approval, so that we can disregard men's honour and dishonour, their evil and their good reports. Let us be protected by the armour of righteousness on the right hand and on the left. Sensitize us so that we always strive to remain in your will. Let us account it a very small thing to be judged by any human court, for you are the one who judges us. *2 Cor.* 6:4, 7, 8; *1 Cor.* 4:3, 4.

5. May you be pleasant and cheerful in your duty.

Lord, enable us to be always joyful. Let us rejoice in the Lord always, for you continually repeat your encouraging word to us, 'Rejoice!' Let us go on our way in the duties of life rejoicing. Let us eat our bread with joy and drink our wine with a merry heart, for you have accepted our works despite their deficiencies. *1 Thess.* 5:16; *Phil.* 4:4; *Acts* 8:39; *Eccles.* 9:7.

Let us have that cheerfulness of heart which does a person good like a proper medicine. Deliver us from that heaviness of spirit which makes the heart stoop, and that sorrow of the world which works death. Give us grace to serve you, the Covenant Lord our God, with joyfulness and gladness of heart as we enjoy the abundance of all things that come from your hand. As kings of the earth give thanks to you, let us continually sing about the ways of the Lord. For great is the glory of our God. *Prov.* 17:22; 12:25; *2 Cor.* 7:10; *Deut.* 28:47; *Psa.* 138:4, 5.

6. May you fulfil every duty required by every situation of life, every event of providence, and every relation in which you stand.

Enable us to enjoy the goodness of a good day, and in a troublesome day to consider what you may be teaching us. Help us understand that you have set the one kind of day over against the other so that we may never presume to know the future. In all our experiences, help us add self-discipline to our understanding, while we wait patiently on you. *Eccles.* 7:14; *2 Pet.* 1:6.

Give us grace to remain contented in the specific calling to which you have called us. In all our ways let us acknowledge your control, trusting that you will continue to direct our steps. Let those who are servants when you call them be your freemen. Let those that are free when called by Christ be Christ's servants. *1 Cor.* 7:24; *Prov.* 3:6; *1 Cor.* 7:21, 22.

In every relationship let us dwell together in unity, that the dew of Mount Hermon, far to the north, may descend on Mount Zion down in the south. In the marriage relationship, let husband and wife live out their lives as heirs together of the grace of life, so that their prayers will never be hindered. *Psa.* 133:1, 3; *1 Pet.* 3:7.

Help us show proper respect to all people. Let us love the brotherhood, fear God and honour the king. Let us be subject to governmental powers, not only because of the threat of wrath in case of rebellion, but also for the sake of our own conscience. *1 Pet.* 2:17; *Rom.* 13:1, 5.

7. May you be made altogether complete in your duty.

Teach us the way laid out for us by your laws, and we shall hold to it to the end. Give us understanding, and we shall keep your commandments. We pledge that we shall observe your law with our whole heart. Make us go in the path of your commandments, for we delight in them. Incline our hearts toward the keeping of your testimonies, rather than to passions inspired by covetousness. *Psa.* 119:33-36.

Inspire us to agonize in our prayers for one another, that we may all come to complete maturity. Let us be brought to our fullness in all the will of God. Let all our ways be directed by your commandments, for we shall never be ashamed if we are careful to keep them all. *Col.* 4:12; *Psa.* 119:5, 6.

Strengthen us with all might by your Spirit in our inner being in accordance with the riches of your glory. Let Christ make his home in our hearts by faith. As we are rooted and grounded in love, make us able to comprehend with all the saints the breadth and length and depth and height of the love of Christ which surpasses human knowledge. Let us be filled with all the fullness found in you as God. Let us live in fellowship with the divine nature, since we have escaped the present world order with its corrupting desires. Let the love of Christ constrain us not to live for ourselves, but for him who died for us and rose again. *Eph.* 3:16-19; *2 Pet.* 1:4; *2 Cor.* 5:14, 15.

Ask the Lord to Enable You To Grow in Grace Every Day

Lord, help us retain a firm hold on Christ our head, by whom the whole body of believers is nourished and knit together through its ligaments and sinews. Sustain us in our spiritual growth. Enable us to grow in grace and in the knowledge of our Lord and Saviour Jesus Christ. Help us hold firmly to your way in righteousness, and grow stronger and stronger with hands that stay clean. Let our path be as the first gleam of morning's light, which shines more and more brightly until the perfect day dawns. *Col.* 2:19; *2 Pet.* 3:18; *Job* 17:9; *Prov.* 4:18.

Be as the refreshing dew of the morning to us, that we may flourish as the lily and send our roots down deeply as the cedar of Lebanon. Let our branches spread out in every direction, and our beauty be as the olive tree. Let the Sun of Righteousness rise and shine on us with healing rays under its wings, that we may go forth every morning as calves leaping from the stall. *Hos.* 14:5, 6; *Mal.* 4:2.

We have not yet attained to the likeness of Christ. We are by no means already perfected. Help us forget past attainments that we may stretch forth and reach out to those things that are ahead of us, which is the prize of the high calling of God in Christ Jesus. *Phil.* 3:12-14.

1. May the Lord give abundant grace when you undergo the crosses and afflictions of this world.

We understand that we are born for trouble just as surely as the sparks of a fire fly upward. But deliver us in six troubles, and in seven let no ultimate evil touch us. As the eternal God, be our refuge. Let your everlasting arms be always underneath us. Do not bring accusations against us forever, or the breath of life you have created in us might faint and fail. *Job* 5:7, 19; *Deut.* 33:27; *Isa.* 57:16.

When we are pressured from every angle, keep us from despair. When we are perplexed, let us not lose hope. When we are sorrowful, let us keep on rejoicing. If we have nothing, help us to remember that in Christ we possess all things. Let us be strengthened with all might according to your glorious power so that we can manifest all patience and longsuffering as we joyfully give thanks to the Father. Let your commandments be the theme of our songs in the house of our pilgrimage. Let your revelations about yourself, which we claim as our permanent possession, always be the reason our hearts can rejoice. *2 Cor.* 4:8; 6:10; *Col.* 1:11, 12; *Psa.* 119:54; *Psa.* 119:111.

2. May God preserve you from the calamities that always threaten your life and your well-being.

Covenant LORD, you are our hiding place and our defence. Under your wings we seek shelter from the storms of life. Your truth is our shield and solid defence against all assaults. Keep us from being afraid of the nighttime terror, or the threatening arrow that flies at us by day. Since the Covenant LORD is our refuge and the Most High our only security, allow no evil to touch us, no plague to come near our home. Make a thick and thorny hedge surround us, our family and all that we possess. Take sickness away from us. Let none of these diseases or plagues touch us. *Psa.* 91:2, 4, 9, 10; *Job* 1:10; *Exod.* 23:25; 15:26.

As the one who preserves your people, be our keeper, for you never slumber or sleep. Be our shade at our right hand, so the sun will not beat down on us by day or the moon by night. Preserve us from all evil. Preserve our souls. Preserve our going out and coming in from this time forth and even forevermore. *Psa.* 121:4-8.

3. May the Lord supply you with the provisions, supports and comforts you need each day, as you receive them with a humble spirit of submission to the will of God.

Lord, you have told us that godliness includes a guarantee for the present life as well as for the life to come. You have promised that if we seek first the kingdom of God and its righteousness, all other things like food, clothing and shelter will be provided for us. So we cast all our care about these things on you, the one who cares for us. For as our heavenly Father you know we need all these things. *1 Tim.* 4:8; *Matt.* 6:33; *1 Pet.* 5:7; *Matt.* 6:32. O Lord, preserve us all along the way as we make our pilgrimage through this world. Give us bread to eat and clothes to wear. Let us finally come to our heavenly Father's house in peace. If you will do these things for us, then we solemnly swear that we will always give you the tithe, and you as our Covenant Lord will always be our God. *Gen.* 28:20-22.

Bless us in the city and bless us in the country. Let our basket and our bowl be blessed. Bless us when we come in, and bless us when we go out. Let your gracious providence order all the events of our life so that they all work together for our good. Fulfil this promise to all those that love you, the ones you have called according to your good purpose. *Deut.* 28:3, 5, 6; *Rom.* 8:28.

Give us the ability to keep trusting you while we are busy doing good. Let our whole lives be lived out in the land you promised us. Satisfy us with the daily feeding that comes from your own hand. Let our righteous lifestyle shine as a brilliant light, and our just dealings as noonday brightness. Protect us from the scourge of the tongue. Let us never fear disaster when it comes near us. Make a solemn covenant for us that includes even the stones of the field. Let the beasts that roam the earth be at peace with us. Let your shalom — your all-embracing peace — surround our tent. When we take stock of our cattle, let us find nothing missing. *Psa.* 37:3, 6; *Job* 5:21, 23, 24.

Let your face as the Lord our God shine with your pleasure on us. Prosper every effort we make to advance your kingdom. Establish the work of our hands so that they count for eternity. Send us your saving favour. Give us success in all we attempt to do for you. *Psa.* 90:17; 118:25.

Let our sons be as healthy, maturing plants throughout their youth. Let our daughters be as cornerstones designed to grace a palace. Let our storehouses be full to the brim with all kinds of provisions. Let no one break into our homes. Let none of your people get dragged into slavery. Let no anxious cry of distress be heard in our streets. How happy are the people that receive these blessings from the Lord. How blessed are the people who have the Covenant LORD as their God. *Psa.* 144:12-15.

Pray for Grace to Persevere to the End

1. May the Lord prepare you for whatever lies before you between this day and the grave.

Lord, deliver us from every evil work. Preserve us until we arrive in your heavenly kingdom. Keep us from stumbling along the way. Continue to sanctify us so you can present us before yourself as totally faultless and with immeasurable joy at your glorious coming. Let the hearts of each of us come to the fullest possible expression of love toward one another and toward all men. Let our inmost being be confirmed as blameless in holiness before you as our Father when our Lord Jesus Christ reappears with all his saints. *2 Tim.* 4:18; *Jude* 24; *1 Thess.* 3:12, 13.

Lord, you have told us that Satan desires to possess all of us so he can sift us as wheat. Let your intercession prevail for each and every one of us so that our faith never fails. Preserve us from the evil one, since the time has not yet come for us to be taken out of this world. Sanctify us through your truth, for your word is truth. *Luke* 22:31, 32; *John* 17:15, 17.

Help us to keep calling on you as long as we live. Until we die, let us never lose our personal integrity. Sustain us so we can hold firmly to our righteous way of life. As long as we live, do not let our own hearts reproach or condemn us. Help us to keep building ourselves up in our most holy faith. Move us so that we pray in the Holy Spirit. Show us how to keep ourselves in your love. Encourage us to look expectantly for the mercy of our Lord Jesus Christ that will eventually bring us into the full experience of eternal life. *Psa.* 116:2; *Job* 27:5, 6; *Jude* 20, 21.

2. May God preserve you in the hour of your death and sustain you through your dying moments.

Merciful Lord, remind us regularly that we have an end. Let us be fully aware of the strict limitation of the days of our life. Let us consider just how frail we are, that our days are no broader than the measurement of a handbreadth stretched from thumb to little finger. Help us fully grasp that every man at his best is nothing more than a breath, and that our days on earth fade away like a fleeting shadow. Teach us to make a careful count of the number of our days that might remain, so we can keep our hearts focused on seeking wisdom. Give us special grace to consider carefully our final end, for there can be no hope of continuing forever in this world. *Psa.* 39:4, 5; *1 Chron.* 29:15; *Psa.* 90:12; *Deut.* 32:29.

Make us fully and properly clothed in preparation for your return. Make us ready to meet you with our lights burning, for the Son of Man will come at a moment that we cannot anticipate. Keep us eagerly waiting all the days of our hard service until our change comes. Then you will call, and we will answer you. *Luke* 12:35, 40; *Job* 14:14, 15.

Bring us to our grave in full strength like the stacking of harvested grain in its season. Satisfy us with life whether it be longer or shorter, and continue to show us your salvation. Stay right next to us when we walk through the shadow-filled valley of death, so that even then we will fear no evil. Let your rod and your shepherd's staff comfort us. Let goodness and mercy follow us all the days of our life, and let us dwell in the house of the Lord forever. May your mercy and your truth stay with us until the end. Redeem our lives from the power of the grave. Take us to yourself. Guide us through this life by your counsel, and afterward take us to glory. *Job* 5:26; *Psa.* 91:16; 23:4, 6; *2 Sam.* 15:20; *Psa.* 49:15; 73:24.

3. May the Lord prepare you for heaven so that in due time you may be a full possessor of eternal life.

Father, we give unending thanks to you for qualifying us to share in the inheritance of the saints who live forever in the brilliance of heavenly light. You have worked transformation in us and given us the binding pledge of your Holy Spirit as the first instalment of our eternal inheritance. Now let our mortality be swallowed up in life. *Col.* 1:12; *2 Cor.* 5:4, 5.

Let the way we live in this world reflect the life of heaven. Let us constantly look for the Saviour, the Lord Jesus Christ, who shall transform our humble bodies that they may take on the form of his glorious body, according to the power of him who is able to subdue all things to himself. *Phil.* 3:20, 21.

Work graciously in us so that we commit ourselves to think constantly about things above, not things on the earth. Let our life be hid with Christ in God. When Christ who is our life is fully revealed, let us be manifest with him in glory. When he appears, let us be made like him, for then we shall see him as he is. Let us gaze on his face in righteousness. When we awake from the sleep of death, let us be satisfied when we take on his likeness. *Col.* 3:2-4; *1 John* 3:2; *Psa.* 17:15.

When this life fails, let us be welcomed into everlasting habitations. How we long for that eternal city that has stable foundations, whose architect and builder is God! Let us comfort one another as we contemplate being together forever with the Lord. For in that day we shall see as we are seen, and know as we are known. *Luke* 16:9; *Heb.* 11:10; *1 Thess.* 4:17; *1 Cor.* 13:12.

In the meantime, help us to comfort ourselves even as we encourage one another with words that remind us of our glorious hope for the future. Since we have this hope, let us purify ourselves even as Christ is pure. May our Lord Jesus Christ himself, and God our Father, who has loved us and given us everlasting consolation and good hope through grace, encourage our hearts and establish us in every good word and work. *1 Thess.* 4:18; *1 John* 3:3; *2 Thess.* 2:16, 17.

4

Thanksgiving

Thanksgiving

☙❧

GIVE THANKS TO GOD FOR THE MERCIES HE HAS SHOWN YOU, AND FOR THE MANY BLESSINGS HE DAILY BRINGS INTO YOUR LIFE

We approach the throne of grace not only to seek God's favour, but to give him the glory due to his name. We give him glory by honouring him for his infinite perfections as the one and only living and true God. We also glorify him by gratefully acknowledging the many manifestations of his goodness to us. He gladly accepts our thanks, and regards himself as glorified by them if they arise from a humble heart aware of its own unworthiness to receive any favour from God. Our thanks must come from the heart, a heart that shows genuine appreciation for his gifts, but always loves the Giver more than the gift.

☙❧

Praise God That You Have So Many Reasons to Thank Him, and for the Encouragements He Has Given You To Offer This Sacrifice of Praise

O Lord, to you we give thanks. Your wondrous works proclaim that you are among us in all your glory. The revelation of your name as the ever-present 'I AM' declares that you are always near. So let us bless the Lord. Let all that is within us bless his holy name. Let our souls bless the Lord and never forget any of his benefits. *Psa.* 75:1; *Exod.* 3:14; *Psa.* 103:1, 2.

We praise you, O Lord, for glorifying you is the most important thing we can do. Praise is pleasant, a beautiful thing for the upright. In every way it is good to give thanks to you, our Covenant LORD, and to sing praises to your name, O Most High God. We will proclaim your covenant love in the morning and your faithfulness every night. We shall exalt you, our God the King. We will bless your name forever and ever. Every day we will bless you. We will constantly pour forth every memory we have of your great goodness, and joyfully sing of your righteousness. *Psa.* 147:1; 92:1, 2; 145:1, 2, 7.

Let us sing to the Lord a new song, and praise him in the assembly of the saints. Let the Israel of God rejoice in the one that made him. Let the children born in Zion be joyful in their King. Let the saints rejoice over God's glory. Let the high praises of God be in their hearts and come forth from their mouths. As long as we live we will bless the Lord. We will sing praise to our God while we have any being. Then when we have no existence on earth, we hope to have a being in heaven that will praise him even better. *Psa.* 149:1, 2, 5, 6; 146:2.

We come into your presence through Jesus Christ to offer the sacrifice of continual praise. We present the fruit of our lips to you, giving thanks to your name, for he who offers praise glorifies you. You have declared that proper praise will please you more than the sacrifice of an ox or bull that has horns and hoofs. *Heb.* 13:15; *Psa.* 50:23; 69:31.

We constantly remember your covenant love. We gladly declare the praise you deserve for all the ways you have dealt so bountifully with us. We will rehearse the great goodness you have lavished on the house of Israel. You have poured out all these blessings on us according to your mercies and the abundance of your covenant love. *Isa.* 63:7.

Thank God for the Goodness Inherent in His Nature

We give thanks to you, the God of gods, the Lord of lords, for your covenant love endures forever. Your goodness is your glory, and your glory is your goodness. In your kindness you are gracious to undeserving sinners according to the abundance of your grace. You manifest your mercy to the rebellious who have lived in debauchery. You show your mercy to whom you choose to show mercy, even to degenerate idol-worshippers like ourselves. All your works praise you and your saints bless your holy name. *Psa.* 136:2, 3; *Exod.* 33:19; *Psa.* 145:10.

You are gracious and full of compassion, slow to anger and abounding in covenant love. You have told us that you do not delight in afflicting the children of men. Though you cause them grief, you have compassion according to the greatness of your unfailing love. You take great pleasure in those that fear you, the ones who hope in the love you manifest through your covenant. *Psa.* 145:8; *Lam.* 3:32, 33; *Psa.* 147:11.

Thank God for the Many Concrete Manifestations of His Goodness to This Fallen World

His goodness is clearly seen in his gracious orderings of the world as it now is as well as his provisions for redemption that extend into the life to come. Consider his goodness toward the whole of his creation and toward humanity in general.

Thank you for demonstrating your mercy by causing your sun to shine on the evil and the good. You graciously send rain on the just and the unjust. We thank you for the arrival of every new day. We see with our own eyes that you have stretched out the heavens like a vast curtain where you have pitched a tent for the sun, which shines forth as a bridegroom coming out of his chamber and rejoices as a strong man to run a race. *Matt.* 5:45; *Psa.* 104:2; 19:4, 5.

When we consider the heavens, the work of your fingers, the sun, the moon and the stars which you have ordained, we stand in awe that you have shown such care for us. For what is man that you should give any consideration of him? You bless us with the light of the sun that is a pleasant thing for our eyes. May all glory go to the Father of light, who commands the morning and causes the dawn to know its place. You have never left yourself without witness among the nations. For you have provided all the peoples of the world with abundance, giving them rain from heaven and fruitful seasons on earth, providing them with food to eat and filling their hearts with joy and gladness. *Psa.* 8:3, 4; *Eccles.* 11:7; *James* 1:17; *Job* 38:12; *Acts* 14:17.

We honour you for the way you cover the heavens with clouds, and prepare rain for the earth. You make grass grow on the mountains. You give food to the wild beasts and the young ravens which cry out to you. You cause it to rain in the wilderness where there is no man. You satisfy even the desolate wastelands. *Psa.* 147:8, 9; *Job* 38:26, 27.

We bless you when we see how you show your care for the earth by watering it. You enrich the soil with the river of God which is full of water as it flows down from heaven. You provide grain, and water the earth's ridges abundantly. You settle its furrows and soften it with showers. You bless its sprouts and crown the year with your bounty. Our carts are heavy with abundance. You make springs pour forth water in the valleys, creating rivulets that run among the hills. They give drink to every beast of the field. The birds of the air nest by the waters, singing among the branches. *Psa.* 65:9-11; *Psa.* 104:10-12.

We stand in awe as we consider that you laid the foundation of the earth so that it will never be moved. You set boundaries for the seas so they will never again flood the earth. You shut up the sea with bars and doors, saying, 'Up to this point you shall come, but no farther. Here your proud waves shall stop.' You have held to your oath when you swore that the waters of Noah would never again overwhelm the earth. You remain faithful to your covenant commitment that so long as the earth continues, seed-time and harvest, cold and heat, summer and winter, day and night shall not cease. Your covenant of the day and of the night has never been broken. You give the sun for a light by day, and the moon and the stars for lights by night. *Psa.* 104:5, 9; *Job* 38:8, 10, 11; *Isa.* 54:9; *Gen.* 8:22; *Jer.* 33:20; 31:35.

We marvel at your abundant provision for every living thing. Every creature waits on you to give them their food at the right season. Whatever you give them they gather. You open your hand in blessing, and they are filled with good things. You hide your face and they are terrified. When you take away their breath, they die and return to dust. Then you renew the face of the earth. You send out your Spirit and they are created. This your glory shall endure forever, and you will rejoice in your own works. *Psa.* 104:27-31.

You cause grass to grow for the cattle, and plants for man to cultivate. You enable man to bring forth food from the earth – wine that gladdens his heart, oil that makes his face shine, and bread to strengthen his heart. You give life and breath to every living thing. The whole earth is full of your gracious love. *Psa.* 104:14, 15; *Acts* 17:25; *Psa.* 119:64.

We praise you that though the heaven, even the highest heavens are yours, you have given the earth to the children of men. As one generation of mankind passes away, another generation comes. By your grace and your goodness you have not blotted out this corrupt and guilty race of humanity from under heaven. You have put all things under their feet, and made them have dominion over the works of your hands. So the fear and the dread of mankind is on every beast of the earth and on the birds of the air. You have delivered them all into his hands. For you have shown your favour toward man, and have delighted in the sons of men. *Psa.* 115:16; *Eccles.* 1:4; *Deut.* 29:20; *Psa.* 8:6; *Gen.* 9:2; *Prov.* 8:31.

※

Give Thanks for God's Purpose and Plan of Redemption Praise Him for the Goodness of His Redemptive Grace

We have expressed our thanks to God for his blessings in the present life. But we must especially declare our thanks for his blessing that will continue into the life to come. Praise him for his redemptive favours to his covenant people, the Israel of God, the church of our Lord Jesus Christ. As Israel of old rehearsed the mighty acts of God on their behalf, so let God's people today review with thanksgiving the many workings of God's grace in planning and perfecting his redemptive work through Christ.

1. Give thanks for God's grand design for man's redemption when he was seen as lost and devastated by sin.

How overwhelmed with thankfulness we should be for the mystery of your wisdom by which you determined the way for man's redemption before time began. How wondrously did your kindness and love appear, O God our Saviour! For it was not by any works of righteousness that we have done, but by your mercy you saved us. We had destroyed ourselves, but in you and you alone was our help. When we were cast out in an open field and no eye pitied us, you saw us polluted in our own blood. Then you said to us, 'Come alive!' Indeed, you were the only one who could say to us, 'Come alive!' And that time was a time of love. *1 Cor.* 2:7; *Titus* 3:4, 5; *Hos.* 13:9; *Ezek.* 16:5, 6, 8.

When the redemption of the sinful soul was so costly that no price could be sufficient payment for its ransom, you found a way that we might be delivered from going down to the pit. When no one could give a ransom for his brother or redeem him by any means, you were pleased to provide a proper payment. When we were about to die and were as water spilled on the ground which cannot be gathered up again, then you devised a way so that the banished might not be forever expelled from your presence. *Psa.* 49:8, 9; *Job* 33:24; *2 Sam.* 14:14.

You did not spare the angels that sinned but cast them down to hell. You destroyed the cities of Sodom and Gomorrah while saving Lot. You have reserved the ungodly for judgment. Yet you have provided salvation for your people. You have spoken concerning your polluted people, 'Do not destroy it altogether, for a blessing is still possible for some in it.' *2 Pet.* 2:4, 6, 7, 9; *Isa.* 65:8.

2. Stand in awe when you consider the eternal purposes and plans of God concerning the redemption of his people.

How great is our unending obligation to give thanks to you, O God. For from the beginning you chose us to be saved through the sanctifying work of the Spirit. In every generation there continues to be a saved remnant according to the election of your grace. We marvel that you have chosen us in Christ before the foundation of the world that we should be holy and blameless before you. For in love you predestined us to be your adopted children through Jesus Christ according to the good pleasure of your will, to the praise of your glorious grace. How amazing it is that you have lavished this saving grace on us as you united us to your Most Beloved Son. *2 Thess.* 2:13; *Rom.* 11:5; *Eph.* 1:4-6.

Heavenly Father, in the wonder of your perfect plan for saving a great number of lost people from the corruption of this depraved world, you gave those who were yours to your beloved Son. Yours they were, and you gave them to Christ. This has been and continues to be your purpose, that of all those you have given him he should not lose a single one of them, but should raise them up at the last day. *John* 17:6; 6:39.

3. Give glory to God for the appointing of a perfect Redeemer for his chosen people.

We bless you for providing a Son of Man, the second Adam, who could keep your law perfectly on our behalf. For when through the disobedience of the one man Adam the many were made sinners, by the obedience of the one man Jesus Christ the many have been made righteous. When no satisfaction for sin could be found in sacrifice and offering, then your eternal Son responded by saying, 'Look on me! I have come to do your will, O God. You have provided a body for me so I can submit in perfect obedience to your will.' It had all been written about him in the divinely inspired scroll. He found his greatest pleasure in doing your will. Indeed, your law was written on his heart. So he learned the depth of what it meant to be obedient to your will, becoming obedient to the point of death, even death on a cross. *Rom.* 5:19; *Heb.* 10:5-7; *Psa.* 40:7, 8; *Heb.* 5:8; *Phil.* 2:8.

You placed your help for us on a mighty man, one you chose in his prime from your people. You found David your servant, and you anointed him with your holy oil, the oil of gladness above his companions. You promised that your saving hand would rest on him, and your arm would strengthen him. You declared that he would hold the position of your firstborn, exalted above the kings of the earth. *Psa.* 89:19, 20; *Heb.* 1:9; *Psa.* 89:21, 27.

We give thanks that you as the Father judge no man, but have committed all judgment to the Son, that all may honour the Son as they honour you. For just as you, the Father, have life in yourself, so you have authorized the Son to have life in himself. You have given the Son authority to execute judgment, because he is the Son of Man. For you love the Son, and have entrusted all things into his hand. *John* 5:22, 23, 26, 27; 3:35.

We gladly acknowledge that Jesus is the Christ, the prophesied Servant of the Lord whom you uphold, your Chosen One in whom your soul delights. We hail him as your beloved Son, the one in whom you have declared yourself to be totally satisfied. In your grand design, your Son embodies in himself the covenant that assures redemption for your people. For through him we are no longer under the obligations of law, but under the merciful provisions of the covenant of grace. We stand in awe that this is the way you loved this hell-deserving world, that you gave up your one and only Son as an atoning sacrifice for sin, that whoever believes in him will never perish, but already possesses everlasting life. *Isa.* 42:1; *Matt.* 17:5; *Isa.* 49:8; *Rom.* 6:14; *John* 3:16; *1 John* 2:2.

Give Thanks for the Manifestation of God's Grace under the Old Covenant

1. Thank the Lord for the ancient indications of his gracious design toward a fallen humanity.

We stand in thankful amazement when we hear that as soon as man had sinned, you graciously promised that the seed born of the woman would crush the serpent's head. We marvel that Jesus Christ was portrayed as the lamb of God that takes away the sin of the world by all the sacrifices offered according to the law of Moses. We wonder that in your eternal purpose he was slain before the foundation of the world. *Gen.* 3:15; *John* 1:29; *Rev.* 13:8.

We rejoice that though the elders of old did not experience the fulfilment of the promise in their own day, yet they received the testimony from you that they were declared righteous by faith in the Saviour to come. We express our deepest gratitude to you for the promise made to Abraham that in his seed all the families of the earth would be blessed. You also promised Jacob that the ruler among your people would never be taken away from the descendants of Judah until the Promised One came who would possess the lordship. For the promise was that the peoples of all the earth would obey him. With these promises the patriarchs rejoiced to see Christ's day, and they saw it and were glad. Today their gladness is ours. *Heb.* 11:2, 4, 39; *Gen.* 12:3; 49:10; *John* 8:56.

2. *Give thanks for the many glorious instances of God's favour to the church under the old covenant.*

O our promise-keeping God, we adore you for the wisdom and goodness by which you brought a tender vine out of Egypt. You drove out the unbelieving nations before it and planted it. You prepared a broad space for it, and caused it to take deep root so that it filled the land. They never possessed the land by their own sword, and their own arm could not save them. No, it was your right hand, your mighty arm, and the radiance coming from your glorious presence. For you looked constantly with your gracious favour on them. *Psa.* 80:8, 9; 44:3.

We owe you so much for preserving the divine oracles for your people in the old covenant scriptures. They were the first to possess the blessing of adoption as your sons. They saw the radiance of your glory. To them belonged the covenant, the receiving of the law, the proper regulations of worship and all your promises. We ourselves can solemnly affirm that both then and now not one word of all your good promises has ever failed, even though you stated them so long ago through your servant Moses. *Rom.* 3:2, 9:4; *1 Kings* 8:56.

We thank you that at different times and in various ways you spoke in the past to our forefathers by the prophets. Thank you for raising up these holy men of God who spoke as they were moved by the Holy Spirit and prophesied of the grace that was to come. They gave clear testimony about the suffering of Christ and the glory that would follow before any of those things had happened. They were not speaking for themselves only, but they were ministering those great truths to us as well, truths so great that even angels desire to look into them. We especially bless you that you have provided even better things for us, that they should not be brought to their complete perfection without us. *Heb.* 1:1; *2 Pet.* 1:21; 1 Pet. 1:10-12; *Heb.* 11:40.

Give Thanks for the Accomplishment of Redemption by the Son of God

1. Give thanks for the Father's commitment with the Son to redeem lost sinners.

Heavenly Father, we bless you that you were in Christ reconciling the world to yourself. You did not impute our trespasses to us, even though we were guilty. Now you have committed to us the word that reconciles sinful men to you, the holy God. *2 Cor.* 5:19.

You have given David's descendant Jesus, the ultimate heir of the Davidic covenant, as a witness to the peoples, a leader and commander for the nations. By your good purposes he was sanctified, sealed and sent into the world. As the Father who sent him, you never left him alone, for he always did everything that pleased you. Glory to God in the highest heavens, and on earth may there be peace through Jesus Christ toward men on whom his good pleasure rests. *Isa.* 55:3, 4; *John* 10:36; 8:29; *Luke* 2:14.

We adore you that your very essence is love, and that you made your love evident to us by sending your one and only Son into the world that we might live through him. Even though we did not love you, you loved us and gave your Son as an atoning sacrifice for our sins. We give thanks to you that the hour has come for you to glorify your Son. For you have granted him authority over all humanity that he may give eternal life to as many as you have given him. *1 John* 4:8-10; *John* 17:1, 2.

2. *Never cease to wonder at the mysterious and miraculous incarnation of the Son of God.*

We give all honour to you, our great God, that when the fullness of time had come, you sent your Son to be born of a woman, born under the law, that he might redeem those that were condemned by the law. We praise you that the eternal Word was made flesh and tabernacled among us. When this one who was firstborn in rank came into the world, all the angels of God were given the charge to worship him. We thank you that chosen witnesses saw his glory, the glory that belongs inherently to your one and only Son, who was full of grace and truth. Undeniably great is this mystery that creates God-centered living, that you the eternal God were manifested in the flesh. *Gal.* 4:4, 5; *John* 1:14; *Heb.* 1:6; *Acts* 10:41; *1 Tim.* 3:16.

We bless you that Jesus was born of a virgin and came into the world that he might bear witness to the truth. We believe and are sure that he is the Christ, the Holy One of God. Without reservation we accept the fact that he is the one that had been prophesied as the Coming One. So we will never look for any other person to save us. *Matt.* 1:22, 23; *John* 18:37; 6:69; *Matt.* 16:16; 11:3.

We thank you that the Son of Man came into this world to seek and save the lost. He came that we might have life, and have it more abundantly. We rejoice that the Son of God was manifested so that he might destroy the works of the devil. Lord, we receive it as a faithful saying and worthy of unqualified acceptance, that Christ Jesus came into the world to save sinners, even the greatest sinner among us. *Luke* 19:10; *John* 10:10; *1 John* 3:8; *1 Tim.* 1:15.

We bless you that since the children of God participate in the mortality of flesh and blood, he also took on the same mortal substances so that by death he might destroy the one that has the power of death, who is the devil. For he did not take on himself the nature of angels, but our human nature. In all things he was made like his brothers, that he might be a merciful and faithful High Priest in offering worshipful service to you. So he was able to present himself as a sacrifice for the sins of the people to remove your wrath. Having been tested in every way, he is not ashamed to call believers his brothers. *Heb.* 2:11-14, 16, 17; 4:15.

3. May God's name be magnified for the holy life Jesus lived, for his illuminating teaching, and the glorious miracles he worked to confirm the truths he taught.

We bless you for the confidence we have that Jesus came as a teacher sent by you. For no man could do the miracles he did unless you were with him. In these last days you have spoken to us by your Son, whose teaching did not originate with him, but from you, the one who commissioned him. He spoke as a person with divine authority. So we come and learn from him that even he is meek and humble in heart, for then we find rest for our souls. *John* 3:2; *Heb.* 1:2; *John* 7:16; *Matt.* 7:29; 11:29.

We honour you for letting him leave us an example, that we should follow his steps. He never sinned once. He never told a single lie. He never returned insult with insult. His meat and drink was to do your will, the perfect will of his Father. He was holy, blameless, undefiled, separated from every evil done by sinners. Let our souls be armed with the same attitude, having the same firmness of will set against sinning. Help us to be in this world, but not of this world, that we may have confidence in the day of judgment. 1 Pet. 2:21-23; *John* 4:34; *Heb.* 7:26; *1 Pet.* 4:1; *John* 17:16; *1 John* 4:17.

We join our own testimony to the witness of his works that you as the Father sent him into this world to be the Saviour of sinners. For by his power the blind received their sight, the lame walked, lepers were cleansed, the deaf heard, the dead were raised, and the poor had the gospel preached to them. Even the winds and the waves obeyed him. We glorify you, the God of Israel, for these clear confirmations that without any doubt this one was the Son of God. *John* 5:36; *Matt.* 11:5; 8:27; 15:31; 27:54.

4. Rejoice at the great encouragement Jesus gave to poor sinners to come to him while he was on earth.

We bless you that Jesus Christ did not come to call the righteous, but sinners to repentance. For he had authority on earth to forgive sin, and he continues to have that same authority. He came into this world to save his people from their sins. He is the Lamb of God who by the sacrifice of himself takes away the sin of the world. To his great honour, not to his shame, he is the friend of scandalous public officials, prostitutes and abusive drunkards. *Matt.* 9:6, 13; 1:21; *John* 1:29; *Matt.* 11:19.

We thank you for the gracious invitation he gives to those who are weary and heavy laden to come to him for rest. We express our deepest gratitude for the assurance he has given us that he will never cast out anyone who comes to him, whatever might be the circumstances. We rejoice in his gracious offer that any thirsty soul may come to him and drink until he is fully satisfied. *Matt.* 11:28; *John* 6:37; 7:37; 4:14.

5. Express your deepest awe at the full satisfaction Christ made to the justice of God for man's sin by the blood of his cross. Rejoice at the triumphs of the cross and all the benefits that flow to you by the dying of the Lord Jesus.

How amazing it is that you have displayed the depths of your love to us! For while we were still continuing as sinners, Christ died for us. You are love, and this is love, not that we loved you, but that you loved us. In your love you sent your Son to be the atoning sacrifice for our sins, and not for ours only, but for the sins of the whole world. For by the death of your Son we have been reconciled to you. We give thanks that by your gracious design he tasted death for all, that through death he might destroy him that has the power of death, that is the devil. *Rom.* 5:8; *1 John* 4:8, 10; 2:2; *Rom.* 5:10; *Heb.* 2:9, 14.

Father, we bless you that by one offering Jesus has consecrated forever those that are being sanctified. For he has finished transgression, made an end of sin, made reconciliation for iniquity, and has brought in everlasting righteousness. He has redeemed us from the curse of the law by being made a curse for us. For what the law could not do in that it was weak through fallen human nature, you have done by sending your own Son in the likeness of that same fallen human nature. *Heb.* 10:14; *Dan.* 9:24; *Gal.* 3:13; *Rom.* 8:3.

We give thanks that he was wounded for our transgressions and bruised for our iniquities. For the chastisement that alone could bring peace between us and you as our God fell on him, and by his stripes we are healed. For you have laid on him the iniquity of us all. How amazing it is that for our sakes you were pleased to bruise him and to put him to grief. We praise you that at the appointed time he arrived as a high priest to put away sin once and for all by the offering of himself. For by the eternal Spirit he presented himself without blemish to you, and by his own blood entered once into the holy place, having obtained eternal redemption for us. *Isa.* 53:5, 6, 10; *Heb.* 9:11, 26, 14, 12.

We rejoice that he has stripped rulers and authorities of their power, boldly exposing them and publicly parading his victory over them in his cross. For he has blotted out all the documentation of our violations of your ordinances which testified against us. He got rid of that condemning record by nailing it to his cross. For he himself is our peace, who has broken down the wall that divides Jew from Gentile, having united the two by creating in himself one new humanity. He has reconciled us both to you in one body, having slain the hostility between the two of us by the cross. *Col.* 2:14, 15; *Eph.* 2:14-16.

How incomprehensible is the height, the depth, the length and breadth of the love of Christ which surpasses human knowledge! How great is that love with which he has loved us! For he has loved us whatever the cost might be to himself, and washed us from our sins in his own blood. He has made us kings and priests to you, our God. Worthy is the Lamb that was slain, to receive power, and riches, and wisdom, and strength, and honour, and glory and blessing. For he was slain and has redeemed us to you by his blood. *Eph.* 3:18, 19; 2:4; *Rev.* 1:5, 6; 5:9, 12.

6. Honour Christ for his resurrection from the dead on the third day.

We give all praise and honour to you, O Christ, that even as you were delivered for our offences, so you rose again that we might be pronounced righteous. We lift up our hearts in thankfulness that you were declared with power to be the Son of God by the resurrection from the dead. For though you were dead, you are now alive, and live for evermore. You have the keys of death and hell. Having been raised from the dead, you will never die again, for death has no more dominion over you. *Rom.* 4:25; 1:4; *Rev.* 1:18; *Rom.* 6:9.

O Lord Christ, we rejoice that you have risen from the dead, and have become the firstfruits of believers that have fallen asleep in you. For as all in Adam died, so all united to you shall be made alive. You had to be raised as the firstfruits; then we who belong to you will be raised when you appear in your glory. *1 Cor.* 15:20, 22, 23.

Father in heaven, we honour you that you would never allow your Holy One to see decay. Instead, you delivered him from the birth-pains of death, because it was impossible for him to be held back by its power. We rejoice that you publicly declared to all the house of Israel that the very same Jesus that they crucified is both Lord and Christ. We affirm our faith that Christ died and rose again so that he might be Lord both of the dead and the living. So whether we remain awake or fall asleep in death, we know that united with him we will keep on living. *Acts* 2:31, 24, 36; *Rom.* 14:9; *1 Thess.* 5:10.

7. Worship Christ for his ascension into heaven, where he continues to sit as sovereign at God's right hand.

Thanks be to God that our Lord Jesus has ascended to his Father and our Father, to his God and our God. Lord Jesus, we honour you that by your ascension to your throne on high you led into a new captivity those who had been captive to Satan.

In your exalted position you have received gifts both from men and for men, even from and for the rebellious. For you are seated on the right hand of the throne of the Majesty in the heavens, with angels, authorities, and powers being subject to you. *John* 20:17; *Psa.* 68:18; *Eph.* 4:8; *Heb.* 8:1; *1 Pet.* 3:22.

We give thanks that in your ascension you have gone before us to prepare a place for us, so we can live forever with you in your Father's house. Though we cannot follow you now to the place where you have gone, yet we look forward to following you to that place when you come again to receive us to yourself. We rejoice that when you return we will be forever where you are. For as our forerunner you have entered heaven itself for us, now appearing in the presence of God as a Lamb that has been slain, standing in the midst of God's throne. *John* 14:2, 3; 13:36; *Heb.* 6:20; *Rev.* 5:6.

8. Express your everlasting gratitude to God for the intercession which Christ continually makes on your behalf by virtue of the satisfaction made by his sacrifice for your sins.

We thank you that since Christ has borne in himself the sins of many, he now makes continual intercession for the transgressors. We rejoice that he prays not only for those that were given him while he was on earth, but for all those throughout the world and across the ages who have believed on him through his apostles' word. We join him in his prayer that in him we all may be united as one. *Isa.* 53:12; *John* 17:20, 21.

We give thanks that we have an advocate with you, the eternal Father, even Jesus Christ the righteous. For he is able to save to the uttermost all of us who come to you by him, since he lives forever to make intercession for us. We continually avail ourselves of the mediation of our High Priest who was taken from among men and ordained for men in matters that concern their relation to you, the Almighty God. For he has offered all the gifts and sacrifices necessary to remove sin. He continues to show compassion to the ignorant and those who have strayed from the way. So for us he has become the author of eternal salvation to all who obey him. *1 John* 2:1; *Heb.* 7:25; 5:1, 2, 9.

9. Give glory to Christ our Redeemer for his exalted position at God's right hand where he rules over heaven and earth.

Our Lord Jesus Christ, we honour you for humbling yourself and becoming obedient to the point of death, even the death of the cross. We glorify you, gladly acknowledging that God has highly exalted you and given you a name above every name, so that at the name of JESUS every knee shall bow and every tongue confess (as we do at this time) that Jesus Christ is Lord, to the glory of God the Father. We submit ourselves totally to you, the one to whom all authority has been given both in heaven and on earth. We honour you as the one that God has set over all the works of his hands. We rejoice that the Father has exalted you so that all things are under your feet, and you are crowned with glory and honour. *Phil.* 2:8-10; *Matt.* 28:18; *Heb.* 2:7-9.

We acknowledge you, O Christ, as King of kings and Lord of lords. We recognize that the Ancient of Days has given you dominion and glory, a kingdom and an everlasting dominion which shall never be destroyed. We understand that the governance of God's eternal, Messianic kingdom is on your shoulders, and that your name is Wonderful Counsellor, Mighty God, the Everlasting Father, the Prince of Peace. We rejoice that the expansion of your peaceful government shall never come to an end. *Rev.* 19:16; *Dan.* 7:13, 14; *Isa.* 9:6, 7.

Heavenly Father, we rejoice that you have set Jesus as King on your holy, heavenly hill of Zion. We give thanks that he shall reign over the house of Jacob forever. We affirm that he shall reign until he has overcome all opposing rule, authority, and power, until you have made all his enemies his footstool.

We look forward to that consummating day when he shall deliver the kingdom to you as the Father, so that you may be all in all forever. *Psa.* 2:6; *Luke* 1:33; *1 Cor.* 15:24, 25, 28.

10. Thank the Lord for the hope he has given you that he will return in glory to judge the world.

Lord, we thank you for the hope that one day soon you will gather together your elect from the four winds of heaven, so that the righteous will shine forth as the sun in the kingdom of their Father. According to your promise, we look for a new heavens and a new earth where righteousness thrives. Since we look for such things, give us diligence so that we will be found spotless, blameless, and at peace with you. *Matt.* 24:31; *2 Pet.* 3:13, 14.

Teach us to live with a sense of accountability, knowing that you have appointed a day in which you will judge the world in righteousness by that man whom you have ordained. By raising him from the dead, you have given assurance to all people in every generation of the certainty of that coming judgment day. For in the day the Lord Jesus is revealed from heaven with his mighty angels in flaming fire, he will take vengeance on those that have not loved you, the one true living God, and have not obeyed the gospel of our Lord Jesus Christ. Yet we look forward to the day when he shall come to be glorified in his holy people, and marvelled at when his glory is manifest in all those who believe. *Acts* 17:31; *2 Thess.* 1:7, 8, 10.

We expect that one day soon you shall send forth your angels to root out of your kingdom everything that causes people to stumble into sin, and everyone who by his lifestyle disregards your law. So we earnestly pray, Come Lord Jesus! Come quickly, and come soon! *Matt.* 13:41; *Rev.* 22:20.

11. Give special thanks for God's grace in sending the Holy Spirit to sustain you beyond the days of Christ's bodily presence on earth.

We express our unending gratitude to you that when our Lord Jesus departed from this earth he sent another Supporter that will live in us forever. We know him as the Spirit of truth, who gives all glory to the Son as he takes that which belongs to him and makes it plain to us. We praise you that after Jesus had been exalted to your right hand, he received from you as his Father the promised Holy Spirit, which he has poured forth on all kinds of people as rivers of living water. *John* 14:16, 17; 16:14; *Acts* 2:33; *John* 7:38.

May you receive all glory for the signs, wonders, miracles, and gifts of the Holy Spirit by which you gave public testimony to the great salvation you were working in the world. May people of all nations call you blessed. For just as earthly, evil parents know how to give good gifts to their children, so you as our heavenly Father give the Holy Spirit to all that ask you. We give you thanks for the Holy Spirit of promise, the guarantee of our eternal inheritance, who remains as ours until the full redemption of those who are your purchased possession. *Heb.* 2:4; *Luke* 11:13; *Eph.* 1:13, 14.

Give Thanks for the Establishment of the Church in the World

1. All glory to God for the covenant of grace made with us in Jesus Christ.

We thank you that in Jesus Christ you have made an everlasting covenant with us, even the confirmed mercies you promised to David. Thank you for all the privileges of that covenant, as well as the seals you have ordained to confirm its promises. For though the mountains depart and the hills are removed, this covenant of your peace shall never be changed. We honour you that Jesus Christ is the Mediator of this better covenant, which is founded on better promises. For though you chasten our transgression with the rod, and our iniquity with stripes, still you will never completely take away your lovingkindness, and will never allow your faithfulness to fail. You will not break your covenant, and you will never modify any word that has gone out of your mouth. *Isa.* 55:3; 54:10; *Heb.* 8:6; *Psa.* 89:32-34.

We stand amazed that you, the eternal God, have confirmed your covenant by an oath-bound commitment. You demonstrated as clearly as possible the consistent character of your purpose to the heirs of your promise. So by joining your personal oath to your word of promise, we have received the strongest possible confirmation of your intention to fully redeem us by these two unchangeable commitments. Knowing it is impossible for you to lie, we have found refuge for our souls by seizing the promised hope you have set before us. *Heb. 6:17-19.*

We rejoice in the confirming character of our baptism, your appointed seal of the righteousness which is by faith, just as circumcision served under the old covenant. We receive by faith this assuring sign of both the forgiveness of our sins and the gift of the Holy Spirit. We claim by faith this promise made to us and to our children. By faith all of us also drink the cup of the Lord's Supper as symbol and seal of receiving the remission of our sins by the blood of the new covenant, which was poured out as a sacrifice for many. *Rom. 4:11; Gal. 2:11, 12; Acts 2:38, 39; Matt. 26:28.*

2. Thank the Lord for recording his eternal Word in the written form of Scripture, and for preserving his Word in its purity and entirety up to the present day.

We wonder at the privilege we have to search the Scriptures, your holy Word, for in them we come to possess eternal life. We see clearly that all Scripture is given by inspiration of God, that it testifies of

Christ, and is profitable for doctrine, for reproof, for correction, and for instruction in righteousness. *John* 5:39; *2 Tim.* 3:16.

We understand that everything recorded in the Scriptures in earlier days was written to instruct us who live today. Enable us to live in hope through patience and the encouragement that comes through the Scriptures. With our whole hearts we embrace the prophetic word which is now made even more certain, as a light shining in a dark place. For the vision of your glory does not come to us as the words of a book scaled shut. Instead, we hear and read about your amazing works in our own mother tongue. *Rom.* 15:4; *2 Pet.* 1:19; *Isa.* 29:11; *Acts* 2:11.

Father, though many prophets and kings longed to see the truths about your wondrous way of redemption, they were not able to do so. But we thank you, Lord of heaven and earth, that these saving realities that remained hidden from the wise and prudent are now clearly revealed to simple babes like us. Father, we praise you, for that was what seemed good in your sight. *Luke* 10:21, 24.

3. Accept with gratitude the directions God has set down for the well-being of his church.

We are humbled that you have willingly declared your word, your laws, and your ordinances for your people, the Israel of God. You have not favoured any other community in this way, for no other people have known your commandments in the way you have revealed them to us. You have established your tabernacle among your people, so that you dwell among us. You have set your sacred place of worship in our midst. You have declared that you will meet with your people, the true children of Israel. *Psa.* 147:19, 20; *Rev.* 21:3; *Ezek.* 37:26; *Exod.* 29:43.

We consecrate all our abilities for service in your kingdom to our Lord Jesus the Christ. For after he ascended on high, he gave multiple and mani-fold gifts for ministry. Lord Jesus, you have poured out your Spirit for the equipping of prophets and apostles, evangelists, pastors and teachers. You fully equip each and every person consecrated to you for their distinctive work as servants for maturing your body, the church. You have assured us that you will continue to pour out your Spirit until we all come into the unity of the faith and the full knowledge of you, the Son of God. We delight in your abundant provisions for the perfecting of a people who will display the full maturity found in the completeness of Christ. We rejoice in your promise to be with us always, even to the end of the age as we continue to make more and more disciples. Be with us as we teach the nations to observe all the things you have commanded. *Eph.* 4:8, 11-13; *Matt.* 28:19, 20.

We thank you that from the time of the world's creation the Sabbath came into existence for the blessing of humanity. As you yourself rested, you sanctified a rest-day for us. You commanded your people to do all their work in six days, and to consecrate one whole day in seven as a time for delighting in you. You anticipated the eternal Sabbath-rest by the many forms of your holy Sabbaths, so that there still remains a Sabbath for the people of God. *Mark* 2:27; *Gen.* 2:3; *Exod.* 20:8-11; *Isa.* 58:13, 14; *Lev.* 25:1-13; *Neh.* 9:14; *Heb.* 4:9.

4. Give glory to God for establishing Christianity throughout the world, and for planting a church true to the gospel despite all the opposition of the powers of darkness.

We thank you that the true gospel of Jesus Christ has been preached to all nations to bring about the obedience of faith according to your commandment. We praise you that you have made this weapon of gospel truth mighty through God for the tearing down of the world's strongholds, so that we have watched Satan fall as lightning from heaven. Though this gospel has been preached in the face of constant conflict, it has grown and prevailed mightily. We rejoice to see multitudes turn from idols that they might serve you, the living and true God, while they wait for the consummating moment when your Son will return in glory. *Rom.* 16:25, 26; *2 Cor.* 10:4; *Luke* 10:18; *1 Thess.* 2:2; *Acts* 19:20; *1 Thess.* 1:9, 10.

Salvation and strength, the kingdom of our God and the power of his Christ have now come. The exalted Redeemer has ridden forth armed with his bow, crowned with his diadem, conquering and to conquer. So whole nations have been born into your eternal kingdom in a day. *Rev.* 12:10; 6:2; *Isa.* 66:8.

5. Give God the glory for preserving Christianity in this fallen world up to the present day.

We marvel at your preserving grace. For though the enemies of your chosen people have afflicted them from their earliest days, though they have afflicted them many times over, yet they have not prevailed against them. Ploughmen have ploughed across their back, making long furrows. Yet as the righteous Lord you have cut them free from the binding cords of the wicked. We see clearly that Jesus Christ has built his church on a rock, and the gates of hell cannot prevail against it. For his seed shall endure forever, and his throne shall last as long as heaven endures. *Psa.* 129:1-4; *Matt.* 16:18; *Psa.* 89:29.

6. Express your personal appreciation to God for the good examples set by those who have gone to heaven before you.

We give you thanks for all those members of the church triumphant in heaven who in their turn approved themselves before you by their great patience in afflictions and distresses. When they were brought before governors and kings for Christ's sake, they faithfully gave their witness to the truth. You put words in their mouths that displayed a wisdom that all their adversaries could not withstand or contradict. All day long many have faced death for Christ's sake. They were treated as sheep for the slaughter. Yet in all these things they were more than conquerors through you, the one who has loved us. *2 Cor.* 6:4; *Luke* 21:12, 13, 15; *Rom.* 8:36, 37.

We praise you that our forefathers in Christ have overcome the accuser of the brethren by the blood of the Lamb and by the word of their testimony. We stand in reverent awe that by your grace they did not love their lives even to the point of death. Thank you for the cloud of witnesses that encompass us and cheer us on. Thank you for those who lived by faith in previous days. They have obtained a good report, and as a result of their faith and patience they are now inheriting the promises. Lord, enable us to imitate them as they imitated Christ. *Rev.* 12:10, 11; *Heb.* 12:1; 11:1, 2; 6:12; *1 Cor.* 11:1.

7. Thank God for the communion of the saints which we enjoy because of our common faith, hope, and love.

We give you praise that so long as we walk in the light we have fellowship one with another. We rejoice in the grace and peace that we share with everyone, everywhere, who calls for salvation on the name of Jesus Christ our Lord. Continue to join us together, since you are both their Lord and ours. We are one body though we are many, since we all receive our nourishment from the same bread of life. Though there are many different kinds of gifts, ministries, and services, you are one and the same God, one and the same Lord, and one and the same Spirit who energizes us all. *1 John* 1:7; *1 Cor.* 1:2, 3; 10:17; 12:4-6.

We thank you that all your children scattered across every continent are one in Christ who is the head of the body, his church. Thank you for all our brothers and companions in the tribulation, the kingdom, and the patient endurance that are ours in Jesus. *John* 11:52; *Col.* 1:18; *Rev.* 1:9.

Thank the Lord for the Personal Application of the Saving Work of Christ in Your Life

1. Praise God that he has not abandoned you in your sin, and has provided your conscience as a constant restraint.

We bless you that you have not given us over to a depraved mind, and that our consciences are not seared. We thank you that you have not pronounced your judgment over us by saying, 'They have pledged their loyalty to idols. Let them alone!' We thank you for that your law has been written in our hearts, and that our own consciences bear witness against us, sometimes accusing and at other times excusing us. *Rom.* 1:28; *1 Tim.* 4:2; *Hos.* 4:17; *Rom.* 2:15.

2. Praise God for the saving change worked in you by the Holy Spirit.

Almighty Redeemer, have you by your grace transferred us out of the kingdom of darkness and brought us into the kingdom of your beloved Son? Have you called us into fellowship with Jesus Christ and brought us near to yourself by his blood, even though by nature we were estranged from you? Then may you receive all glory. O Lord Jesus, when the devil, like a well-armed strong man, guarded his fortress in our hearts so that his goods were peacefully secured, you came against him as one who was stronger than he. You took away all the defensive armour in which he trusted, and divided up the plunder as you wished. Not to us, O Lord, not to us, but to your name we give all the glory. *Col.* 1:13; *1 Cor.* 1:9; *Eph.* 2:13; *Luke* 11:21, 22; *Psa.* 115:1.

We continually give thanks for all those to whom the gospel has come not only in word, but in power, in the Holy Spirit, and with convincing certainty. O Lord God, you have loved us with an everlasting love. With the bonds of love and kindness you have drawn us to yourself, and with the bands of love you have eased the yoke of sin off our shoulder. *1 Thess.* 1:2, 5; *Jer.* 31:3; *Hos.* 11:4.

3. Express your unending gratitude for the forgiveness of your sins and the peace of your conscience.

We give thanks to you for the redemption we have through Christ's blood. We praise you for the full forgiveness of our sins according to the riches of your grace which you have lavished on us, for you forgave all our iniquities and healed all our diseases. In love you delivered our souls from the pit of destruction, for you cast all our sins behind your back. *Eph.* 1:7, 8; *Psa.* 103:3; *Isa.* 38:17.

You brought us into the howling wilderness and stripped us of all our earthly comforts as a way of leading us to repentance. Yet in our utter barrenness you spoke words of comforting reassurance to us. Then you returned us to the luscious vineyards we had lost, and transformed our valley of Achor into a door of hope. *Hos.* 2:14, 15.

4. Give God the glory for the powerful influence of divine grace in sanctifying and preserving you, in preventing you from falling into sin, and in strengthening you to do your duty.

We lift up our testimony to your grace that has worked mightily in us even until today. You keep giving us the reviving nourishment we need, and so we continue to stand. In the day when we cried out, you answered us and enabled us to stand firm with strength in our souls. You have not snuffed out the smouldering wick or snapped off the splintered cane. As you have admonished us, you have not despised the day of little things. Our feet almost tripped, our steps almost slipped. But you held us up by your right hand. Your shield protects us, and you stoop down to lift us up. *Acts* 26:22; *Psa.* 138:3; *Matt.* 12:20; *Zech.* 4:10; *Psa.* 73:2, 3; 18:35.

Keep us from ever forgetting the guidelines you have provided for our life, for you have revived us through them. Unless we had delighted in your law, we would have perished many times over in our troubles. But your commandments have inspired our songs wherever we have camped throughout life's pilgrimage. Unless you had been our help, our souls would have been condemned to silence very quickly. But when we felt that we had lost our footing, your covenant love held us up. Despite the multitude of our disturbing thoughts, your reassurances brought joy to our souls. *Psa.* 119:92, 93; 94:17-19.

5. Refresh yourself through your close fellowship with God and your sense of his favourable attitude toward you.

We have been more than satisfied with the abundance of pleasures found in our fellowship with you. You have let us drink from your river of delights. The life-giving fountain flows from you, and in your light we see light. You have brought us to your holy mountain, and made us joyful in your house of prayer. We have found it to be our greatest blessing to draw near to you, our Saviour and our God. *Psa.* 36:8, 9; *Isa.* 56:7; *Psa.* 73:28.

We have every reason to say that one day in your courts is better than a thousand days spent anywhere else. It is far better for us to be a mere doorkeeper in your house than to dwell in the tents of wickedness. For you, the Covenant Lord our God, are a sun and a shield. You always give grace and glory. No good thing will you ever withhold from those who walk with a heart fully committed to you. O Lord of hosts, how blessed is the man who trusts in you! *Psa.* 84:10-12.

6. Thank the Lord for his gracious answers to your prayers.

O Lord, we love you because you have heard our prayers and have answered us. We will call on you as long as we live. Out of the depths we called to you. You heard our vows and allowed us to share in the inheritance of those who fear your name. *Psa.* 116:1, 2; 130:1; 61:5.

Even before we called you answered us. While we were still speaking you said, 'Here I am!' What other people has had God so near to them, a God who carefully considers everything his people ask in prayer? Lord, you have heard the desire of the humble. You will encourage our heart by listening with your ear. *Isa.* 65:24; 58:9; *Deut.* 4:7; *Psa.* 10:17.

Blessed be God, who has not rejected our prayer. For we have prayed, and have gone our way without having a sad face any longer. *Psa.* 66:20; *1 Sam.* 1:18.

Consider the Goodness of the Lord Shown to You through All the Varying Seasons of Your Life

1. Give thanks that he has made you capable of knowing, loving, serving, and enjoying him; for he has not made you like the beasts that perish forever.

We praise you that we are fearfully and wonderfully made. You have made us just a little lower than the angels. You have crowned us with glory and honour. For there is a spirit within man, even the breath of the Almighty, that gives him understanding. Our bodies are capable of being the temples of the Holy Spirit, and our souls of having the Spirit of God dwell in them. Let us therefore glorify you with our bodies as well as with our spirits, which are yours. You have formed us for yourself that we might declare your praise. *Psa.* 139:14; 8:5; *Job* 32:8; *1 Cor.* 6:19, 20; 3:16; *Isa.* 43:21.

2. Give thanks that he preserves you day after day and year after year.

We praise you that we did not die while still in our mother's womb. We did not give up our spirit as we were being born. For you ordered that our mother's knees should receive us and her breasts should provide us with life's nourishment. You judged us as transgressors from the womb. Yet by your power we were safely born, and were sustained from the moment we emerged from the womb. *Job* 3:11, 12; *Isa.* 48:8; 46:3.

You maintain the life of our souls and keep our feet from slipping. Lord, who is like you, delivering the poor and needy from the person that is too strong for him. For you preserve our bones so that not a single one of them is broken. We lie down in undisturbed sleep and wake up refreshed, for you see to it that we rest safely. You charge your angels to preserve us in all our ways. They bear us up in their hands to keep us from dashing our foot against a stone. They are all serving spirits, commissioned to minister good to the heirs of salvation. *Psa.* 66:9; 35:10; 34:20; 3:5; 91:11, 12; *Heb.* 1:14.

3. Gratefully remember the divine interventions that have delivered you from sickness and many other threats to your well-being.

We marvel when we recall those times when there might have been a single step between us and death. It has often appeared that we have received the sentence of death within us. Yet in your love you have delivered us from the pit of corruption. We have stood at the gates of the grave and expected to be deprived of the remainder of our years by the shortening of our days. But you have delivered us and cast all our sins behind your back. *1 Sam.* 20:3; *2 Cor.* 1:9; *Isa.* 38:10, 17.

When the sorrows of death encompassed us and the pains of the grave seized us, we called on the name of the Lord. Even in those dire circumstances we were led to declare, 'Gracious and righteous is the Lord. Our God is merciful.' We have been brought down very low, but you have helped us. You have delivered our souls from death, our eyes from tears, and our feet from stumbling. We will therefore live out the rest of our lives before the you in the land of the living. *Psa.* 116:3-6, 8, 9.

4. Thank God for the supports and comforts that have made your pilgrimage through life easier and more pleasant.

Blessed be the Lord who daily bears my burdens. You make me lie down in green pastures. You lead me beside still waters. You prepare a bountiful table for me in the presence of my enemies. You anoint my head with oil. My cup overflows. Your lamp has been continually shining on my head. By your light I have walked through darkness. Your intimate friendship has been an integral part of my home. You may have sent me out without a purse, a backpack or an extra pair of shoes. But did I ever lack anything? Nothing, Lord. *Psa.* 68:19; 23:2, 5; *Job* 29:3, 4; *Luke* 22:35.

You have allowed us to enjoy things in abundance. You have put plenty into our hands. Time after time we have eaten to the full and delighted in your great goodness. We remember with gratitude all the ways that you have led us through this wilderness. So we must stop and set up a memorial stone which we will name Ebenezer, for up until now the Lord has helped us. *1 Tim.* 6:17; *Neh.* 9:25; *Deut.* 8:2; *1 Sam.* 7:12.

5. Offer thanks to God for success in your callings, encouragement in your relations, and convenience in your places of residence.

We are amazed that you have supplied us with adequate strength for every new challenge in life. You have ordered our ways so that they have been perfectly suited for us. You have blessed the work of our hands and established it as useful to your kingdom. Though our beginning was humble, you have prospered us greatly. With nothing more than a staff we passed over this Jordan, and now we have become two companies. For you have graciously determined that solitary souls should expand into families. *Psa.* 18:32; *Job* 1:10; 8:7; *Gen.* 32:10; *Psa.* 68:6.

Our houses have been safe from fear. No rod of God has rested on us. The voice of rejoicing at your deliverances has resounded throughout our home day after day. If we have enjoyed life with our wife, found deep satisfaction in her, and she has been to us as a lovely deer, a graceful doe, we must give you thanks. For every part of this creation means no more to us than what you make it to be. *Job* 21:9; *Psa.* 118:15; *Eccles.* 9:9; *Prov.* 5:19.

6. Honour your sovereign Lord for the share he has given you of the public plenty and peace

Every time we eat our bread in quietness we bless you for the good land you have given us. Your eyes are always attentive to the needs of this land from the beginning of the year to its end. You have maintained peace along our borders and filled us with the finest grains from our fields. We will rehearse your righteous acts, for we are free from the whizz of arrows shot by archers whenever we go to draw water. We thank you that the governing authorities set over us are your ministers to us for good. They have been appointed to seek the welfare of our people, maintaining peace for the generation to come. *Deut.* 8:10; 11:12; *Psa.* 147:14; *Judg.* 5:11; *Rom.* 13:4; *Esther* 10:3.

7. Thank the Lord for the support he gives you when you are under affliction. Praise him for the benefit you receive even from your trials.

You comfort us in all our tribulation. You are fully aware of our trials, and sympathize with our souls in all their troubles. Even when we are like a city under siege, you display the awesome nature of your covenant love. When our afflictions abound, make our consolations abound even more. *2 Cor.* 1:4; *Psa.* 31:7, 21; *2 Cor.* 1:5.

All our troubles bring grief rather than joy at the time. Yet let them eventually yield the peaceable fruit of righteousness and prove to be for our profit, that we might participate in your holiness. We admit that it was good for us to be afflicted, since through our afflictions we got a better grasp of your commandments. For before we were afflicted, we kept going astray. But now we keep your word. *Heb.* 12:10, 11; *Psa.* 119:67, 71.

We find ourselves in distress over and over again through numerous trials. Sovereign Lord, make all the trials of our faith result in praise, honour and glory to you at the appearing of Jesus Christ. We have not seen him, yet we love him. Even now we still do not see him. Yet continuing to believe, help us to rejoice with a joy so great and glorious that it cannot come to full expression. Keep us longing for the consummation of our faith, which will be the full salvation of our souls. *1 Pet.* 1:6-9.

8. Give honour to God for the fulfilment of all his promises to you.

O Lord, you have consistently done good to your servant in perfect accord with all your promises. You have been true to your covenant, the word you ordained for the benefit of a thousand generations. Not one word has failed of all the good promises you swore to David your servant, and to Israel your people. *Psa.* 119:65; 105:8; *1 Kings* 8:56, 66.

So what shall I repay to the Lord for all his benefits to me? He has delivered my life from death, my eyes from tears, and my feet from stumbling. I will drink from the cup of salvation and call on the name of the Lord. For the Lord is good, his mercy is everlasting, and his truth endures across the generations. *Psa.* 116:12a, 8, 12b, 13; 100:5.

Let us bless the Lord at all times. Let his praise be in our mouths continually. Let us sing to the Lord as long as we live. Let us rejoice in the hope that we will shortly be with those blessed ones who dwell in his house above. For they still are praising him, and do not rest day or night from saying, 'Holy, holy, holy, is the Lord God Almighty.' *Psa.* 34:1; 104:33; *Rev.* 4:8.

9. Be inspired to look eagerly toward the prospect of eternal life, when time shall be no more.

Thank you for the crown of everlasting life which you have promised to those who love you. Keep us looking forward to the inheritance that is incorruptible, undefiled and will never fade away, which is reserved in heaven for us. *James* 1:12; *1 Pet.* 1:4.

Constantly stimulate us to live with the hope of eternal life, which you, the God who cannot lie, have promised to all true believers. By your grace we already have this eternal life abiding in us. Encourage us to keep seeking the better country, since we have no continuing city in this world. Help us to set our hope on the heavenly city that has foundations, whose architect and builder is God. *Titus* 1:2; *1 John* 5:13; *Heb.* 11:16; 13:14; 11:10.

5

Intercession

Intercession

INTERCEDE FOR OTHERS IN
YOUR PRAYERS TO GOD

*O*ur Lord Jesus Christ has taught us to pray not only
*with others but also for others. The Apostle Paul
has directed us to intercede always for all the saints with
all prayer and supplication in the Spirit. Many of his
prayers as recorded in his epistles are offered on behalf of
his fellow-believers and friends.*

*We must not think that when we are in this part of
prayer we may be any less fervent, or even indifferent,
simply because we ourselves are not immediately concerned. Instead, a holy fire of love both to God and man
should make our devotions more warm and lively as we
pray for others.* Eph. 6:18.

Pray That Grace Will Become Active among People and Places Where It Has Not Yet Begun Its Work

Lord, teach transgressors your ways and let sinners be converted to you. Let the disobedient be turned to the wisdom of the just. Prepare a people for the Lord. Let those that are still dead in trespasses and sins be made alive. Say to them, 'Live!' Issue your command to them, saying, 'Live!' Then that moment shall be a time of love. *Psa.* 51:13; *Luke* 1:17; *Eph.* 2:1; *Ezek.* 16:6, 8.

Open their eyes, and turn them from darkness to light. Deliver them from the power of Satan, that they may receive forgiveness of sins and an inheritance among those who are sanctified. By the blood of the covenant set the prisoners free from the waterless pit. Let them return to the stronghold as prisoners of hope. Let your word prevail by pulling down Satan's fortifications. Cast down all vain imaginations, and every haughty opinion that exalts itself against the knowledge of God. Let their every thought be made captive to Christ. *Acts* 26:18; *Zech.* 9:11, 12; *2 Cor.* 10:4, 5.

Pray to the Lord of the Harvest for the Worldwide Spread of the Gospel

1. Intercede for the whole world of mankind in its lostness from God.

O God our Saviour, we pray for all men as we have been taught, believing that it is good and acceptable in your sight to pray in this way. You would have all men to be saved and come to the knowledge of the truth as it is in Jesus. For he gave himself as a ransom for all kinds of people. *1 Tim.* 2:3-6.

Gracious Lord, look with compassion on the world that lies under the control of the evil one. Cast out the prince of this world who has blinded the minds of people who do not believe. Make known your way of salvation throughout the earth, that all the nations may praise you. Let those that live without God and without hope in the world be transformed and enlisted in your service. Let all nations experience your power to save. Let them be glad and sing for joy, for you shall judge the peoples righteously as you govern the nations of the world. Clearly display your salvation and your righteousness before all nations. Let the ends of the earth witness the greatness of your salvation. *1 John* 5:19; *John* 12:31; *2 Cor.* 4:4; *Psa.* 67:2, 3; *Eph.* 2:12; *Psa.* 67:3, 4; 98:2, 3.

Give to your Son the nations as his inheritance, and the uttermost parts of the earth as his possession. You have said it is too easy a thing for him to raise up the fallen tribes of Jacob and restore the preserved in Israel. So you have given him the larger task of being a light to the Gentiles and bringing salvation to the ends of the earth. Let all the kingdoms of this world become the kingdoms of our Lord and of his Christ. *Psa.* 2:8; *Isa.* 49:6; *Rev.* 11:15.

2. Earnestly pray for the spread of the saving gospel of Christ among all nations and the expansion of his church by the constant conversion of many.

Let the gospel of Christ be preached among all nations to all peoples. For how shall anyone believe in him if they have not heard? How shall they hear without preachers? How shall they preach unless they are sent? We pray for your sovereign help in the spread of the gospel, for who else can thrust forth labourers except you, the Lord of the harvest? Let the people who walk in darkness see a great light. Let light dawn on those who live in the regions of death's gloomy shadow. *Matt.* 24:14; *Rom.* 10:14, 15; *Matt.* 9:38; *Isa.* 9:2; *Matt.* 4:16.

As the Lord of the harvest, add to your church every single day the ones being saved. Give us faith to enlarge the place of our tent, and expand the curtains of our dwelling. Make us bold to lengthen our cords even as we strengthen our stakes. Bring your saved seed from the east and gather them from the west. Say to the north, 'Give them up', and to the south, 'Do not hold them back!' Bring your sons from far-off places, and your daughters from the ends of the earth. Let their flocks be accepted on your altar, and let them bring glory to your magnificent house. Let them fly as clouds across the sky, and as doves to their nests. *Acts* 2:47; *Isa.* 54:2; 43:5, 6; 60:7, 8.

May sweet-smelling incense be presented to you along with their pure offerings. From the rising of the sun to its going down, let your name be great among the nations. Let the offering of the peoples be acceptable to you, having been sanctified by the Spirit. Let the earth be full of the knowledge of the Lord as the waters cover the sea. *Mal.* 1:11; *Rom.* 15:16; *Isa.* 11:9.

3. Make a special plea for God's ancient covenant people the Jews, that they may see Jesus as their promised Messiah.

LORD of the Covenant, our heart's desire and prayer for Israel is that they may be saved. Let them look with faith on him whom they have pierced. Let them turn to the Lord so that the veil blinding their hearts may be taken away. Let the branches which are broken off not continue in unbelief. Let them be grafted back into their own olive-tree. Though blindness has happened to part of Israel, let the fullness of the Gentiles come in, so that the fullness of the Jews may also be realized. In this marvellous manner, let all Israel be saved. *Rom.* 10:1; *Zech.* 12:10; *2 Cor.* 3:16; *Rom.* 11:23-26.

4. Intercede for the ancient churches of Asia and Africa, as well as the Reformation churches of Europe, that have suffered large setbacks.

Let the churches of Asia, Africa and Europe that were once golden candlesticks remember the height from which they have fallen. Let them repent and do the things they did when the gospel first came to them. Let the Lord Jesus delight to walk in their midst once more. Restore to them their saving judges as at the first, and their wise counsellors as at the beginning. Purge away their dross, and take away all their impurities. Return them from their captivity as streams breaking forth in the desert-lands of the south. *Rev.* 1:11, 12; 2:1, 5; *Isa.* 1:25, 26; *Psa.* 126:4.

5. Pray for the spread of the gospel to every corner of this vast world. Plead for God's mercy to extend to each and every continent, including North America, South America, Australia and Antarctica.

From pole to pole, and from the River to the ends of the earth let the peoples come to believe that Jesus is the Lamb of God, the only one who takes away the sin of the world. Let desert tribes bow before him and his enemies lick the dust. Commission special servants of yours to preach the gospel in places where Christ has never been known. Consecrate people from all the various nations of the world as an offering acceptable to you, sanctified by the Holy Spirit. *Psa.* 72:8, 9; *John* 1:29; *Rom.* 15:20, 16.

6. Pray for the conviction and conversion of atheists, hardened sinners, profane scoffers, and those that disgrace Christ by their immoral lives even while professing faith.

Show fools their folly when they say 'There is no God.' For their atheism makes them corrupt and leads them to practise abominations. Teach transgressors your ways, and let sinners be converted to you. Graciously give them repentance that will enable them to acknowledge the truth as it is in Jesus. Lead them into the way of truth that produces godly living. Mercifully enable them to deliver themselves out of the snare of the devil. *Psa.* 14:1; 51:13; *2 Tim.* 2:25; *Eph.* 4:21; *Titus* 1:1; *2 Tim.* 2:26.

Lord, maintain the honour of the Scriptures, the law, and your own testimony to the truth. Enlighten those who speak contrary to the Word, for they have no light in themselves. Magnify your Name and your Word above all things. Magnify the law, magnify the gospel, and make both glorious and honourable in the sight of men. Let those that are like sheep going astray return to Jesus Christ the Shepherd and Overseer of our souls. *Isa.* 8:20; *Psa.* 138:2; *Isa.* 42:21; *1 Pet.* 2:25.

Let people who will not be convinced by the Word be won over by the lifestyle of Christians. As they hear the truth of your word, let them be convicted of their sin. Disclose the secrets of their heart by the proclamation of your prophetic word. Bring them to the point of worshipping you as they are forced to admit that you are truly in the assembly of believers. *1 Pet.* 3:1; *1 Cor.* 14:24, 25.

Pray for Christ's Church and Kingdom

1. Pray to the Lord for the well-being of his church throughout the world in all aspects of its life.

Save your people, O Lord, and bless those who are your inheritance. Since a door large with promise has swung open for the gospel, let your word have free course in every place, and let it be glorified. *Psa.* 28:9; *1 Cor.* 16:9; *2 Thess.* 3:1.

Nourish your people. Keep lifting them up. Make them strong. Grant them the blessings of peace. Let your favour encompass them as a protecting shield. Do good to Zion according to your good pleasure. Build up the walls of Jerusalem. May peace reside within her walls, and prosperity in her palaces. For the sake of our brothers and fellow believers, we pronounce our benediction: 'May God's peace rest on her.' *Psa.* 29:11; 5:12; 51:18; 122:7, 8.

We pray not for the world, but for all that you as the Father have given to the Son, that they may be one even as you and the Son are one. Since there is one body, one Spirit, one hope to which we are called, one Lord, one faith, one baptism, and one God and Father of us all, let all Christians be joined in one heart and one way. *John* 17:20, 21; *Eph.* 4:4-6; *Jer.* 32:39.

Allow us to see the good of gospel-Jerusalem all the days of our life. May your peace rest on gospel-Israel. Give us good reason to answer the messenger of any nation or people that threatens your kingdom, 'The Lord has founded Zion. His afflicted people will always find secure refuge in her.' May your grace rest on all those who love the Lord Jesus Christ in sincerity, for you know the ones who are yours. Let everyone that claims the name of Christ shun every form of unrighteousness. *Psa.* 128:5, 6; *Isa.* 14:32; *Eph.* 6:24; *2 Tim.* 2:19.

2. Ask the Lord to pour out his Spirit on the church in a fresh and powerful way. Entreat him to unleash the power of true godliness. Plead for the revival of apostolic Christianity, and the correcting of everything that has gone wrong in the church.

Lord Christ, pour out your Spirit on your churches from your exalted throne in heaven. Revive your great work of restoration in the midst of the years. In the midst of the crumbling of earthly kingdoms make known your great redemptive plan, and preserve the lives of your people. Let our times be times of reformation. Let our revival be supported and encouraged by all that are upright in heart. *Isa.* 32:15a; *Hab.* 3:2; *Heb.* 9:10; *Psa.* 94:15.

Let the kind of religious devotion that is pure and undefiled before you, our compassionate

Father, flourish and prevail everywhere. Bring in your true kingdom among men, which is not focused on eating and drinking but on righteousness, peace, and joy in the Holy Spirit. Then the wilderness will become a fertile field, and judgment will once more be founded on righteousness. *James* 1:27; *Rom.* 14:17; *Isa.* 32:15b, 16.

Let whatever might be lacking in your church be set in proper order. Let every plant that has not been planted by you, our heavenly Father, be weeded out. Come to your temple like a refiner's fire and the strongest lye-soap. Purify the sons of Levi and all the seed of Israel. Purge them as gold and silver, that they may present a righteous offering that pleases you as in days of old. *Titus* 1:5; *Matt.* 15:13; *Mal.* 3:1-4.

3. Plead with the Lord to break the power of all the enemies of his righteous kingdom, and defeat all their Satan-inspired schemes.

Let all those in authority who set themselves against you and your anointed Messiah plot in vain. As the God who sits enthroned in heaven, laugh at them. Let your Anointed One rule them with a rod of iron whenever they take counsel together saying, 'Let us break their chains and fling from us their fetters.' Call them up short in your wrath, and terrify them in your fury. *Psa.* 2:1-5, 9.

When anyone opposes you and your gospel, give them exactly what they deserve. Give them a miscarrying womb and dry breasts. Make them like whirling dust and chaff before the wind. Cover their faces with shame, that they may turn and seek you in your true essence as revealed in your name. Let everyone know that you are the Most High God. For your self-revealing name is the Great I Am who reigns sovereignly over all the earth. *Hos.* 9:14; *Psa.* 83:13, 16-18.

Sovereign Lord, strike fear in the hearts of your enemies, that the nations may know themselves to be nothing more than mortal men. Whenever the proud enemies of your church deal proudly, make it plain that you are far greater than any of them or their gods. Let those that hate your holy Mt Zion be shamed and turned completely around. Let them be as a sprig of grass on a roof-top that withers before it grows. Let no weapon formed against your church prosper. Let every tongue that declares a judgment against her be condemned. *Psa.* 9:20; *Exod.* 18:11; *Psa.* 129:5, 6; *Isa.* 54:17.

Make gospel-Jerusalem an immovable stone with razor-sharp edges for all peoples. Though the nations of the earth take on a military formation against it, let those that attempt to cast off that burden be sliced to pieces. Let all your enemies perish, but let those that love you be as the sun when it goes forth in its strength. *Zech.* 12:3; *Judg.* 5:31.

Let the man of sin be slain by the breath of your mouth, and destroyed by the brilliance of your coming. Let those that have long been under the power of a strong delusion to believe the lie be enlightened. Let those who are perishing come to love the truth. Let Babylon, that epitome of a whole culture opposed to God, completely collapse and sink like a millstone into the sea. Let the kings of the earth that have dedicated their power to supporting oppressive, beastly structures in society be either destroyed or transformed to participate in the blessings of the new Jerusalem. *2 Thess.* 2:3, 8-11; *Rev.* 18:2, 21; 17:17; 21:24.

4. Ask the Lord to send relief to churches suffering under oppression. Entreat him to provide support, comfort, and deliverance for everyone who is being persecuted for righteousness' sake.

Let us identify with those that are imprisoned for the testimony of Jesus as though we were imprisoned with them. Let us be as one with those who suffer from severe oppression, remembering that we also live in a body that can be abused. Send them relief from heaven above. Deliver your saints from hateful enemies too strong for them. Bring them out into an expansive place where your blessings abound. Do not let the domineering rod of the wicked rest on the lot in life appointed for the righteous. Preserve the righteous from being tempted to respond in sinful ways to their mistreatment. *Heb.* 13:3; *Psa.* 18:16, 17, 19; 125:3.

Awake, O mighty arm of the Lord. Stir up yourself and show forth your strength. Intervene as in ancient days, as in earlier generations. Make the depths of the sea an escape route for the ransomed of the Lord. Arise in rapid response to the oppression of the poor and the groaning of the needy. Make them safe from those that ridicule them. *Isa.* 51:9, 10; *Psa.* 12:5.

Strengthen the patience and faith of your suffering saints. Enable them to live in hope and quietly wait for your salvation. Do not let those who have been oppressed return in disgrace from their mistreatment. Let the poor and needy come back praising your name. Let the salvation of Israel come down from the heavenly Mt Zion. Let Jacob rejoice and Israel be glad because you have restored your people from their captivity. Let the appointed year of your redemption come, the year of retribution in which you uphold the cause of Zion. *Rev.* 13:10; *Lam.* 3:25, 26; *Psa.* 74:21; 14:7; *Isa.* 63:4; 34:8.

Arise, Lord! Have mercy on Zion. Let this day be her favoured time, her appointed hour, for even her stones are precious to us. Even her dust stirs our pity. Build up Zion, and manifest your glory in her.

Listen to the prayer of the destitute. Do not ignore their pleas. Restrain your impending judgments. How can your people endure any more, for they are so small. For the sake of your own glory, make your face shine with favourable smiles on your desolated sanctuary. *Psa.* 102:13, 14, 16, 17; *Amos* 7:5; *Dan.* 9:17.

Let the sorrowful sighing of the prisoners alert you to their need. According to your great power, sustain those that are appointed to die for your name's sake. Let those whose teachers have been removed to some obscure corner set their eyes once more on the people you have given to instruct them in your ways. Even though they have had to eat the bread of adversity and drink the water of affliction, give them relief very soon. *Psa.* 79:11; *Isa.* 30:20.

5. Pray with great earnestness for the healing of the unhappy divisions within the church.

Because of the divisions among us, there are great searchings of heart, for there are three against two, and two against three in one house. But is this breach as wide as the sea that cannot be healed? Is there no balm in Gilead? Is there no physician there? Why then is there no healing of the wound of the daughter of your people? Lord, heal the divisions among us, for because of them whole nations quake. *Judg.* 5:16; *Luke* 12:52; *Lam.* 2:13; *Jer.* 8:22; *Psa.* 60:2.

We beg in the name of the Lord Jesus Christ that there may be no divisions among us. Let us be perfectly joined together with the same mind and the same purpose. Lord, keep us from judging one another and looking down on one another. Enable us to earnestly pursue the things that make for peace and the things by which each one of us may edify another. Let us do nothing out of rivalry or empty conceit. Instead, let us always regard others as higher than ourselves. Let our generous consideration of others be noted by all men, since we understand that the Lord himself is always nearby and soon to come. *1 Cor.* 1:10; *Rom.* 14:3, 19; *Phil.* 2:3; 4:5.

May the God who fosters endurance and encouragement enable us to live in harmony with one another, in accord with our oneness in Christ Jesus. With one heart and mouth may we glorify the God and Father of our Lord Jesus Christ. May you confirm our unity in the salvation we hold in common, even as we contend earnestly for the faith. Let us live in peace, that you, the God of love and peace, may be with us. *Rom.* 15:5, 6; *Jude* 3; *2 Cor.* 13:11.

6. Pray for all the ministers of God's Word and sacraments.

Teach your ministers how they ought to behave in your house, which is the church of the living God.

Let them never preach themselves, but always and only Christ Jesus the Lord. Inspire them to exert themselves so that they receive your approval for their work. Make them tireless labourers who will never need to feel ashamed, since they handle your word of truth with precise accuracy. *1 Tim.* 3:15; *2 Cor.* 4:5; *2 Tim.* 2:15.

Make them mighty in the Scriptures. Raise up men of God who have the competence that comes from being thoroughly equipped for every good work. In all things let them be a model of good works. Let them not be corrupted in what they teach. Make them serious, sincere, and well balanced in whatever they say, so they will never need to be contradicted. *Acts* 18:24; *2 Tim.* 3:17; *Titus* 2:7, 8.

Convict them of the importance of devoting themselves altogether to the public reading of Scripture, to exhortation, and to teaching, rather than being distracted by so many other things that are good in themselves. Show them repeatedly that they must give themselves over to prayer and the ministry of the word. Let them be absorbed in the few things critical to an effective ministry. Enable them to keep a close watch on themselves and their doctrine, for in practising constant self-scrutiny they will save both themselves and the people who hear them. *1 Tim.* 4:13; *Acts* 6:4; *1 Tim.* 4:15, 16.

Put the word you want them to say in their mouth, so that they may speak boldly as they openly declare the mystery of the gospel. Let them speak out fearlessly as they ought to speak. Make every one of your preachers a capable minister of the new covenant. Let their ministry not focus on the letter engraved in stone, which kills by its demands of perfection among fallen sinners. Instead, let them minister in the Spirit, the one who gives life. Lord, show mercy to your ministers, so they can be faithful. *Eph.* 6:19, 20; *2 Cor.* 3:6; *1 Cor.* 7:25.

Let the bow in their hands remain steady, and their arm remain limber because of the overarching hand of the Mighty One of Jacob, the Shepherd, Israel's Stone. Let the ministers of your word be full of power, justice, and might by the Spirit of the Lord, to show your people their transgressions and the house of Jacob their sins. Let them not labour in vain. Keep them from spending their strength for nothing. Let your hand be with them, that many may believe through their ministry and turn to you. *Gen.* 49:24; *Mic.* 3:8; *Isa.* 58:1; 49:4; *Acts* 11:21.

Keep them sound in the faith. Tutor them so they always speak things that promote sound doctrine. Let them instruct with meekness those that oppose themselves. Keep your servants from striving. Help them to be gentle in their dealings with all kinds of people. Make them capable teachers who are always patient. *Titus* 1:13; 2:1; *2 Tim.* 2:24, 25.

Make them good examples to all believers by everything they say and do. Let their words and deeds manifest the generosity of love, the fullness of the Spirit, the consistency of faith, and the virtue of purity. Let these ministers of the new covenant that bear your vessels be fully consecrated as they offer priestly service to you. Inscribe this declaration on their foreheads: 'Holy to the Lord.' *1 Tim.* 4:12; *Isa.* 52:11; *Rom.* 15:16; *Exod.* 28:36.

Pray for the Nations of the World

Lord, you govern the nations. Who would dare not to stand in awe of you, O King of all kingdoms? You sit on your throne determining what is right. Judge the world in righteousness, and administer justice to all peoples. *Psa.* 22:28; *Jer.* 10:7; *Psa.* 9:4, 8.

Hasten the day when you will make wars cease in every corner of the earth. Let one nation never again lift up its sword against another. Let them beat their swords into ploughs and their spears into pruning-hooks. Bring in that glorious day when nations will study war no more. *Psa.* 46:9; *Isa.* 2:4.

In the days of this long succession of earthly monarchs, as the God of heaven set up your kingdom that can never be destroyed, which is the kingdom of Christ the Lord. Frustrate whatever self-serving schemes may be in the hearts of the nations that would oppose his perfect rule of righteousness. Let your purposes stand and the intentions of your heart be fulfilled throughout all generations. Make kings foster fathers and queens nursing mothers to the Israel of God. *Dan.* 2:44; *Prov.* 19:21; *Psa.* 33:10, 11; *Isa.* 49:23.

Offer Special Prayers for Your Own Land and Nation

1. Thank God for his mercies to your land.

Lord, thank you for planting us on a fruitful hill rather than making the wilderness our habitation or the barren desert our home. Our land yields abundant harvests. You have treated our nation so graciously. We have heard with our ears and our fathers have told us of the work you did for them in earlier days. By your special favour we have experienced for ourselves exactly what previous generations told us. Help us to regularly remind ourselves of your mercy to our land whenever we gather together for worship. *Isa.* 5:1; *Job* 39:6; *Psa.* 85:12; 85:1; 44:1; 48:8, 9.

How gracious you have been to give us such a pleasant land. It is rightly called 'Immanuel's land'. Though we have abused it terribly, it remains a Valley of Vision. For you have set up your tabernacle among us, and your sanctuary remains in our midst. Because of your continual blessing, each family lives safely under its own vine and fig tree. Peaceful security stays with us as we travel back and forth. *Jer.* 3:19; *Isa.* 8:8; 22:1; *Ezek.* 37:26, 27; *1 Kings* 4:25; *2 Chron.* 15:5.

In your loving concern, set over us a good government that practises justice and opposes corruption. Give us governmental leaders who will be a terror to all those who do evil, and will praise and protect those who do good. *1 Kings* 10:9; *Rom.* 13:3.

2. Humble yourself before God for national sins that could easily provoke his wrath.

We are a sinful people, a people weighed down with guilt. We and our children are utterly corrupt. We have good reason to weep before you over the abominations regularly committed among us. Because so much iniquity abounds, the love of most has grown cold. Yet in your grace you have not forsaken us. *Isa.* 1:4; *Ezek.* 9:4; *Matt.* 24:12; *Jer.* 51:5.

3. Pray earnestly for God's mercy toward your nation.

(i) Humbly ask God for the manifestation of his favour toward your nation, since every blessing depends on his grace.

O Saviour of your people in time of trouble, do not be a stranger in our nation. Do not be like a traveller that turns aside for just a night. Instead, come and make your permanent residence among us. Our national iniquities testify against us. We have sinned against you. Yet for the glory of your own name do not forsake us. *Jer.* 14:7-9.

Bring genuine repentance to this people for their sins, O Covenant LORD, God of hosts. Cause your face to shine with favour toward us. Demonstrate your binding love to your covenant people as you bless their land. Let your salvation be always near those who fear you, that glory may dwell in our land. Let mercy and truth meet together. Let righteousness and peace kiss each other. Let truth spring up out of the earth, and righteousness come down from heaven. Let righteousness go before you to determine the way of your dealing with our nation. Give the best for our people, whatever that might be. *Psa.* 80:3; 85:7, 9-13.

(ii) Pray that the gospel will always continue among your nation, and the means of grace remain available to all your people. Ask the Lord to allow a door to remain open in your nation for the spread of the saving gospel of Christ.

Let the ruling throne of Christ be apparent among us as an unbroken dynasty that lasts forever through the establishment and maintenance of his church and his kingdom. Let your sovereignty that governs all nations bring blessing to our people. Let the lampstand of Christ's church in the midst of our nation never be removed from its place, though we deserve that it should. For your people have left their first love. Never do to us as you did to Shiloh, where you first set your name and then removed it. Let our people never know what a famine of the Word of God means. Do not force the people of this land to wander from sea to sea and from the river to the ends of the earth seeking some word from you. *Psa.* 45:6; *Jer.* 17:12; *Rev.* 2:4, 5; *Jer.* 7:12, 14; *Amos* 8:11, 12.

Be the stability of our times and the source of our saving experiences. Let the fear of the Lord be for us the key that opens your treasures of wisdom and knowledge. Let the righteous flourish among us. Let those who fear you continue in our land as long as the sun and moon endure. Throughout the generations to come let there be abundance of peace, so that children yet to be born may praise the Lord throughout our land. *Isa.* 33:6; *Psa.* 72:5-7; 102:18.

(iii) Pray for the outward peace and tranquillity of your nation, and the continuation of its liberty. Ask for God's abundant blessing on the fruitfulness of your land.

Make peaceful relations be our governor, righteousness the supervisor of our businesses. Let violence never be heard in our streets, invasion or devastation along our borders. Let our national boundaries have the reputation of inviting visitors with the words, 'Come in here to find the good news of salvation proclaimed openly'; 'Enter here and be free to offer your praise to God.' Never let our land be termed 'Forsaken' and 'Desolate'. Show your delight in blessing your people in this land. Display your special love to them as those to whom you are married. Let a song be sung by your people in this nation when you manifest yourself as their wall of defence. Let the city of God in heaven find a reflection of its righteousness in our cities. Let people who maintain truth feel completely welcome as they enter our cities, towns, and villages. *Isa.* 60:17, 18; 62:4; 26:1, 2.

Let righteousness which exalts a nation abound among us. Deliver us from national sins which are a disgrace to any people. Let our peace be as the deep waters of a river and our righteousness as the mighty waves of the sea. *Prov.* 14:34; *Isa.* 48:18.

Never make our heavens as brass and our earth as iron. Do not take away our corn and our wine in their seasons. Give us rain moderately in its proper season, both the early and the later rains. Let our land yield her increase, and our trees their fruit. Reserve the appointed weeks of harvest for us, giving us fair weather in all the various seasons of the year. Let us eat our bread in peace and be fully satisfied, living safely in our land. *Deut.* 28:23; *Hos.* 2:9; *Joel* 2:23; *Jer.* 5:24; *Lev.* 26:4, 5.

Abundantly bless our provisions. Satisfy our poor with bread. When they gather in their harvest, let them eat and give you the praise you deserve. Do not blow away what our hands have gathered. When we expect much do not let it end up being very little. Heap your blessing on our blessings, that all nations may call us blessed, a land filled with delights. *Psa.* 132:15; *Isa.* 62:9; *Hag.* 1:9; *Mal.* 3:10, 12.

Be a wall of fire around your people in our land. Be the glory in our midst. Let the gospel be our glory, and let a canopy protect its honour. Create for your people a cloud to cover them in the heat of the day, and a flaming fire to give light and protection for them by night. May peace be within our borders and security within our walls. Let your people rejoice whether their travels take them far away, or they stay near to home. Let them invite all nations to come and worship with them at your holy mountain. *Zech.* 2:5; *Isa.* 4:5, 6; *Psa.* 122:7; *Deut.* 33:18, 19 .

(iv) Offer your petitions for God's blessing on all efforts to reform your nation's lifestyle and to suppress all its vices.

Let reformation begin with your church. Let the Redeemer come to Zion, turning away ungodliness from Jacob. Let the filth of Jerusalem be purged from your chosen remnant by a purifying, burning spirit of judgment. *Rom.* 11:26; *Isa.* 4:4.

O righteous God who tests the hearts and motives of men, let the wickedness of the wicked come to an end, and establish the purposes of the just. Motivate many to rise up on your behalf against those who practise evil. Help them to stand up for you against all workers of iniquity. Let those that are striving against sin never become weary or faint in their determination. *Psa.* 7:9; 94:16; *Heb.* 12:3, 4.

Let the mouth of all that promote oppression be shut. Display your covenant faithfulness to the poor and needy by multiplying their families like flocks as you free them from their affliction. Execute your righteous judgments so that the infection caused by any plague may be stopped. Banish the name of every idol from our land. Purify the lips of the peoples that they may call on your name and serve you shoulder to shoulder. Exalt your people above all nations by making them a holy people to you, the Covenant LORD our God. Let them be praised, made famous and held in honour by all people. *Psa.* 107:41, 42; 106:30; *Zech.* 13:2; *Zeph.* 3:9; *Deut.* 26:19.

(v) Pray for the protection of your people as they enter the conflict against evil and untruth when it manifests itself within your own nation, among your national neighbours, and throughout distant countries.

We thank you for faithful witnesses for Christ who live in jeopardy of their lives as they stand in the frontline of the battlefield on behalf of gospel truth throughout the nations of the world. Give them all the skills and instincts necessary for the conflict that confronts them. Train their hands for the battle and their fingers for the fight. Let your salvation be their shield. Let the powerful interventions of your right hand sustain them. Cover their heads against the mortal dangers that fly at them in the day of battle. *Judg.* 5:18; *Psa.* 18:34, 35; 140:7.

Give us your help in all our conflicts, for any deliverance that comes by human help is utterly useless. Let us do valiantly through your strength, for you yourself will tread down our enemies. In your good providence appoint our deliverers. Make ungodly nations like dust to our sword, and like driven stubble to our bow. *Psa.* 60:11, 12; *Isa.* 41:2.

Let us be a happy people, unique in being saved by you, O Lord. Position yourself so you can be our defensive shield and our brilliant sword. Make our enemies flee in panic when they see that you are fighting for us against them. Rise, Lord, and let your enemies be scattered. Let all those that hate you flee before you. Then return, O Lord, to the many thousands of your people that sojourn as strangers through this hostile world. *Deut.* 33:29; *Exod.* 14:25; *Num.* 10:35.

(vi) Pray for all those who work as public servants throughout your land.

Counsel our policymakers. Teach our governors wisdom. Give them an abundant share of the spirit of wisdom, understanding and knowledge that belong to Christ our sovereign Messiah. Make them quick to demonstrate that they understand the importance of fearing the Lord. Do not silence the lips of trustworthy advisors. Do not take away the discernment of the aged. In this day and age, do not let the things that could bring peace to your people be hid from our eyes. *Psa.* 105:22; *Isa.* 11:2, 3; *Job* 12:20; *Luke* 19:42.

Make it clear that you stand in the assembly of the politically powerful, that you judge the judges. Let the leaders of the nations recognize that they live under the sovereignty of the God of Abraham. Let the flags of the world's nations symbolize that they acknowledge your rule, so that you may be greatly exalted. *Psa.* 82:1; 47:9.

(vii) Pray specifically for magistrates, judges, and supreme court justices of the land.

Direct those that preside judicially over us to make just decisions, ruling in the fear of God. Let them always remember that they judge not for man but for you, the God who presides over them in their judgments. Let the fear of the Lord continually rest on them. *2 Sam.* 23:3, 4; *2 Chron.* 19:6, 7.

Appoint as our judges people who are capable of handling their responsibilities well. Make them incorruptible men of truth, fearing God and despising bribery. Let justice roll on like a river, and righteousness as a mighty stream that never stops flowing. *Exod.* 18:25; *2 Chron.* 19:7; *Amos* 5:24.

Empower our magistrates to retain their integrity. Enable them to defend the widow and fatherless, do justice for the afflicted and needy, and deliver the poor and helpless out of the hands of wicked men. Let our rulers never be a terror to those who do good works but always to those who do evil. *Psa.* 82:3, 4; *Rom.* 13:3; *1 Pet.* 2:14.

Offer Specific Prayers for the Various Ages and Conditions of Men

1. Remember the special needs of those that are young and just now setting out in the world.

Lord, help those that are young to remember their Creator in the days of their youth. Keep them from the vanity which comes with childhood and the early stages of life. Restrain them from walking according to the impulses of their heart and the sights that appeal to their eyes. Let them carefully consider that as God you will call them to account for every unwise thing they do and every idle word they speak. Encourage the young to be sober in their judgments. Let your word abide in them, that they may be strong to overcome the wicked one. *Eccles.* 12:1; 11:9, 10; *Matt.* 12:36; *Titus* 2:6; *1 John* 2:14.

Let Christ possess the multitude of our youth that emerge like dewdrops from the womb of the morning. Let him be formed in hearts that are still young. Protect those that are just now setting out in the world. Preserve them from the corruption that is in the world through uncontrolled desires. Let those who have been well educated in your truth hold on firmly to sound doctrine. Encourage them to continue living and believing according to the things they have learned, since they know well the reputation of the people who have taught them. *Psa.* 110:3; *Gal.* 4:19; *2 Pet.* 1:4; *Titus* 1:9; *2 Tim.* 3:14.

2. Pray for those that are old in view of their special testings.

Some among us are old disciples of Jesus Christ. Lord, give them satisfaction and fulfilment as they bring forth good fruit for Christ in their old age. Demonstrate to them and to us that you are upright, and never forsake your faithful servants. Be their rock of stability through all the changes of life, for not one instance of unrighteous dealing can be found in you. *Acts* 21:16; *Psa.* 92:14, 15; 37:28; 92:15.

Now the days full of trouble have come. Now the years have come when people say there is no pleasure in them. Let your consolations delight their souls. Let them keep bearing fruit in old age. Let them stay fresh and green. Make them glad for as many days as you have afflicted them. Abundantly bless them for as many years as they have seen trouble. For you have promised that even to our old age you will never change. You are always the same. You will keep carrying us when our hair turns grey. You are the one who has made us, and you are the one who will bear us up, sustain us, and deliver us even to the very end. *Eccles.* 12:1; *Psa.* 94:19; 92:14; 90:15; *Mal.* 3:6; *Isa.* 46:4.

You have raised us up from our youth. You have repeatedly displayed your wondrous works to us. Now when we are old and grey-headed do not leave us. Do not cast us off in our old age. Never fail us when our strength fails. Let every grey head be a crown of glory attained by a righteous life. Let us know for certain the one we have believed. Confirm our confidence that you are able to keep our souls until that great final day. *Psa.* 71:6, 17, 18; *Prov.* 16:31, 2 *Tim.* 1:12.

3. Do not neglect to pray for the rich and prosperous in this world, for they need prayer as much as anyone else. In fact, considering how hard it is for the rich to enter the kingdom of God, they may need our prayers more than other people.

You have surprised us by teaching that it is extremely hard for those who are rich to enter the kingdom of heaven. Yet you have also taught us that things impossible with men are possible with you. Lord, keep those that are rich in the present world from being arrogant or trusting in uncertain riches. Give them grace to put their hope in you, the living God who generously provides us with everything we enjoy. Show them how to do good and how to be rich in good works. Make them always ready to distribute among others the material blessings you have given them. Give them a willingness to share, that they may store up for themselves a firm foundation in readiness for the age to come. Enable them to take hold of life that is truly life. *Matt.* 19:24, 26; *1 Tim.* 6:17-19.

4. Never fail to pray for the poor and those who are afflicted with many needs in this world. For they are always present among us, and we must not miss any opportunity to minister to them in Christ's name.

Loving Father, make us always ready to give even a cup of cold water in your name to those who are in need. If the poor have ever come to our door and we have not cared for them, let us experience your righteous judgments. *Matt.* 10:42; *Job* 31:16-22.

Many are the troubles that may come to the righteous, including poverty. Gracious Lord, deliver them out of them all. Make those that are poor in this world rich in faith and heirs of your eternal kingdom. Give them abundant grace to receive the gospel in all its fullness. *Psa.* 34:19; *James* 2:5; *Matt.* 11:5.

5. Pray for your enemies and those that hate you.

Lord, help us to love our enemies, to bless those that curse us, and to pray for those that persecute us. Father, forgive those who would even murder us, for they have no comprehension of what they are doing. Do not hold them accountable for their malice against us. Work in us an attitude of forbearance and forgiveness in love. Whenever we come before you in prayer, let us forgive others that you our heavenly Father may forgive us. Make even our enemies be at peace with us because our ways are pleasing to you. *Luke* 6:27, 28; 23:34; *Acts* 7:60; *Col.* 3:13; *Mark* 11:25; *Prov.* 16:7.

Let the peaceful relations of Messiah's kingdom come to its fullest realization. Let the wolf and the lamb lie down together. Let no one hurt or destroy anyone else in all your holy mountain. Cure the people of the north in Ephraim from their jealousy toward the people of the south in Judah, and keep Judah from harassing Ephraim ever again. *Isa.* 11:6, 9, 13.

6. Never forget to pray for your friends and those that love you.

Let everything go well with all those that we love in the truth. Let their bodies stay in good health. But especially let their souls prosper. *3 John* 2.

May the grace of the Lord Jesus Christ be with their spirits. *Philem.* 25.

6

*Prayers for
Particular Occasions*

Prayers for Particular Occasions

✿

OFFER SPECIAL PRAYERS FOR PARTICULAR OCCASIONS RELATED TO BOTH PUBLIC AND PRIVATE LIFE

*G*od has given you the duty as well as the privilege of bringing each and every thing that concerns you before him in prayer. But beyond a duty and a privilege, specific prayer about particular situations in life is God's own remedy against troubling cares. He has given directions that in everything by prayer and supplication with thanksgiving you should make your desires known to him rather than being anxious about anything. As part of your boldness in your approach to him, you are encouraged to be very specific in presenting your case. The petition should correspond to the problem, the pain and the grief. Not that God needs you to explain your situation to him, for he knows it far better than you ever could. Instead, he wants you to acknowledge him in all your ways, wait patiently on him for his direction for your every step, and bring all your desires into submission to his more perfect plan and purpose. Never presume to dictate to him the programme you have laid out for your life. Instead, as you offer up your desires to him, gladly submit to his infinite wisdom as you humbly give expression to your needs, desires, and burdens. Ask him to do whatever he judges to be best for his glory, your good, and the worldwide spread of the saving gospel of Christ. Phil. 4:6; Heb. 10:19; 2 Chron. 6:29; Prov. 3:6; Psa. 37:23.

Now consider particular occasions for offering up prayers to God. These petitions include prayers for the regular course of the day, prayers for your life in Christ's church, prayers for the life of the community, prayers for the sick in body, prayers for people with spiritual problems, and prayers for people facing special challenges.

❦

Pray for the Regular Course of the Day

1. Begin your morning with prayers to God your Saviour.

Gracious Lord, we lift up our voice to you the moment we wake up. In the earliest hours of the morning we direct our prayer to you. We turn our eyes toward heaven, for our soul waits for you more than people who anxiously watch for the morning. We sing out loud of your mercy in the morning, for you have guarded us throughout the night. *Psa.* 5:3; 130:6; 59:16.

Daytime belongs to you. Night-time is also yours. You have established light and its source in the sun. You have commanded the light of the morning to appear once more. You have caused the dawn's light to stretch out its rays to take hold of the ends of the earth. In its light the earth takes shape like clay under a seal. *Psa.* 74:16; *Job* 38:12-14.

As the morning dawns, let the Dawn of Salvation shine on us from heaven above. Refresh us with the forgiveness of our sins that comes through your tender mercies. Let the Sun of Righteousness arise with healing under the wings of his spreading rays. Let our path be as the dawning light which shines brighter and brighter until it reaches the brilliance of noonday. Only because of your mercy have we not been consumed. Your compassions never fail. They are new every morning. Great is your faithfulness. Though weeping may endure for a night, joy comes in the morning. *Luke* 1:77, 78; *Mal.* 4:2; *Prov.* 4:18; *Lam.* 3:22, 23; *Psa.* 30:5.

Thank you for letting us lie down and sleep at night. Unlike the Son of God on earth, we have a place to lay down our head. We have not been forced to wander in deserts and mountains, in dens and caves of the earth. We have slept comfortably rather than tossing back and forth until dawn. You have not appointed wearisome nights to us. We do not murmur as we lie down, 'When will this miserable night be gone?' Our bed comforts us, and our sleep erases every distressful thought. As a sign of your love, you grant the gift of sleep. We go to bed, sleep through the night, and wake up again. You have brought the dawn's light once more to our eyes, so that we have not slept the sleep of death. *Psa.* 3:5; *Luke* 9:58; *Heb.* 11:38; *Job* 7:3, 4, 13; *Psa.* 127:2; 13:3.

O Lord, preserve us from the pestilence that stalks in darkness and from the evil purposes of the rulers of the darkness of this world. Keep us safe from the devil as he goes about like a roaring lion seeking someone to devour. We praise you that you never become drowsy. You never fall asleep. For you are the only one who can protect your chosen people. As long as you keep us, we are perfectly safe. *Psa.* 91:6; *Eph.* 6:12; *1 Pet.* 5:8; *Psa.* 121:4, 7.

Let us say with your servant David, 'When I wake up, I am still with you.' Our eyes look in anticipation toward the watches of the night, for then we have opportunity to meditate on your word. Yet vain thoughts still lodge inside us. Pardon our sins. In the morning let us hear your words of covenant love, for we trust in you. Let us know the way in which we should walk this day, for we put our life in your hands. Teach us to do your will, for you are our God. Let your gracious Spirit lead us on a level pathway. *Psa.* 139:18; 119:148; *Jer.* 4:14; *Psa.* 143:8, 10.

Keep us from all evil throughout this day. Lord, preserve our souls. Preserve us in our going out and our coming in. Charge your angels to protect us. Let them bear us up in their hands so that we will not bruise our foot on a stone. Give us grace to do the work of the day in its day, as the duty of the day requires. *Psa.* 121:7, 8; 91:11, 12; *Ezra* 3:4.

2. Conclude your day with prayers to God your Preserver.

Blessed be the Lord, who daily bears our burdens. This day you have preserved us once more in our going out and our coming in. So we will lie down and sleep in peace, for you make us dwell in safety. Put a hedge of protection about us, our home, and everything that is ours. Let your angels encamp around us to deliver us, that we may lie down without anything to make us afraid. Even when we approach the sleep of death, enable us to commit our spirits into your preserving hands in peace. *Psa.* 68:19; 121:8; 4:8; *Job* 1:10; *Psa.* 34:7; *Job* 11:19; *Psa.* 31:5; *Acts* 7:59; *Luke* 23:46.

O Lord, you make everyone who witnesses the beginning and ending of the day to marvel at your wonders. Wherever morning dawns and evening fades you call forth spontaneous shouts of joy. We go out to work when the day dawns, and return to rest in the evening. In the same way, let our souls return and rest in you, for you have dealt bountifully with us. Let our sleep be sweet to us. For by it you call us from our work and our labour, and tell us to rest for a while. *Psa.* 65:8; 104:22, 23; 116:7; *Jer.* 31:26; *Mark* 6:31.

Open our ears when you warn us in our subconscious through dreams as deep sleep falls on us in the night. Let your night-time warnings turn us from wrongdoing, keep us from pride, and deliver us from the pit of destruction. Give us your counsel, and let our heart instruct us at night-time. Examine us throughout the night. Enable us to commune with our own hearts on our beds and be at rest. *Job* 33:15-18; *Psa.* 16:7; 17:3; 4:4.

Father, just as you have given us this day our daily bread, so forgive us the trespasses of this day. Let us praise you as we remember you on our bed. Help us to focus our meditations on you through the long hours of the night. As you manifest your pleasure to your saints, let us be joyful in your glorious reality and sing aloud on our beds. *Matt.* 6:11, 12; *Psa.* 63:5, 6; 149:4, 5.

3. Before a meal, ask God's blessing.

Lord, you give food to all flesh, for your covenant love endures for ever. The eyes of all wait on you. You open your hand and satisfy the desire of every living thing. You give meat to those who fear you, for you remember your covenant love forever. You are our life, the one who determines the length of our days. You are the God who has fed us all our life up to this day. You give us richly all things to enjoy, though we serve you very poorly. You have given us every kind of vegetation and meat for our food as well as all kinds of fruit from trees. You have allowed us to enjoy as food everything that lives on the earth. *Psa.* 136:25; 145:15, 16; 111:5; *Deut.* 30:20; *Gen.* 48:15; *1 Tim.* 6:17; *Gen.* 1:29; 9:3.

In accordance with the good news proclaimed by Christ, keep us from calling anything unclean that you have made pure. Help us to stop thinking that what goes into a man can defile him, since Jesus our Lord has declared all foods clean. Free us from the corruption that comes out of our heart. Let us refuse nothing of your good creation, since you created it to be received with thanksgiving by those who believe and know the truth. *Acts* 10:15; *Mark* 7:18-23; *Matt.* 15:11; *1 Tim.* 4:3, 4.

We readily admit that we are not worthy of the least crumb that falls from the table of your good providence. You might justly take away from us the basic necessities of bread and water. It would be perfectly right for you to make us eat our bread and drink our water under the strictest rationing, and in the most appalling circumstances. For when we have been fully fed and satisfied, we have forgotten you, our God and our Maker. Pardon our inexcusable sins of ingratitude. Do not let the table where we eat our meals become a snare and a trap for us, when it should be the daily source of our well-being. *Matt.* 15:27; *Isa.* 3:1; *Ezek.* 4:16; *Deut.* 32:15; *Psa.* 69:22.

Help us to remember that everything must be consecrated by the Word of God and prayer. Constantly remind us that man does not live by bread alone, but by every word that proceeds out of your mouth. As we follow our Master's example, let us look up to heaven and pray for your blessing on our food. Demonstrate the richness of your grace by placing your fullest blessing on our provisions. Satisfy the poor of our land with the sustaining bread they need. *1 Tim.* 4:5; *Matt.* 4:4; 14:19; *Psa.* 132:15.

God forbid that we should be blemishes at the love-feasts of believers, feeding ourselves without any awareness of the possibility of eating and drinking damnation to ourselves. Keep us from making a god of our belly. Guard our hearts so that they are never overwhelmed by dissipation or drunkenness. Whether we eat or drink, or whatever we do, help us to do everything to your glory. *Jude* 12; *1 Cor.* 11:29; *Phil.* 3:19; *Luke* 21:34; *1 Cor.* 10:31.

4. After you have eaten, give thanks to God.

What a blessing it is that we have enough food to eat until we are full. We bless you for the good land you have given us. You are Lord of all, and you give food to the hungry. You prepare an abundant table for us even in the presence of our enemies. You anoint our head with oil, and our cup overflows. Put the spirit of your generosity in us so that we will be moved to send portions to those who have nothing to eat. *Deut.* 8:10; *Psa.* 146:7; *Psa.* 23:5; *Neh.* 8:10.

Especially we bless you for the Bread of Life which came down from heaven. O Father, you gave him for the life of the world. Lord, give us that bread every day. Give us the wisdom to labour less for food which perishes, and more for the nourishment of our souls that will endure throughout this life and the life to come. You are the portion of our inheritance, you are our cup. You have secured our inheritance. We have every reason to declare, 'Our boundary lines have marked out pleasant places for us. The Lord has granted us a most generous inheritance.' If only you would allow us to be among the blessed ones who will eat bread in your kingdom and feast on the hidden manna. *John* 6:33, 34, 27; *Psa.* 16:5, 6; *Luke* 14:15; *Rev.* 2:17.

5. Before departing on a journey, pray for God's protection.

Lord, watch over us as we travel. Let nothing evil happen to us. Give us a prosperous journey by your will. Wherever we go, let us be surrounded with your favour as with a protecting shield. Help us always to remember the ways of wisdom you have taught us, so we can move through this life safely as we travel. Keep us from tripping in the pathway, or injuring ourselves by stumbling over a stone. *Gen.* 28:20; *Psa.* 91:10; *Rom.* 1:10; *Psa.* 5:12; *Prov.* 3:19, 21, 23; *Psa.* 91:12.

May the Father himself, together with the Son, direct our way to the people and places where we can serve him best. Teach us how to order all our affairs with discretion. Give us success in whatever mission you send us on. As the God who watches over all your people, watch over us so that we make no plans to harm one another while we are separated from each other. Show us the consistency of your covenant love even as we travel as strangers to distant places. *1 Thess.* 3:11; *Psa.* 112:5; *Gen.* 24:12; 31:49, 52.

6. When you return safely from a journey, give thanks to the Lord.

Blessed be the LORD of the Covenant, the God of Abraham. You have never forgotten to display your love and your truth, for you always guide us by your providential appointments to the people and places that are just right for us. All my bones, the foundational structures of my whole being, raise their testimony. Lord, who is like you, for you preserve all my bones. Not a single one of them is broken. O God, you are the one who undergirds me. You devise the perfect way for my life. *Gen.* 24:27; *Psa.* 35:10; 34:20; 18:32.

Pray for Your Life in Christ's Church

1. On the evening before the Lord's Day, prepare yourself through prayer.

Though the sun will rise tomorrow in the same way it does on every other day of the week, let us remember that tomorrow is the Sabbath of the Lord. Help us to recognize that it is a high day, blessed, holy and honourable to you. Give us an abundance of grace to sanctify the day even as you have sanctified it from creation. Do wonders among us tomorrow. Enable us to set our minds on a proper work of preparation, since the Sabbath is now drawing near. *Exod.* 16:23; *John* 19:31; *Isa.* 58:13; *Gen.* 2:3; *Josh.* 3:5; *Luke* 23:54.

When you saw everything you had made in six days, you declared that all was very good. But despite the perfections of our first father, we have all offended in many ways. Yet as we come to worship in repentance and trust in Christ's blood, wash not only our feet, but also our hands, our head, and our heart. Cleanse us so we can teach transgressors your ways. Let us use this day to the fullest, encircling your altar, declaring our thanksgiving and recounting all your wondrous works. *Gen.* 1:31; *James* 3:2; *John* 13:9; *Psa.* 51:3, 7, 13; 26:6, 7.

Give us rest from all our works for this whole day. Let us leave all our worldly cares at the bottom of your holy hill as we go up the mountain to worship you. Then let us return refreshed to our labours. *Heb.* 4:10; *Gen.* 22:5.

2. On the morning of the Lord's day, consecrate yourself to God.

May we be in the Spirit on the Lord's Day! May we call the Sabbath a delight as we honour the Son of Man, who is Lord of the Sabbath. Let us not go our own ways, seek our own pleasure, or speak our own words throughout this day. *Rev.* 1:10; *Mark* 2:28; *Isa.* 58:13.

We glorify you for blessing us as we join the prophesied Coming One in your house on the day you have appointed for presenting our sacrificial offerings to you. Thank you for making your light shine on us by allowing us to see one more of the days of the Son of Man, the second Adam. We testify that in our experience one day in your courts is better than a thousand days spent anywhere else. *Psa.* 118:26, 27; *Luke* 17:22; *Psa.* 84:10.

Father, Lord of heaven and earth, we thank you that as we participate in your ordinances on this holy day, the things which have remained hidden from the wise and prudent are now revealed to us babes. For it was good in your sight for our eyes to see and our ears to hear the truths about you and your redemption that many prophets and kings desired to see and hear, and never did. But now life and immortality are brought to light for us by the gospel. *Luke* 10:21-24; *2 Tim.* 1:10.

3. As you begin your public worship on the Lord's day, remember that you are being led by the one God, the Great Shepherd of the sheep who presides over all the masters of Christian assemblies. Deut. *6:4;* Heb. *13:20;* Eccles. *12:11.*

Our help is in the name of the Lord who made heaven and earth. We come together to give glory to the great I Am, the Covenant Lord who in six days made heaven and earth, the sea and everything in them. You rested the seventh day after you had completed your work of creation. Therefore you have blessed this Sabbath day and made it holy. Let us be your new creation, your own workmanship, created in Christ Jesus for doing good works. As the Creator-God, you commanded light to shine out of darkness on the first day of the world. Now shine in our hearts on this first day of the week. Give us the light of the knowledge of the glory of God as it radiates from the face of Jesus Christ. *Psa.* 124:8; *Exod.* 3:14; 20:11; *2 Cor.* 5:17; *Eph.* 2:10; *2 Cor.* 4:6.

We have come together to give glory to the Lord Jesus Christ as we sanctify this Sabbath day to his honour. For this is the Lord's day in which he proved his lordship over heaven and earth by his resurrection from the dead on the first day of the week.

Lord Christ, you are the stone the builders rejected, but now you have become the chief cornerstone of the Messianic kingdom. This is the Lord's doing, and it is marvellous in our eyes. This is the consummation-day you have made, let us rejoice and be glad in it. For you are the first and the last, who was dead and are alive forever more. *Rev.* 1:10; *Matt.* 28:1, 6; *Psa.* 118:22-24; *Rev.* 2:8.

Today let us experience the power of Christ's resurrection. As we have been buried with him in the likeness of his death, let us also walk in newness of life just as Christ was raised from the dead as a public display of the Father's glory. Let us be seated with him in heavenly places. Let us enjoy resurrection life as we seek the things above where Christ is seated at the right hand of the Father. *Phil.* 3:10; *Rom.* 6:4, 5; *Eph.* 2:6; *Col.* 3:1.

Let us today give glory to the Spirit of grace that has been poured out on all people. Let us celebrate the giving of that consummate promise of the Father. Let us rejoice in the full manifestation of your power by the coming of the Spirit on the same day of the week that Christ rose from the dead. Especially on this day fill us with the Holy Spirit. Let the fruit of your light, as brought by Christ and his Spirit, be manifest in us with all goodness, righteousness, and truth. *Acts* 2:17; 1:4, 8; *Lev.* 23:15, 16; *Acts* 2:1, 4; *Eph.* 5:18.

O God, you are to be greatly feared in the company of your holy ones. All who draw near to you must come in worship with deepest reverence and godly fear. For you, our God, are a consuming fire. You have warned us that you must be held in sacred honour among all those who come near you. Make yourself the object of our fear and our reverent awe. May you be glorified before all the peoples of the world. You have given us the sign of your Sabbath that we might know that you are the Lord who sanctifies us. Sanctify us by your truth that we may sanctify you in our hearts. *Psa.* 89:7; *Heb.* 12:28, 29; *Lev.* 10:3; *Isa.* 8:13; *Ezek.* 20:12; *John* 17:17.

As we assemble together, we testify to our communion with the universal church. Though we are many, yet we are one. For we worship one and the same God, the Father from whom are all things, and for whom we exist. We worship one Lord Jesus Christ, through whom are all things, and through whom we exist. We worship by the energizing work of one and the same Spirit, who distributes to each person individually as he will. We walk by the same rule, and look toward the same blessed hope, which is the glorious appearing of our great God and Saviour Jesus Christ. *1 Cor.* 10:17; 8:6; 12:11; *Gal.* 6:16; *Titus* 2:13.

4. At the baptism of adults, join heaven in rejoicing over one sinner who repents.

Lord, we praise you that you have always included foreigners with your people as legitimate recipients of the covenantal seal. From the first day of its institution in the days of Abraham, the father of all believers, you welcomed people from every nation into your covenant community. How wonderful it is that you ordered that anyone from any tribe or nationality could become a full participant in all your covenant promises by confessing the God of Israel and receiving the sign of the covenant. Thank you for letting us live in the day in which you have brought the old covenant sign of circumcision to its fullest realization by the simpler seal of baptism. We rejoice that by your authority as the resurrected and reigning Christ, you commanded that disciples from all nations should be baptized in the name of the Father and of the Son and of the Holy Spirit. Thank you that at the reconstitution of your covenant people on the day of Pentecost, you ordered the baptism of 3,000 people. We praise you for moving people from numerous nations to embrace the apostolic message of repentance and faith in Jesus as Lord and Christ, at that special moment of the baptism of the Spirit from heaven. We rejoice that you have openly indicated that people from all nations should receive baptism as equal participants in the covenantal promise of the Holy Spirit. *Gen.* 17:10-12; *Exod.* 12:48; *Col.* 2:11, 12; *Phil.* 3:3; *Matt.* 28:19; *Acts* 2:41; 10:34, 35, 47.

Now in this glorious age of worldwide gospel proclamation we praise you for the baptism of additional converts who give a credible profession of their repentance and faith in Christ as their personal Lord and Saviour. As you have appointed, let the baptismal water symbolize and seal their union with Christ and his people, and their cleansing from sin and the corruption that is in the world by the washing of water. Claim them as your own from this day forward. Deliver them from the kingdom of darkness and transfer them into the kingdom of the Son you love. *Ezek.* 36:25; *Acts* 22:16; *1 Cor.* 6:11; *Eph.* 5:26; *Heb.* 10:22; *Col.* 1:13.

5. At the baptism of children, claim God's covenant promises.

God of Abraham, Isaac, and Jacob, we thank you that you made your ancient covenant with believers and their children as an everlasting covenant to a thousand generations. We rejoice that as you ordained circumcision as the old covenant seal for believers and their children, so you have instituted baptism as the new covenant fulfilment of that seal. As Joshua of old made covenantal commitments for himself and his house, give us strength as new covenant believers to do the same. Now, O LORD of the Covenant, make good your ancient covenant to be a God to believers and their children. Let this blessing of Abraham come equally on all peoples on earth, for your promise is still to us and to our children. *Gen.* 17:7; *Psa.* 105:8-10; *Gen.* 17:10; *Col.* 2:11, 12; *Phil.* 3:3; *Josh.* 24:15; *Acts* 16:15, 33; *Acts* 3:25; 2:39.

Lord Jesus, you took infants into your arms and blessed them. You have directed us to bring little children to you and not to hinder them. For you have said that the kingdom of God belongs to such as these. Blessed Jesus, take these children into the arms of your grace and power, put your hands on them and richly bless them. *Luke* 18:15, 16; *Mark* 10:14-16.

O God, all souls are yours, the souls of parents and the souls of their children. Turn the hearts of the fathers to their children and the hearts of the children to their fathers. Let these children be a living sacrifice, holy and acceptable to you. They are conceived in sin, but a fountain has been opened to cleanse from sin and impurity. Wash these children in that fountain. By their baptism let them be consecrated to the Father, the Son, and the Holy Spirit. Let these children grow up to be vessels of honour, sanctified, useful to the Master and prepared for every good work. *Ezek.* 18:4; *Mal.* 4:6; *Rom.* 12:1; *Psa.* 51:5; *Zech.* 13:1; *Matt.* 28:19; *2 Tim.* 2:21.

Pour your Spirit on our seed, your blessing on our children, that they may flourish like grass in the meadow and like willows by flowing streams of water. In accord with your everlasting covenant, let our descendants be famous among the nations and our offspring among the peoples. Let the nations acknowledge that we are a people blessed by the Lord. Let our children declare, 'I am the Lord's.' Let them boldly inscribe your name on their hands and claim for themselves the name of the Covenant Lord. *Isa.* 44:3, 4; 61:8, 9; 44:5.

6. Before celebrating the Lord's Supper, prepare yourself for the special manifestation of God's grace.

Gracious Lord, you have invited us to participate in the fulfilment of that ancient Passover feast of your chosen people. Help us to prepare everything in the private upper room of our intimate communion with you. Teach us to wash one another's feet as we remember your example. Enable us to eat in readiness for your coming, with our belt tightened about our waist, our shoes on our feet, and our staff for travelling in our hand. Let us eat in haste, knowing that the Lord is about to pass over in judgment. Let us eagerly accept the open invitation to eat wisdom's bread and drink the wine she has mingled. Increase our hunger and thirst after the righteousness that comes only by remaining in intimate communion with Christ the true vine. Though we are totally unworthy to be your guests, you have invited us to the marriage supper of the Lamb. Adorn us with the necessary wedding garment of Christ's imputed righteousness so we will not be ejected from the celebration. May the good and merciful Lord pardon everyone that prepares his heart to seek the Covenant LORD of his fathers, even though he has not perfectly kept the law of purification required for participating in the Passover. Hear our prayer and prepare your people. *Matt.* 26:17-19; *John* 13:3-5; *Exod.* 12:11; *Prov.* 9:5; *Matt.* 5:6; *John* 15:5; *Rev.* 19:9; *Matt.* 22:11-13; *2 Chron.* 30:18, 19.

7. During the celebration of the Lord's Supper, make the most of this moment of special grace.

Let this cup that blesses bring us into a united participation in the benefits of Christ's blood. Let this bread which we break bring us into a united participation in the benefits of Christ's body. By this thanksgiving celebration let us continually proclaim the Lord's death until he comes. *1 Cor.* 10:16; 11:26.

By the celebration of this feast, let us be joined to the Lord in an everlasting covenant. Let us become one spirit with him. Make us partakers of Christ as we are strengthened in the sacrament so that we can hold firmly the beginning of our confidence steadfast to the end. Let Christ's flesh be true nourishing meat to us. Let his blood be refreshing drink. By faith let us eat his flesh and drink his blood, that he may live in us and we in him. Through this sacrament let us find abundance of life in him. Let the cross of Christ, which is an obstacle to faith for the Jews and foolishness to the Greeks, be your wisdom and your power to us. *Jer.* 50:5; *1 Cor.* 6:17; *Heb.* 3:14; *John* 6:55-57; *1 Cor.* 1:23, 24.

Let this sacrament of the Lord's supper be to us a sealing confirmation of the remission of sins, the gift of the Holy Spirit, and the promise of eternal life. In view of all your blessings, let us lift high this symbolic cup of salvation, and praise your name as our Covenant LORD. *Acts* 2:38; *1 John* 2:25; *Psa.* 116:12, 13.

8. After celebrating the Lord's Supper, renew your vows to God.

Lord, enable us to remain faithful to this covenantal bonding to Christ which we have received through this sacrament. As the oath of the covenant binds us in our obligations to you, so preserve this solemn commitment of our hearts, and confirm our loyalty to you. Let us joyfully sing your praise even as we fulfil our vows to you day after day after day. Let us hold fast to what we have received so that no one can ever take away our crown. *1 Chron.* 29:18; *Psa.* 56:12; 61:8; *Rev.* 3:11.

Let us bear about in our bodies the dying of our Lord Jesus, so that the life also of Jesus may be manifested in our mortal bodies. For to us to live is Christ. Give us grace to walk in Jesus Christ just as we have received him. Let our lifestyle give glory to his gospel in everything we do and say. *2 Cor.* 4:10; *Phil.* 1:21; *Col.* 2:6; *Phil.* 1:27.

9. At a service of ordination to the gospel ministry, offer special prayers for the pure proclamation of the Word.

Let the ministry of the Word of God be committed to faithful men who may be fully capable of teaching others. Make them burning and shining lights. Make it apparent that none other than Christ Jesus himself put them in the ministry. Keep reminding us that we must not lay hands of ordination too quickly on anyone. *2 Tim.* 2:2; *John* 5:35; *1 Tim.* 1:12; *1 Tim.* 5:22.

Let those who are ordained treat their ministry with all seriousness, so that they fulfil every aspect of it. Let them remember that they have received their call to the ministry from the Lord. Let them always lead a disciplined life and patiently endure all the different trials that inevitably will come. Make them work hard at evangelizing. Help them discharge all the many duties of their ministry. Let those who preach repentance and remission of sins in Christ's name be endowed with power from on high. Make them good ministers of Jesus Christ who constantly nourish themselves in the truths of the faith and hold firmly to sound doctrine. *Col.* 4:17; *2 Tim.* 4:5; *Luke* 24:47, 49; *1 Tim.* 4:6.

Pray for God's Blessing on
All Aspects of Life in the Community

1. On the occasion of a marriage, ask the Lord Jesus to be personally present.

Let believers who marry always marry in the Lord. Let the Lord Jesus grace every Christian wedding by his presence. Let him turn the commonplace things like water into the rich wine that flows from his redemptive work as it restores all things to their pristine beginnings. Let husband and wife each promote the salvation of the other. Bless them so that they live in holy love. Let them dwell together in God, and God in them. *1 Cor.* 7:39; *John* 2:2, 3, 5-10; *1 Cor.* 7:16; *1 John* 4:16.

Let the husband live with his wife as a man who understands her well. Let the wife be as a fruitful vine by the side of their home, a helper who corresponds to him. Let them live together as joint heirs of the grace of life, that their prayers may not be hindered. Prepare them for the world to come and their resurrection, where people will neither marry nor be given in marriage. *1 Pet.* 3:7; *Psa.* 128:3; *Gen.* 2:18; *Luke* 20:35.

2. On the occasion of a funeral, ask the Lord to enable you to reflect soberly about your life.

Lord, let us find that it is better to go to the house of mourning than to the house of feasting. For death is the destiny of everyone, and the living should take it to heart. Let us be wise to consider the outcome of our life, for we must all be gathered to our people. Help us to keep reminding ourselves that except for those who continue in this life until Christ returns, all of us will fall asleep in death as it has happened to our relatives, friends, and neighbours. Prepare us to follow those who already have fallen asleep in Jesus, though we cannot go to the place prepared for us right now. *Eccles.* 7:2; *Deut.* 32:29; *Num.* 27:13; *1 Thess.* 4:15; *John* 14:2; 13:36.

We know that you will bring us to death. But let us not see death until by faith we have clearly seen the Lord Christ as our Redeemer. Then let us depart in peace according to your word. Prepare us for the demolishing of this earthly tent in which we now live by making us confident that we have a building from you, a house in heaven not made by human hands that will last for eternity. *Job* 30:23; *Luke* 2:26, 29; *2 Cor.* 5:1.

Let us live with the assurance that our Redeemer lives, and that in the end he shall stand on the earth, perhaps even on the dust of our grave. For though our body is destroyed, yet in our flesh we shall see you. We shall see you for ourselves with our own eyes, and no stranger shall see you in our place. *Job* 19:25-27.

3. When rain is lacking, come before the Lord with special confessions and petitions.

You have held back the rain from us. You have caused it to rain on one city and not on another. Yet we have not returned to you as would have been expected. Heaven has been shut up and there is no rain because we have sinned against you. But now we confess your name, and turn from our sins. Hear from heaven, forgive our sin, and let rain fall again on our land. *Amos* 4:7, 8; *1 Kings* 8:35, 36.

Graciously give us the early and later rains. We depend on you and no other, for no gods of other peoples have the power to give rain. Heaven cannot of itself send its showers. We wait on you, for you alone can make rain. *Zech.* 10:1; *Jer.* 14:22.

4. When there is too much rain, ask the Lord to be gracious.

You have sworn that the waters of Noah will never again return to cover the earth. Yet you continue to load thick clouds with moisture, and disperse the lightning through the clouds. Let the rain you send show your loving care toward our land rather than coming for our correction. Let it not be a sweeping rain that leaves no food. *Isa.* 54:9; *Job* 37:11-13; *Prov.* 28:3.

5. When a plague of infectious disease strikes your land, cry out for the Lord's mercy.

Bless our bread and our water, and take sickness from our land. Deliver us from the pestilence that threatens to engulf us. Command the destroying angel to put his sword into his sheath. Be moved to pity when you see our calamity, and restrain your hand of judgment. *Exod.* 23:25; *Psa.* 91:3; *2 Sam.* 24:16.

6 In the event of large calamities, earnestly seek the Lord's face.

O Lord, sometimes you bring judgment by fire. We mourn over the destruction you have brought through the flames. Mercifully declare that we will not be utterly consumed by the fire. Hear our prayer as you did in the case of Moses, and let the fire be quenched. *Amos* 7:4; *Lev.* 10:6; *Amos* 7:5, 6; *Num.* 11:2.

Lord, you hold the wind in the hollow of your hand, and bring it out of your storehouses as you will. Even stormy winds fulfil your word. Preserve us and our homes. Keep us from being buried in their ruins, as were Job's children. *Prov.* 30:4; *Psa.* 135:7; 148:8; *Job* 1:19.

Intercede for People with Bodily Weaknesses

1. Pray for the sick.

Lord, while on earth you demonstrated that all of us should show our concern for the sick by bringing them to you. Be with the elders of our church that they may pray in faith for the sick. Help us to bring the sick to you in faith, since you have promised that the prayer of faith will save the sick and you will raise them up. *Mark* 2:2-5; *Acts* 5:15, 16; *James* 5:14, 15.

Our Lord Jesus, when you were on earth, people with all kinds of diseases and bodily weaknesses were brought to you and you healed them all. Lord, you still have the same power over bodily infirmities. You are like a man in authority who says to his servants, 'Go!', and they go; 'Come!' and they come; 'Do this!' and they do it. Lord Christ, speak the word and the sick shall be healed. Show us that you still empathize with our weaknesses. By prayer we bring our sick friends to you and lay them expectantly before you. *Matt.* 4:23, 24; 8:8, 9; *Heb.* 4:15; *Luke* 5:18.

Let those who suffer understand that affliction does not simply rise out of the dust or spring on its own out of the ground. Yet man is born to trouble as surely as the sparks fly upward. Let the afflicted seek you in their weakness more than physicians, knowing that the issues of life and death belong to you. Deliver those who are yours in times of trouble. Preserve their lives. Sustain them on their sick bed. Restore them to full health. Be merciful to them and heal them even though they have sinned. Turn to them and have mercy on them. Bring them out of their distresses. Look mercifully on their affliction and their pain. Forgive all their sin. *Job* 5:6-8; *2 Chron.* 16:12; *Deut.* 32:39; *Jer.* 21:8; *Psa.* 41:1-4; 25:16-18.

Gracious Lord, do not rebuke the people you love in your wrath. Do not chasten them in your burning anger. Have mercy on them, for they are weak. Heal them, for the bones of their bodily frame are trembling. Return in your mercy and deliver their souls. Save them because of your unfailing love. Bring to them no greater trial than you yourself will enable them to bear. *Psa.* 6:1-4; *1 Cor.* 10:13.

Keep those who are sick from despising your chastening. If you are chastening them, let them not lose heart when you rebuke them. Let them endure the rod of your discipline and continue in their devotion to you, the one who has appointed it. As an amazing sign of your grace, let them kiss the rod and accept the punishment of their iniquity. In the submissive spirit of King David, let them recognize that you, their Lord, are the source of their rebukes. Let them live in the expectation that you will see their distress and grant them good for their evil. *Heb.* 12:5; *Mic.* 6:9; *Lev.* 26:41; *2 Sam.* 16:11, 12.

Lord, show them why you contend with them. In their affliction lead them to humble themselves before you as the God of their fathers. Help them to repent and turn from every evil way. Let your discipline keep them from being condemned with the world. By the sickness of the body and the sadness of the soul let the heart be made better. *Job* 10:2; *2 Chron.* 33:12; *Jer.* 18:11; *1 Cor.* 11:32; *Eccles.* 7:3.

When you chasten a man for sin with your rebukes, you consume his treasured possessions like a moth, for every man is a mere breath. Remove your stroke from those that are about to be consumed by the blow of your hand. Turn your piercing gaze from them that they may be cheerful once more before they fade away and are no more. Show your uprightness and your grace to those that are chastened with pain on their bed, for their bones have endured the severest pains so that they cannot stand the thought of food. Deliver them from going down to the pit, for you have found for them a ransom. *Psa.* 39:10, 11, 13; *Job* 33:19-24.

Make your face shine on them. Save them for your mercy's sake. As the God who comforts the downcast, give them your comfort. Let their soul dwell at ease even while the body lies in pain.

Consider the weakness of their bodily frame. Remember that they are nothing but dust. May the eternal God be their refuge. May his everlasting arms be underneath them. *Psa.* 31:16; *2 Cor.* 7:6; *Psa.* 103:14; *Deut.* 33:27.

When an illness continues for a long time:
Lord, let patience have its perfect work. Let those who have spent a long time in the furnace of affliction continue hoping and quietly waiting for your salvation. Let suffering produce patience, and patience experience, and experience a hope that will never let anyone be disappointed. Enable them to regard their heaviest affliction as light and momentary since it achieves for them the superabundance of eternal glory. *James* 1:4; *Lam.* 3:26; *Rom.* 5:3-5; *2 Cor.* 4:17.

If recovery seems fairly certain:
Lord, let those you have tried come forth like gold. Let them live so they can praise you. In your love deliver them from the pit of destruction, and cast all their sins behind your back. Restore them to full health and let them live. Speak the word and they shall be healed. Say to them, 'Live!' Yes, say to them, 'Live!', and that will be a time when you manifest your love. *Job* 23:10; *Psa.* 119:175; *Isa.* 38:16, 17; *Matt.* 8:8; *Ezek.* 16:6, 8.

We pray in the spirit of your Son during his suffering: Father, if it be possible let this cup of suffering pass away from us. Yet not as we will, but as you will. Let the will of the Lord be done. Fulfil your purpose for us. Your mercy, O Lord, endures for ever. Do not forsake the work of your own hands. But whether we live or die, let us be the Lord's. *Matt.* 26:39; *Acts* 21:14; *Psa.* 138:8; *Rom.* 14:8.

If they appear to be at the point of death:
The flesh and heart appear to be failing. Lord, be the strength of their heart and their everlasting portion. Be clearly present in the valley of death's shadow as the good shepherd with your guiding rod and supporting staff. Do not fail them or forsake them now. Be an ever-present help in their time of greatest need. Into your hands we commit their spirit, since you are the one who has redeemed it. Let the angels carry this soul of your loved one into Abraham's comforting embrace. Let it be presented to you without spot or wrinkle or any other blemish. Lord Jesus, receive this precious soul. Let it join the fellowship of the spirits of just men made perfect. The moment the soul is absent from the body, let it be present with the Lord. This very day let it be with you in paradise. Let it be forever comforted and perfectly free from sin. Prepare us to follow after this our loved one, just as believers without number have

done in earlier ages. Let us be together forever with the Lord, where there shall be no more death and where all tears shall be wiped away. *Psa.* 73:26; 23:1, 4; *Heb.* 13:5; *Psa.* 46:1; 31:5; *1 Pet.* 4:19; *Luke* 16:22; *Eph.* 5:27; *Acts* 7:59; *Heb.* 12:23; *2 Cor.* 5:8; *Luke* 23:43; 16:25; *Rom.* 6:7; *Job* 21:33; *1 Thess.* 4:17; *Rev.* 21:4.

2. Pray for sick children.

Lord, we see death reigning even over those that have not sinned after the likeness of Adam's transgression. But Lord Christ, you have abolished death and admitted even little children into your kingdom. Show your special pity toward sick children even as they are special objects of the loving care of their parents. They come into this world like little flowers. Do not let them be cut down so early in their lives. Let them continue until they have accomplished their work according to the labour of their day. Be gracious to us, and let the children live. Nevertheless, Father, your will be done. But by all means, let their spirits be saved in the day of the Lord Jesus. *Rom.* 5:14; *2 Tim.* 1:10; *Mark* 10:14; *Psa.* 103:13; *Job* 14:2, 6; *2 Sam.* 12:22; *Acts* 21:14; *1 Cor.* 5:5.

3. Pray for women that are about to give birth.

Lord, you pronounced sentence on the woman that was first in transgression, that in pain and sorrow she would bring forth children. But let this treasured maiden of yours be saved in child-bearing. Let her be strong to continue in faith, in loving deeds, and in holiness as she continually displays sound judgment. Enable her to cast her burden on you, her loving Lord, so you can sustain her. Whenever she is afraid, let her trust in you. Let her encourage herself in the Lord her God. Do not let the root dry up that brings forth life, and do not let the branch wither that produces fruit. Let her live before you. Be her rock of refuge and her fortress. Save her in this hour of special need. Graciously deliver her when pain comes on her that she cannot escape. Hasten to help her. Be her Saviour. Do not delay. Let her be safely delivered. Let her quickly forget her anguish because of the joy that a child is born into the world. *1 Tim.* 2:14; *Gen.* 3:16; *1 Tim.* 2:15; *Psa.* 55:22; 56:3; *1 Sam.* 30:6; *Job* 18:16; *Psa.* 71:3; *1 Thess.* 5:3; *Psa.* 40:13, 17; *John* 16:21.

4. When people have recovered from sickness or have been safely delivered at the time of giving birth, give thanks to the Lord along with them.

We praise you, O Lord, because you have lifted up those who have been brought low. You have brought back the ones we love from the edge of the grave. You have preserved their life, so that they did not descend into the pit. You have helped those who were brought very low. You have delivered their souls from death, their eyes from tears, and their feet from stumbling. Now give them grace to walk righteously before you in the land of the living. Receive the sacrifices of thanksgiving from their lips. Stir them up to call on your name and pay their vows to you, the faithful Covenant LORD who has saved them. *Psa.* 30:1-3; 116:8, 9, 17, 18.

The grave cannot praise you, death cannot celebrate you. Those who go down to the pit do not hope in your truth. But the living – they are the ones who praise you, even as we are doing this day. Lord, let none of those who have been delivered from death be as the nine lepers who never returned to give thanks. Let them not be as Hezekiah, who because of his pride failed to repay you for the goodness shown to him when you raised him up from his sick bed. Instead, let them offer proper praise that glorifies you. From this day on, let them order their lives so that they continually experience your salvation. Let the ones you have severely chastened but not delivered to death be the very ones who praise you the most. For you are their salvation. *Isa.* 38:18, 19; *Luke* 17:17, 18; *2 Chron.* 32:24, 25; *Psa.* 50:23; 118:18, 21.

Offer Special Prayers for People with Spiritual Problems

1. Pray for those who are under the conviction of sin and are seeking Christ.

Lord, you know the hearts of those who are seeking the way to Zion. They are lamenting over their distressful situation. They are turning their faces toward you. Do not snuff out the smouldering wick or snap off the splintered cane. Let your justice be victorious in their salvation. They are pricked in the heart for their sin. Graciously teach them the good and the right way, and then lead them in it. *Jer.* 50:5; *1 Sam.* 7:2; *Matt.* 12:20; *Acts* 2:37; *1 Sam.* 12:23.

Manifest Christ as the way, the truth, and the life to those who are asking what they must do to inherit eternal life. As the good shepherd, gather the lambs in your arms and carry them close to your heart. Gently lead them. Help those who believe to overcome their remaining unbelief. *John* 14:6; *Matt.* 19:16; *Isa.* 40:11; *Mark* 9:24.

2. Pray for those that live with doubts and fears about their spiritual state, and tend to be melancholy in mind.

Lord, strengthen the weak hands, and steady the feeble knees. Say to those that have a fearful heart, 'Be encouraged, have no fear.' Answer them with comforting words that are suited to their distress. Say to them, 'Cheer up! Your sins are forgiven. Have confidence! It is I. Have no more fear. For I am your salvation.' Let them hear the voice of joy and gladness, that the bones you have broken may rejoice. *Isa.* 35:3, 4; *Heb.* 12:12; *Zech.* 1:13; *Matt.* 9:3; *Mark* 6:50; *Psa.* 35:3; 51:8.

Rebuke Satan the tempter, the one who constantly accuses the brothers. Covenant LORD, rebuke him, for you have chosen Jerusalem despite the filth of its sin. Let tempted, troubled souls be as brands plucked right out of a blazing fire. Give special help to those who are so overwhelmed with problems that they refuse to be comforted. Be with them when every remembrance of you troubles them. Enable them to trust the final outworkings of your mercy. Let them be confident that in due time they will rejoice in your salvation. Though you slay them, let them keep trusting you. *Zech.* 3:2; *Psa.* 77:2, 3; 13:5; *Job* 13:15.

All your waves and your billows engulf me. The depths of the waters below echo the depths of the waters above as the downpours descend from you.

Yet command your lovingkindness for me through-out the day. Let your song be with me in the night, for I will direct my prayer to you, the God of my life. Though my soul is cast down and deeply disturbed, enable me to continually hope in you. In the end, let me praise you. Let experience repeatedly teach me that you are the source of my good health, and you alone are my God. *Psa.* 42:7, 8, 11.

Refresh the life of an upright spirit in me. Do not cast me away from your presence. Never take your Holy Spirit from me. Restore the joy of my salvation, and put in me a spirit willing to be led by you. Let my tongue sing aloud of your righteousness, and show forth your salvation. Pull me out of this slimy pit, this mire and muck. Set my feet on a rock. Steady my steps and put a new song in my mouth, even praises to my God. Make me glad for as many days as you have afflicted me, for as many years as I have seen trouble. *Psa.* 51:10-14; 71:15; 40:2, 3; 90:15.

Though for a brief moment you have banished your people from your presence, yet in your great compassion restore them to yourself once more. Though you have hid your face from them, have mercy on them according to your everlasting kind-ness. By the blood of Christ purge all guilt from their conscience. Let your Spirit bear firm witness with their spirits that they are your children. *Isa.* 54:7, 8; *Heb.* 10:14, 22; *Rom.* 8:16.

3. Pray with parents whose children are a great concern to them or have become a grief to them.

Lord, give parents the desire of their souls concerning their children, which is to see them walking in the truth. Form Christ in them at a very early age. Let their children know and love you, the God of their fathers. Inspire them to serve you with their whole heart and with a willing mind. Let children be pointed in the right direction as arrows in the hands of their parents, that the parents may count themselves happy to have their quiver full of them. Let children never be arrows that pierce the hearts of their own parents. *2 John* 4; *Gal.* 4:19; *1 Chron.* 28:9; *Psa.* 127:4, 5.

Let foolish children that are the constant grief of their father and the heavy burden of the one that gave them birth be brought to repentance. Turn from his folly the child whose eye mocks his father and scorns obedience to his mother, before the raven plucks it out. Let the profligate son who has been so unprofitable now be beneficial to everyone he happens to meet. Turn the hearts of the children so that they love and respect their fathers. Let the disobedient come to respect the wisdom of the just, so they may be a people ready, prepared for your coming. Make those who have presumed to make themselves great clearly understand the evil of their deeds and their sins. Open their ears so they can hear correction and turn away from their iniquity. *Prov.* 17:25, 30:17; *Philem.* 11; *Mal.* 4:6; *Luke* 1:17; *Job* 36:9, 10.

4. Pray for those who have lost their senses or their memory.

Compassionate Father, look with gentle care on those that may have lost their mental or emotional balance. In their distress they may tend to choose death rather than life. Graciously restore them to their right mind. Deliver them from doing themselves any harm. Whatever afflictions you lay on any of us in this world, preserve our sanity of mind and our peace of conscience. *Job* 27:2; 7:15, 16; *Mark* 5:5; *Acts* 16:28.

Pray for People Facing Special Challenges

1. Pray for people in prison.

Let those that are bound in affliction and iron chains, sitting in darkness and deepest gloom, consider carefully what they should learn from their day of adversity. Let those who have rebelled against your word and despised your counsel have the grace to cry out to you in their trouble. In their captivity lead them to humble themselves and pray and seek your face. Let them repent by declaring, 'We have sinned and done wickedly.' Let them return to you with all their heart and all their soul. Free them from prison that they may praise your name. Transfer them from the bondage of corruption into the glorious liberty of the children of God. Let the Son make them free, so they can be free indeed. *Psa.* 107:10, 11, 13; *Eccles.* 7:14; *1 Kings* 8:47, 48; *Psa.* 142:7; *Rom.* 8:21; *John* 8:36.

Especially be with those who are wrongfully imprisoned, just as you were with Joseph in the prisons of Egypt. Show them great mercy through your providential care even in their confinement. Hear the prayer of those who are cruelly mistreated. Do not regard as worthless those who languish in prison. Let their sorrowful sighing come before you. According to the greatness of your power preserve those that are unjustly appointed to die. *Gen.* 39:20, 21; *Psa.* 69:33; 79:11.

2. Pray for criminals condemned to death who have only a little longer to live.

Gracious and merciful Lord, look with pity on those whose life is to be cut short because of their sins. Give them repentance that leads to salvation even in their last hours, as you did for the thief on the cross. Enable them to acknowledge that they are receiving in their body what they deserve according to your justice. Let them admit that you have done right and they have done wrong. Turn them around so they face the truth in repentance, and they shall be truly turned. Convict them of their wrongdoing that they may smite their chest in anguish over their sin. Let them be ashamed and humiliated when they see that they bear the disgrace of their youth. Let others hear and fear, and stop sinning presumptuously. Enable them to give glory to you by making honest confession before you and men. *Job* 21:21; *2 Cor.* 7:10; *Luke* 23:40-43; *Neh.* 9:33; *Jer.* 31:18, 19; *Deut.* 17:13; *Josh.* 7:19.

Pluck them as brands out of the fire. Let them be delivered from the wrath to come. Show them mercy on that great judgment day. Lord Jesus, remember them now that you have entered into your kingdom. Let them not be hurt by the second death. Deliver them from going down to the pit. Though the flesh be destroyed, let the spirit be saved in the day of the Lord Jesus. As the God of infinite mercy, be merciful to these sinners who have sinned against their own souls. *Jude* 23; *1 Thess.* 1:10; *2 Tim.* 1:18; *Luke* 23:42; *Rev.* 2:11; *Job* 33:24; *1 Cor.* 5:5; *Luke* 18:13; *Num.* 16:38.

3. Pray for those that sail the seas or fly the skies.

Let those that go down to the sea in ships or fly in the skies observe your works and your wonders in the depths and the heights. Let those that do business in great waters and expansive skies acknowledge what a great God you are, a God whom the winds and the waves obey. Let them honour you as the one who has placed the sand as a boundary for the sea by a perpetual decree. Let them trust you, the one who has limited the capacity of the clouds so that the rainwaters can never again flood the mountain-peaks. For though the winds and the waves roar and toss about, they cannot prevail against your purposes. *Psa.* 107:23, 24; *Matt.* 8:27; *Jer.* 5:22; *Gen.* 9:11.

Preserve them through the paths of the seas and the skies. Keep them in perils by waters, perils by robbers, perils by bandits of the sky. If stormy winds arise so that they are at their wit's end, deliver them out of their distresses. Speak the word and calm the storm. Bring them to their desired destination. Let those who are delivered and arrive safely praise you for your goodness and for your wonderful works to the children of men. *Psa.* 8:8; *2 Cor.* 11:26; *Psa.* 107:25-31.

4. Pray for people who have had a death in the family, especially when the head of the family has been lost.

Visit the houses of mourning as our Saviour did while he was on earth. Be a father to the fatherless and a defender of widows as they live in the shelter of your holy dwelling-place. Let the fatherless find mercy with you. Sustain their lives. Let widows who are in real need and left all alone keep focusing their hope in you. Though they are desolate, let them trust in you and continue in prayer night and day. Where fathers and mothers have forsaken their own offspring, may you take up their children and not leave them as orphans. *John* 11:17; *Psa.* 68:5; *Hos.* 14:3; *Jer.* 49:11; *1 Tim.* 5:5; *Psa.* 27:10; *John* 14:18.

Provide comfort to the grieving by assuring them that Christ is the resurrection and the life. Remind them that their relatives are not dead but sleep in Jesus. Reassure them that their loved ones shall be among the first to rise again and return with Jesus in clouds of glory. With these truths encourage them that though they sorrow, they do not sorrow as those who have no hope. Enable them to trust in you, the living God, the Rock of Ages. Despite the sadness of their loss, let them be unashamed to be joyful because of you, the Water of Life. *John* 11:25; *Matt.* 9:24; *1 Thess.* 4:13, 16, 17; *Psa.* 18:46; *John* 4:14.

7

Concluding Our Prayers

Concluding Our Prayers

Conclude Your Time of Prayer by Asking That all Your Prayers Will Give Glory to God the Father, the Son and the Holy Spirit

The Lord commands us to pray always, to pray without ceasing, to be in prayer continually. For we must always delight in the privilege and duty of prayer. We must be constantly committed to it, never grow weary of it, and never put it out of the centre of our lives.

Yet we must come down from this mountain. For our lives cannot be totally consumed with the formal exercises of prayer. Neither may we spend too long in our prayer closet, which would make the privilege of prayer a burdensome task to ourselves as well as to those who join with us. We have other work that demands our attention. Jacob wrestles all night with the angel, but at daybreak he must go, for the journey before him is still long. The prayers of David the son of Jesse must be ended. We must therefore consider how we shall conclude our seasons of prayer.

But how shall we conclude? How shall we make a proper exit from our priestly presence in the Most Holy Place? Even as we complete this privileged session at the throne of grace, we must at the same time consider how we can maintain this intimate relationship with our Lord. Our ongoing conversation with God must retain its vital role in the thoughts and imaginations of our heart.

1. Sum up your requests in a few comprehensive petitions.

Now may the God of peace who escorted Jesus our Lord out from among the dead, that Shepherd of the sheep who established his greatness through the blood of the everlasting covenant, endow you with everything good for doing his will, as he works in us that which is pleasing to him through Christ Jesus, to whom be glory forever and ever. *Heb.* 13:20, 21

May the God of all grace, who has called us to his eternal glory by Christ Jesus, after we have suffered a while, perfect us, establish, strengthen, and fortify us. May the Lord guide our hearts directly into the love that comes from God, and into a patient waiting for Christ. *1 Pet.* 5:10; *2 Thess.* 3:5.

So now, Lord, what is our expectation? Our only hope is in you. We depend on you to be our all-sufficient God. Do for us immeasurably more than all we are able to ask or even think, according to the power that works in us. Supply all our needs according to your riches in glory that are in Christ Jesus. *Psa.* 39:7; *Gen.* 17:1; *Eph.* 3:20; *Phil.* 4:19.

    2. Humbly beg the Lord to accept your poor weak prayers for Christ's sake.

    O our God, let your ears be attentive to the prayers we have offered. Do not turn away the face of Christ your Anointed One, who perfects our prayers in your presence. Remember the mercies shown to David your servant. Remember great David's greater son, even Jesus, who is at your right hand making continual intercession for us. Let yours eyes be open to the supplication of your servants, and to the prayers of your people Israel. Graciously listen to us whenever we call on you. For we are your people and your inheritance. May the God of Israel grant us the things we have requested from him. *2 Chron.* 6:40, 42; *Rom.* 8:34; *1 Kings* 8:51, 52; *1 Sam.* 1:17.

    Lord Christ, you have assured us that whatever we ask the Father in your name he will give it to us. So Father, we make all our petitions in that powerful name which is above every other name in heaven or earth. Make your face shine on us for the sake of the Lord Jesus, the Son of your love, for you always hear him. Be well pleased with us in him. Let the words of our mouths and the meditations of our hearts be acceptable in your sight, O Lord our strength and our redeemer. *John* 16:23; *Phil.* 2:9; *Dan.* 9:17; *Col.* 1:13; *John* 11:42; *Matt.* 17:5; *Psa.* 19:14.

3. Ask forgiveness for anything that has been wrong with your prayers.

Lord, we have not prayed as we should. Who is it that does what is right and never sins? Even when we determine to do good, evil is present with us. Though the will to do good is present, we cannot carry out the good thing we intend to do. So you might justly refuse to hear us even when we make many prayers. *Rom.* 8:26; *Eccles.* 7:20; *Rom.* 7:18, 19; *Isa.* 1:15.

But we have a Great High Priest who bears in himself the guilt of the consecrated service that we present to God. For his sake take away all iniquity from us. Remove all that defiles our sacred service. Do not deal with us according to the folly of our depraved nature. Receive us graciously and love us freely. *Exod.* 28:38; *Heb.* 7:24-26; *Job* 42:8; *Hos.* 14:2.

4. Commit yourself to divine grace in all other serv-ices that lie before you today, and throughout the rest of your life.

Speak, Lord, for your servants are listening. What would you say to your servants? Let us never turn a deaf ear from hearing your law. For then our prayers will be an abomination to you. Instead, may we listen well to you, that you may listen well to us. Enable us to go from strength to strength until we appear before you in Zion. As we pass through the valley of Baca, graciously turn the place of weeping into a wellspring of blessing. Let the rain of divine grace and blessing fill the pools of our pilgrimage to overflowing. *1 Sam.* 3:9; *Josh.* 5:14; *Prov.* 28:9; *Judg.* 9:7; *Psa.* 84:5-7.

Now may the Lord our God be with us as he was with our fathers. May he never leave us or forsake us. May he incline our hearts toward him, to walk in all his ways and to keep his commandments, his laws, and his judgments. May our hearts be wholly committed to the Lord our God all our days, even to the end of our lives. Then may we rest in him, and at the end of time may we arise to possess our allotted inheritance. *1 Kings* 8:57, 58, 61; *Dan.* 12:13.

5. Conclude all your prayers with doxologies that ascribe honour and glory to the Father, the Son, and the Holy Spirit. Then seal up all your praises and prayers with a heartfelt 'Amen!'

Blessed be the Lord God of Israel from everlasting to everlasting. Amen and Amen. Forever blessed be the Covenant LORD, the God of Israel, who only does wondrous things. Blessed be his glorious name forever. Let the whole earth be filled with his glory. Amen and Amen. Indeed, let all the people say, 'Hallelujah! Amen.' *Psa.* 41:13; 72:18, 19; 106:48.

Now to God the Father and our Lord Jesus Christ, who gave himself for our sins that he might deliver us from this present evil world, be glory forever and ever. Amen. To the only wise God be glory forever through Jesus Christ. Amen. *Gal.* 1:3, 5; *Rom.* 16:27.

Now to the king eternal, immortal, invisible, the only wise God, be honour and glory forever and ever. Amen. To him be everlasting honour and power. To him be glory and dominion. Amen. Now to him who is able to keep us from falling, and to present us faultless before his glorious presence with great joy; to the only wise God our Saviour be glory and majesty, dominion and power, before all ages, now and forever more. Amen. To God be the glory in the church by Christ Jesus throughout all ages, world without end. Amen. *1 Tim.* 1:17; 6:16; *1 Pet.* 5:11; *Jude* 24, 25; *Eph.* 3:21.

Blessing and honour and glory and power be to him that sits on the throne and to the Lamb forever and ever. Let the whole creation say, 'Amen and Amen!' We prostrate ourselves before the throne and worship God, saying, 'Amen. Blessing and glory and wisdom and thanksgiving and honour and power and might be to God forever and ever. Hallelujah! Amen.' May salvation and glory and honour and power forever belong to the Lord our God. Hallelujah! Amen. *Rev.* 5:13; 7:11, 12; 19:1, 4.

6. Finalize your prayers by using the form Christ taught his disciples.

Our Father in heaven. May your name be sanctified. May your kingdom come. May your will be done on earth as it is in heaven. Give us today our daily bread. Forgive us our debts as we have forgiven our debtors. Lead us not into temptation, but deliver us from the evil one. For yours is the kingdom and the power and the glory forever and ever. Amen. *Matt.* 6:9-13.

8

The Lord's Prayer
Expanded

The Lord's Prayer Expanded

🕉

An Expansion of the Lord's Prayer Using Expressions from Scripture

While on earth, the Lord Jesus Christ responded to a request from his disciples to teach them how to pray. This simple question, coming from his most intimate disciples, shows just how difficult it is for a fallen humanity to address God in a proper manner. In his response to this request, Jesus did not intend to provide a form of prayer that should be rigidly recited and mindlessly repeated. He was offering a balanced expression of prayer forms that could be employed by individuals but also corporately in worship, as his use of plurals such as 'Our Father', 'Give us', 'Lead us', and 'Forgive us', clearly indicate. At the same time, he was providing a basic pattern for prayer, a sum of all its proper elements, a model by which we may frame our petitions. The expressions he uses are remarkably concise while at the same time vastly comprehensive. So it will be of great benefit to lay open this perfect prayer before us, and observe more carefully its order and substance. By expanding on its various forms and petitions we may learn how to use it more intelligently. The inevitable consequence of a richer comprehension of this model prayer should, with God's blessing, result in our own great personal benefit as well as the coming down from heaven of many potential blessings for our needy world. In the present expansion of the prayer we intend to illuminate the scope and substance of the prayer, always using relevant scriptures with this goal in mind.

Our Father

O Lord our God, without doubt you are our
Father, though Abraham was ignorant of us and
Israel would not recognize us. Your name 'Father'
is from eternity, and from this moment we cry out
as children to you. Have we not all one Father?
Has not one God created us? You are the Father
of our spirits, the one to whom we should be in
subjection and live. You are the Father of lights,
the Father of mercies, and the God of all consolation. You are the eternal Father from whom,
through whom, and for whom are all things. *Isa.*
63:16; *Mal.* 2:10; *Heb.* 12:9; *James* 1:17; *2 Cor.* 1:3; *Isa.*
9:6; *Rom.* 11:36.

You are the Father of our Lord Jesus Christ,
your one and only Son who resides in the heart
of the Father. As the essence of divine wisdom, he
was side by side with you as the master craftsman
of creation. He was daily your delight, even as he
was rejoicing always before you. We wonder at the
fact that in Christ we are your adopted sons. We
adore you as the Father of all believers. We marvel
that you predestined us to be your adopted children
before the foundation of the world. *Eph.* 1:3; *John*
1:14, 18; *Prov.* 8:30; *Eph.* 1:4, 5.

How amazing is the love the Father has lavished on us, that we should be called the children of God! We are astounded that the Lord God Almighty should be to us a father and we should be his sons and daughters. We believe on your name, understanding that you give authority to become the sons of God to as many as receive Christ. We praise you that by your grace we have been born again, not by the will of man, but by you, the eternal Father. Now send the Spirit of your Son into our hearts, and teach us to cry 'Abba, Father'. *1 John* 3:1; *2 Cor.* 6:18; *John* 1:12, 13; *Gal.* 4:6.

We stand in amazement at our privileged position of being your adopted sons. As obedient and genuine children, help us fashion our lifestyle according to the example of the Holy One who has called us. As dearly loved children, let us be followers of you, our Father. As your sons, let us be conformed to the image of your Son, who holds the priority position of firstborn among many brothers. *Gal.* 4:5; *1 Pet.* 1:14-16; *Eph.* 5:1; *Rom.* 8:29.

You are our Father. But shamefully we must ask ourselves, 'How have we given you the honour you deserve as a father?' Lord, give us grace to serve and worship you in a proper way as your children, with reverence and godly fear. We come to you as prodigal children who have wandered from our father's house into a far country. If we continue to live far from you, we will starve to death. But now, Father, we rise up to return to you, for in your house is more than enough food to spare. Father, we have sinned against heaven and before you. We are not worthy to be called your children. Please, just make us one of your hired servants. *Mal.* 1:6; *Heb.* 12:28; *Luke* 15:13, 17-19.

Enable us to come to you with humble boldness and confidence as to a tender father who spares us as a man spares his son who faithfully serves and honours him. Encourage us with the knowledge that you love us as our Father, and that we also have someone who is constantly speaking to you on our behalf. Despite the evil of every earthly parent, they all know how to give good gifts to their children that ask them. So with much more confidence in you as our heavenly Father we ask you to give us the Holy Spirit. Loving heavenly Father, pour out on us the spirit of grace and supplication. *Eph.* 3:12; *Mal.* 3:17; *1 John* 2:1; *John* 16:27; *Luke* 11:13; *Zech.* 12:10.

Our Father in Heaven

You are our Father whose exalted dwelling-place is in heaven. Therefore we lift up our souls to you. You dwell in the heavens above, so we raise our eyes toward you. As the eyes of a servant focus on the hand of his master, and as the eyes of a maiden focus on the hand of her mistress, so our eyes focus on you, O Lord our God. You are a God whom the heaven of heavens cannot contain, and yet we have ready access to you. For we have a high priest who has passed into the heavens above as our forerunner. *Psa.* 115:3; 86:4; 123:1, 2; *1 Kings* 8:27, 28; *Heb.* 4:14, 16.

O God, you are the High and Holy One who inhabits eternity. You dwell in the high and holy place of heaven, but you welcome all those that are of a humble and contrite spirit. Holy and revered is your name. You are in heaven, and we are on earth. So keep us from being rash with our mouth, and let our words be few. We cannot dispute with you. Yet through a mediator we have boldness to enter into the holiest place where you dwell. *Isa.* 57:15; *Psa.* 111:9; *Eccles.* 5:2; *Job* 9:14; *Heb.* 10:19.

Look down from heaven. Observe us from your holy and glorious habitation. Do not hold back your tenderness and compassion toward us. Help us in our helplessness and our distress, since all things are possible with you. Hear us from your holy heavens. Deliver us by the saving strength of your right hand. Send us help from your sanctuary, and give us strength from the heavenly Mount Zion. Since heaven is your home, let our whole way of life be directed from there. Enable us to seek continually the things that are above, not the things on earth. *Isa.* 63:15; *Mark* 9:22, 23; *Psa.* 20:2, 6; *John* 16:28; *Phil.* 3:20; *Col.* 3:1, 2.

May Your Name Be Sanctified

So what is the first petition, the primary request we make of you, our heavenly Father? What do we want you to do for us above all other things? *Matt. 20:32.*

This is the first desire and prayer of our hearts: Father in heaven, let your name be glorified. Let it be treated as holy. Let it be sanctified. Be glorified as a holy God. Fulfil our desire to exalt you, the Lord our God, to worship at your footstool, and to meet with you at your holy hill. Let us praise your great and terrible name, for it is holy. As the High and Holy One, you live in the midst of the praises of Israel. *Rom.* 10:1; *Lev.* 10:3; *Psa.* 99:3, 5, 9; 22:3.

Let us glory in your holy name. Let our hearts rejoice because we have trusted in your holy name. Let us always give thanks and triumph in your praise. Enable us to glorify your name forevermore by praising you with all our hearts. Let us glorify you, our heavenly Father, by bringing forth much fruit. May we have the privilege of being your people, that we may promote your fame, your praise and your glory. As a people uniquely possessed by the Lord, let us show forth the praises of him who has called us out of darkness into his marvellous light. Let it be clear to all that we are your children, the work of your hands, because we sanctify your name as the Holy One of Jacob. Let it be known that we fear the God of Israel, so we may be to the praise of your glory. *Psa.* 105:3; 33:21; 106:47; 86:12; *John* 15:8; *Jer.* 13:11; *1 Pet.* 2:9; *Isa.* 29:23; *Eph.* 1:12.

Lord, cause strong nations to glorify you when they witness the way you help the poor and needy. Let the cities of brutal nations fear you when you devastate their royal palaces. Be magnified across all national borders when you frustrate the plans of the nations. Let them glorify you toward the east, and magnify you as the Lord God of Israel among the western lands beyond the sea. Let all the nations you have made worship you and glorify your name. For you are great and do wondrous things. You are God alone. Let the peoples glorify you for your mercy. Let your name be known among all nations, and let them rejoice with your people. Let your name be magnified among all peoples. Let all the ends of the earth remember your deliverance of the needy so that they will turn to you. Let all the families of the nations worship you. Let them declare your righteousness to a people yet to be born. *Isa.* 25:2-4; *Mal.* 1:5; *Isa.* 24:15; *Psa.* 86:9, 10; *Rom.* 15:9, 10; *Mal.* 1:11; *Psa.* 22:26, 27, 31.

As we have received a gift to serve others, enable us to fulfil our ministry as good stewards of your manifold grace. In all things may you be glorified through Jesus Christ. If we suffer, let us suffer as Christians, glorifying you even in our suffering. Fulfil our earnest expectation and hope, which is that Jesus Christ may always be magnified in our bodies, whether by life or by death. Lord, order all things to your own glory as King of the nations and King of your people. Bring everything to pass according to the perfect design of your own will, that you may magnify yourself. May you be perceived in the eyes of many nations as Lord. Sanctify your great name which has been profaned among the nations. Let them know that you are the Lord when you sanctify your people before their eyes. *1 Pet.* 4:10, 11, 16; *Phil.* 1:20; *Jer.* 10:7; *Rev.* 15:3; *Eph.* 1:11; *Ezek.* 3:23; 36:23.

Lord, what will you do for your great name? For the sake of your name, pour out your Spirit on all flesh. Let the word of Christ dwell richly in the hearts of all who believe in you. Be exalted, O Lord, among the nations. Be exalted throughout the earth. Be exalted above the heavens. Be exalted by your own strength, so that we may sing and praise your power. Do great things with your glorious and everlasting arm to make a glorious and everlasting name for yourself. Let the people magnify your name for ever, saying, 'The Lord of Hosts is the God of Israel, and a God to Israel.' *Josh.* 7:9; *Joel* 2:28; *Col.* 3:16; *Psa.* 46:10; 57:11; 21:13; *Isa.* 63:12, 14; *1 Chron.* 17:24.

Father, glorify your own name. You have glorified
it in the past. Now glorify it once more through the
lifting up of your Son. Glorify your Son that your
Son also may glorify you. Give him a name above
every name, and in every place. In all things let him
have the pre-eminence. *John* 12:28, 22; 17:1; *Phil.* 2:9;
Col. 1:18.

May Your Kingdom Come

Our Father in heaven, for the sanctifying and glorifying of your holy name, let your kingdom come. The kingdom is yours, and you are exalted as head above all. Both riches and honour come from you. You reign over all. In your hand is power and might that can make people great, and give strength to all. We delight to speak of the glorious majesty of your kingdom, for it is an everlasting kingdom. Your dominion endures throughout all generations. You rule perpetually by your power. Your eyes watch over the nations. Do not let the rebellious continue to exalt themselves, but through the greatness of your power let your enemies submit themselves to you. *1 Chron.* 29:11, 12; *Psa.* 145:11, 13; 66:7, 3.

Make it clear that the kingdom is yours, and that you govern the nations. Make it so evident that people are compelled to testify among the nations, 'The Covenant Lord reigns.' Let all men fear you. Let them declare your works, saying: 'Surely he is God who judges throughout the earth.' Make all the kings of the earth know that the God of heaven rules among men. Lead them to acknowledge that the Most High exercises dominion over the empires of men, for he gives authority to anyone he desires.

Let them praise, extol, and honour you as King of heaven. O Lord, all your works are truth and your ways are just. Humble those who walk in pride. *Psa.* 22:28; 146:10; 64:9; 58:11; *Dan.* 4:25, 26, 37.

Let the kingdom of your grace prevail more and more in this fallen world. Yet guard us from thinking your kingdom will come in a form that can be detected by the careful scrutiny of men. Let us by faith see your kingdom in our midst by the presence of Christ. Let his kingdom be like yeast, diffusing its life-giving power until the whole world has been permeated by his gracious rule. Enlighten our minds so we can see his kingdom in this world as a grain of mustard seed, which begins as the smallest of all seeds and yet grows until it becomes the greatest among shrubs. *Luke* 17:20, 21; *Matt.* 13:31-33.

Let the kingdoms of this world become the kingdom of our Lord and of his Christ. Assume to yourself your own great power and reign throughout the world even though the nations rage against you. Set up your throne where Satan's seat of power is located. Let every thought be brought into submission to you. May the law of your kingdom be magnified and honoured by all men. Let your kingdom that does not come in word only, but in power, be set up throughout the world. Stretch forth your mighty sceptre from your throne in the heavenly Mount Zion. Rule in the beauty of holiness. *Rev.*

11:15-18; 2:13; *2 Cor.* 10:5; *Isa.* 42:21; *1 Cor.* 4:20; *Psa.* 110:2, 3.

Satan as a strong man fully armed has been guarding his palace for many long years. His possessions have remained undisturbed. Let Christ, who is stronger than he, now launch his attack. Let Christ strip him of all his armour in which he trusts. Let our Lord Jesus distribute Satan's looted goods as he wishes. Give to the Son of Man dominion, glory, and a kingdom so that all peoples, nations and languages may serve him. Turn over the judgment of the peoples to the saints of the Most High. *Luke* 11:21, 22; *Dan.* 7:13, 14, 22.

Let the kingdom of your grace be manifest more and more throughout our land and in the places where we live. Let your word have free course and be glorified. Do not let your kingdom be taken from us and given over to a nation bringing forth its proper fruits, even though we deserve it. Let your gracious kingdom permeate all our lives, so that our bodies can be proper temples of the Holy Spirit. Let no iniquity have dominion over us. Overturn, overturn, overturn the power of corruption inherent in us. Let the prophesied One, who has the right to rule, come to us. Make us altogether willing in the day of your power. Rule in us by your truth. As people of the truth, enable us to always hear Christ's voice. Let us not only call him 'Lord, Lord', but also do the things he says. Let the love of Christ control and constrain us. Let our eyes be fixed on fearing him, so that we do not sin. *2 Thess.* 3:1; *Matt.* 21:43; *1 Cor.* 3:16; *Psa.* 119:133; *Ezek.* 21:27; *Psa.* 110:3; *John* 18:37; *Luke* 6:46; *2 Cor.* 5:14; *Exod.* 20:20.

Let your glorious kingdom come quickly. Inspire us to believe it is coming soon. Move us to look for the Saviour, the Lord Jesus, to come in the clouds of heaven with power and great glory. Keep us hoping that he will appear soon to inspire our joy. Teach us to love the prospect of his appearing. Let us look forward constantly to the arrival of the Day of God. Make us ready so we can lift up our heads with joy, knowing that our redemption is drawing near. Make us fully conscious of the firstfruits of the Spirit's presence in us, that we may groan within ourselves as we eagerly wait for our full adoption, which is the redemption of our bodies. Arouse within us a desire to depart and be with Christ, which is far better than continuing any longer in our present state. *Rev.* 22:7, 12; *Phil.* 3:20; *Matt.* 24:30; *Isa.* 66:5; *2 Tim.* 4:8; *2 Pet.* 3:12; *Matt.* 24:44; *Luke* 21:28; *Rom.* 8:23; *Phil.* 1:23.

Glorified Jesus, always be with your people, and especially with your ministers who go into the world to make disciples of all the nations. Be with them even to the consummation of the age, just as you promised. You have declared, 'Be sure that I am coming soon.' Even so, Come, Lord Jesus. Come quickly, as soon as the mystery of the Father's working in this world is finished. *Matt.* 28:19, 20; *Rev.* 22:20; 10:7.

May Your Will Be Done on Earth as It Is in Heaven

Father in heaven, as evidence that your kingdom comes, and so that your name may be sanctified, let your will be done on earth as it is in heaven. Do whatever you please in heaven, in earth, in the sea and in all deep places. For your purposes shall stand. You will do all your good pleasure. May it ever be so, holy Father. Not our will, but yours be done. As you have planned, so let it happen. As you have purposed, let it stand. Do all according to the counsel of your own will. Make even those that have not known you serve your purposes. Even when they do not intend to do your will, and do not think in their heart that they are fulfilling your purposes, let them do so nonetheless. *Matt.* 6:9, 10; *Psa.* 135:6; *Isa.* 46:10; *Luke* 22:42; *Isa.* 14:24; *Eph.* 1:11; *Isa.* 10:7.

Father, let your will be done concerning us and all our possessions. We present ourselves as your servants without reservation. You are the Lord. Do whatever you please. May your will be done. Give us the grace to submit to your will in conformity to the example of the Lord Jesus who prayed most earnestly, 'Not as I will, but as you will.' Enable us to say, 'The Lord gave, and the Lord has taken away, blessed be the name of the Lord.' Shall we always accept only good from you and not receive trouble also? *1 Sam.* 3:18; *2 Sam.* 15:26; *Acts* 21:14; *Matt.* 26:39; *Job* 1:21; 2:10.

Father, let the prophetic scriptures be fulfilled that declare your will. Let them never be broken. Heaven and earth will pass away. But do not let the smallest letter or the least stroke of a pen as recorded in your word disappear without being fulfilled. Do what is written in the scriptures of truth. Let your word be forever settled and certain in the heavens. *Matt.* 26:56; *John* 10:35; *Matt.* 24:35; 5:18; *Dan.* 10:21; *Psa.* 119:89.

Lord, you are our Father who is in heaven. Give grace to each of us to know and do your will. It is your will that we should be holy. May the God of peace now sanctify us wholly. Let us be filled with the knowledge of your will in all wisdom and spiritual understanding. Make us perfect in every good work to do your will. Let the time we have spent in the past doing the will of the flesh and walking according to the course of this world be regarded by us as enough and more than enough. From now on, let it always be our food to do your will and to finish your work. Let us not do our own will, but your will as the one who sent us, so that we may be among those who shall enter into the kingdom of heaven rather than being among those beaten with many stripes. *Matt.* 12:50; *1 Thess.* 4:3; 5:23; *Col.* 1:9; *Heb.* 13:21; *1 Pet.* 4:3; *Eph.* 2:2; *John* 4:34; *Matt.* 7:21; *Luke* 12:47.

Lord, give grace to all believers in Christ to know and do your will. Let us clearly discern the good, the acceptable, the perfect will of God. Help us not to be unwise, but understand what your will is. Enable us to stand mature and complete in all the will of God. Help us to serve our generation in accordance with your perfect will. Enable us to do your will, so that we may inherit the promises. Let the word you have spoken concerning your servants be established forever. Do just as you have promised. *Rom.* 12:2; *Eph.* 5:17; *Col.* 4:12; *Acts* 13:36; *Heb.* 10:36; *1 Chron.* 17:23.

Let us rejoice when we realize that your will is done perfectly in heaven. Make us glad that the holy angels do your commandments, always listening to the voice of your word, always looking on the face of you, our heavenly Father. Make us weep when we see that so little of your will is done on earth. How many of the children of men are being led captive by Satan at his will! Make this earth more like heaven. Let your will be done on earth as it is in heaven. How we wish that the saints on earth were more like the angels in heaven! We hope that soon we shall be like the angels of God in heaven. Even now may we, like them, be as a flame of fire doing your will. Let us fly swiftly to accomplish whatever you will for us to do. Let us go straight forward wherever the Spirit goes, in perfect fulfilment of your will. Give us the grace to minister for the good of others as the angels do, so that we may enjoy the privilege of coming into communion with the great host of angels and men in heaven. *Psa.* 103:19, 20; *Matt.* 18:10; *2 Tim.* 2:26; *Matt.* 22:30; *Rev.* 4:8; *Dan.* 10:13; *Psa.* 104:4; *Dan.* 9:21; *Ezek.* 1:9, 12; *Heb.* 1:14; 12:22, 23.

❦

Give Us This Day Our Daily Bread

Our Father in heaven, we have prayed for the sanctifying of your name. We have prayed for the coming of your kingdom, and that your will may be done on earth as it is in heaven. We now implore you to give us this day, and day by day our daily bread. For you have taught us through your Son to seek first the kingdom of God and his righteousness, trusting that all other needful things such as our daily bread will then be given to us. *Matt.* 6:9 11; *Luke* 11:3; *Matt.* 6:33.

Keep deception and falsehood as a way of personal gain far from us. Give us neither poverty nor riches. Satisfy us with the amount of bread you ordain for us. Do not give us too much, for then we may deny you and say, 'Who is the Lord?' Do not give us too little, for then we may steal and take your name in vain. Forgive us whenever we pray selfishly, asking only for daily bread for ourselves. Help us to earnestly pray for the needs of others. Satisfy your poor with bread. Let us despise any gain that might come from oppression. Let us walk in righteousness. Let us keep our hands empty of bribes, so we can fully enjoy your blessing on the highest heights. Let the place of our defence against all the assaults of our enemy be found in a rocky fortification that cannot be penetrated. Give us an adequate supply of bread, and let our supply of water never fail. *Prov.* 30:8, 9; *Psa.* 132:15; *Isa.* 33:15, 16.

Let us never crave for delicacies, since that kind of food distorts the true nature of the godly life. Let us never long to live in luxury, wrongly reasoning that we have not yet received our rightful share of good things in our lifetime. Instead, help us to simply pray for bread that is enough to sustain our life. Guard our hearts from ever desiring food we might get through deception. Make it repulsive to us to even think of drinking stolen waters. Deliver us from wanting to eat the bread of idleness. If it is your will, let us eat the fruit of our labour, the work of our own hands. Give us the grace to work quietly and eat our own bread. Let us be content to have food and clothing so we can honestly say, 'We have all we need, and even more.' *Prov.* 23:3; *Luke* 16:19, 25; *Psa.* 104:15; *Prov.* 20:17; 9:17; 31:27; *Psa.* 128:2; *1 Thess.* 4:11; *2 Thess.* 3:12; *1 Tim.* 6:8; *Phil.* 4:18.

Lord, bless the resources you have given us, and accept the work of our hands. Make us able to provide for our family, for all those who are a part of our household. As far as it is proper, let us leave an inheritance for our children's children. Let the favour of the Lord our God rest on us. Establish the work of our hands for us – yes, the work of our hands, make it endure. Lord, bless our land with the choice things that descend from heaven above, and with the finest yield of the sun and the seasons. But above all, let us have the goodwill of him that dwelt in the bush, even the blessing that rested on the head of Joseph, on the top of the head of him who was prince among his brothers. *Deut.* 33:11; *1 Tim.* 5:8; *Prov.* 13:22; *Psa.* 90:17; *Deut.* 33:13, 14, 16.

But if the fig tree should not bud, and there should be no fruit on the vine; if the labour spent on the olive tree should fail, and the fields should yield no food; if the flock should be cut off from the fold, and there should be no cattle in the stall; yet let us rejoice in our Covenant LORD, and be joyful in the God of our salvation. *Hab.* 3:17, 18.

Father, we do not ask for bread that would be enough for a long time in the future. We only ask that we may have for this day our daily bread. For we would learn not to take any anxious thought about tomorrow. Keep us from worrying about what we shall eat or drink, or what we shall have for clothing. Help us to thrust all our cares on you, knowing that you care for us. Increase our trust in you, our heavenly Father, who knows we need all these things. Teach us to look with faith to you, the one who feeds the birds of the air, even though they never sow a single seed or reap a single grain of wheat. Let us trust that you will be sure to feed us, who are much more valuable than many little birds. *Matt.* 6:11, 31, 32; 10:31.

Forgive Us Our Debts, as
We Forgive Our Debtors

Lord, as we pray every day for our daily bread, we also ask you to forgive our sins. We stand guilty and rightfully condemned before you. We have all sinned, and failed to measure up to your glory. You created and recreated us in your own likeness so we could give glory to your name by living in true righteousness and holiness. But we constantly fall far short of this grand purpose you have for us. In many things we all offend every day. Who can tell how often he breaks your law? If you were to keep a record of our sins, who could stand before you? But there is forgiveness with you, that you may be reverently feared. God be merciful to us sinners. *Rom.* 3:19, 23; *Eph.* 4:24; *James* 3:2; *Psa.* 19:12; 130:3, 4; *Luke* 18:13.

We have wasted our Lord's goods. We have buried the talents you entrusted to us. In our self-centred pride, we have given little or no recompense to you that would correspond to the benefit we have received from you. So we have become large debtors. The Scriptures have declared all of us under sin. We have done evil things that deserve death. We have done things for which your wrath is being poured out on the disobedient. Our debt is more than millions of dollars, pounds or shillings. It is a great debt, and we have nothing to pay. We cannot possibly offer the plea, 'Have patience with us, and we will pay back everything we owe you.' Satan our adversary could justly accuse us before you as our judge, and you could hand us over to the officer to throw us into prison, the prison of hell. There we should stay until we have paid the very last penny, which is utterly impossible. *Luke* 16:1; *Matt.* 25:18; *2 Chron.* 32:25; *Gal.* 3:22; *Rom.* 1:32; *Eph.* 5:6; *Matt.* 18:24-26; *Zech.* 3:1, 3; *Matt.* 5:25, 26.

But may God be praised! You have rebuked Satan, removed the filthy rags of our sin, and clothed us in the festal garments of Christ's righteousness. You have told us that if anyone sins, we have an advocate who will plead with you on our behalf. This advocate is Jesus Christ the Righteous, who has provided an atoning sacrifice to remove your wrath against us for our sins. *Zech.* 3:2, 4; *Gal.* 3:27; *2 Cor.* 5:21; *1 John* 2:1, 2.

Because of the sacrifice of your Son, wipe away all our transgressions. Do not bring us to judgment. Let Christ be the guarantee of our salvation as the one who has restored on our behalf things he never took away. Let him be the one mediator between us and yourself who has laid his hand on both of us. Let us be fully reconciled to you through him. Let the record of chargeable offences that testifies against us be wiped clean. Let it be nailed to the cross of Christ. Forgive all our sins, that we may be brought to life together with him. O Lord, show us the abundance of your mercy, and never remember our sins and iniquities again. *Psa.* 51:1; 143:2; *Heb.* 7:22; *Psa.* 69:4; *1 Tim.* 2:5; *Job* 9:33; *2 Cor.* 5:20; *Col.* 2:13-15; *Heb.* 8:12.

Let us receive the blessing of recovered favour with you. Give us the full assurance that our sins are forgiven. Speak peace to us. Bring joy and gladness to our hearts. Let the blood of Christ your Son wash away all our sin. Purge our consciences from deeds that lead to death so we can find fullness of life in serving you, the living God. *Rom.* 5:11; *1 John* 2:12; *Psa.* 85:8; 51:8; *1 John* 1:7; *Heb.* 9:14.

As evidence that our sins have been forgiven, give us the grace to forgive our enemies. Empower us to love those who hate us, and to bless those who curse us. Let us fully recognize that if we do not forgive others of the wrongs they have done to us, you as our heavenly Father will not forgive our sins. Lord, help us to forgive others, and to do it with our whole heart. If we have a quarrel against anyone, let us forgive just as Christ forgave us. Let us never dare to think that we will repay evil with evil, or avenge ourselves. Let us banish all bitterness, wrath, rage, angry shouting, slander, and all forms of hatred. Give us the grace to be tender and gentle in our dealings with one another. Let us extend full forgiveness to each other just as you have forgiven us for Christ's sake. Make us merciful as you, our own heavenly Father, are merciful, for you have promised that you will show mercy to the merciful. *Matt.* 5:44; *Luke* 6:27, 28; *Matt.* 6:15; *Mark* 11:25, 26; *Col.* 3:13; *Prov.* 20:22; *Rom.* 12:19; *Eph.* 4:31, 32; *Matt.* 5:7; *Psa.* 18:25.

Lead Us Not into Temptation, but Deliver Us from Evil

Lord, a wicked inclination remains in us that is bent toward backsliding. As soon as you forgive our sins, we are ready to return to our foolish ways. So knowing well our weakness, we humbly beg you not only to forgive our sin but to help us stop doing wrong. Lead us not into temptation. We know that no one when he is tempted can ever say, 'I am being tempted by God', for you never tempt anyone to sin. We therefore ask you, Never give us over to the lusts of our own hearts. Never turn us over to the stubbornness of our own wills. Restrain Satan as he roams around like a roaring lion looking for someone to devour. Keep us from being trapped through ignorance of his schemes. Spare us from being turned over to Satan's desire to possess us so that he can sift us like wheat. If you allow him to try us, strengthen us so our faith does not fail. Let not a messenger from Satan harass us. But if constant trials are necessary to keep us from pride, let your grace be sufficient for us. Make us strong where we are weak. Make us more than conquerors through Christ who has loved us. Make us strong in the Lord, since our struggle is not simply against flesh and blood. Reinforce us with your powerful might, since our warfare is against principalities, powers, and the rulers of the darkness of this world. As the God of peace, tread Satan under our feet, and do it soon. Keep us from falling, and present us faultless before yourself at Christ's glorious appearing. *Hos.* 11:7; *Psa.* 85:8; *Job* 34:32; *Matt.* 6:13; *James* 1:13; *Psa.* 81:12; *1 Pet.* 5:8; *2 Cor.* 2:11; *Luke* 22:31, 32; *2 Cor.* 12:7, 9, 10; *Rom.* 8:37; *Eph.* 6:10, 12; *Rom.* 16:20; *Jude* 24.

Lord, keep us from walking right into temptation's way. Knowing our ever-present danger, help us keep on the lookout for the subtleties of sin and Satan. Let us never stop praying. Providentially guide all our affairs so that no temptation comes to us that goes beyond the common experience of mankind. Never let us be tempted beyond what we are able to discern, resist, and overcome through your grace. Do not let stumblingblocks be placed in our way as we travel through life. Keep us from causing fathers and sons, neighbours and friends to perish because we have turned aside from your royal law of love. Let us never be the cause of stumbling for any brother for whom Christ died. Give us the great peace that is the permanent possession of those who love your law. Make us confident that nothing can make us stumble if we live by that law. *Matt.* 26:41; *Neh.* 4:9; *1 Cor.* 10:13; *Jer.* 6:19, 21; *Rom.* 14:13; *Psa.* 119:165.

Lead us into all truth. Teach us, for you are the God of our salvation. Show us your ways and teach us your paths. Lead us in the paths of righteousness for your name's sake. Lead us beside calm waters that have not been troubled by sin. Keep the evil one from attaching himself to us, knowing that he that is in us is greater than he that is in the world. Let us not be trapped by his deceitful ways or wounded by his fiery darts. Let your word permeate all our thoughts so that we can be strong and overcome the wicked one. *John* 16:13; *Psa.* 25:4, 5; 23:2, 3; *1 John* 5:18; 4:4; *Matt.* 13:25; *Eph.* 6:11, 16; *1 John* 2:14.

Answer our prayers for one another that none of us practise any wrongdoing. Let us always do the things that are right before you. Save us from the guilt and power of our sins. Claim us as your possession so that we are redeemed from all vices. Free us from the sin that so easily entangles us as we run the race of faith. Terrify us with your warnings to empty us of all pride of self. Banish lying from us once and for all. Remove every desire to eat the sinners' dainties. Put in our hearts the basic inclination to live according to the limitations of your laws rather than being driven by covetousness. Restrain our lips so that we never speak rashly, as did Moses. Above all, keep your servant from presumptuous sins. Let them never dominate us. Preserve our innocence from large transgressions. *2 Cor.* 13:7; *Matt.* 1:21; *Titus*

2:14; *Heb.* 12:1; *Job* 33:16, 17; *Psa.* 119:29; 141:4; 119:36; 106:33; 19:13.

Preserve us so that nothing evil happens to us and no disaster comes near our dwelling. Let your hand be with us, and keep us from harm. Deliver us from anything or anyone that rises up against us. Show us your marvellous lovingkindness. Defend us as the apple of your eye. Hide us under the shadow of your wings. Be the one to preserve our souls, for we have committed them to you. You have delivered us from deadly perils, you will deliver us in days to come, and we trust that you will provide a final deliverance. Free us from all fears. Let us live out our lives in the security that you alone can provide. Calm us from the dread of evil. Bring us safe at last to your holy mountain where there is no prickling briar, no painful thorn, and nothing to harm or destroy. Let the earth be full of the knowledge of the Lord as the waters cover the sea. *Psa.* 91:10; *1 Chron.* 4:10; *Psa.* 17:7, 8; *2 Tim.* 1:12; *2 Cor.* 1:10; *Psa.* 34:4; *Prov.* 1:33; *Ezek.* 28:24; *Isa.* 11:9.

For Yours Is the Kingdom, the Power and the Glory Forever. Amen

Father in heaven, let your kingdom come. For yours is the kingdom. You are God in heaven, and rule over all earthly kingdoms. Let your will be done, for yours is the power to do your will, and there is nothing too hard for you. Let your name be sanctified, for yours is the glory, and you have set your glory above the heavens. *2 Chron.* 20:6; *Jer.* 32:17; *Psa.* 8:1.

As our sovereign Lord, supply our needs, pardon our sins, and preserve us from evil. For yours is the kingdom, the power, and the glory. You are Lord over all. You richly bless all that call on you. Exercise your full authority as God in pardoning our sins, for none can forgive sins but you alone. Demonstrate that it is your glory to forgive sin and help the helpless. Now help us, O God of our salvation. Purge away our sins for your name's sake. Deliver us for the glory of your name. *Rom.* 10:12; *Mark* 2:7; *Num.* 14:17; *Psa.* 79:9.

Fulfil our desire to give glory to you in all our prayers, for you are great and greatly to be praised. We honour you for establishing your kingdom, for it is an everlasting kingdom that endures through all generations. Demonstrate that the sceptre by which you rule your kingdom is a righteous sceptre, for you love righteousness and hate wickedness. Show your mercy even as you reward every person according to his works. We praise you for your power, for you have a mighty arm. Your arm is strong and your right hand is exalted. Let righteousness and justice provide the foundation of your throne. May covenant love and faithfulness be abundantly evident in your presence. May your glory endure forever. May you rejoice in everything you do. Glory be to the Father, the Son, and the Holy Spirit, as it was in the beginning, is now and ever shall be. Let God be praised in his sanctuary, and praised in the heavenly expanse where his power resides. Praise him for his mighty works, praise him for his surpassing greatness. Let everything that has breath praise the Lord. Praise the Lord. *Psa.* 145:3, 13; 45:6, 7; 62:12; 89:13, 14; 104:31; 150:1, 2, 6.

Conclusion

As we conclude our prayers, we express our confidence that you hear us in whatever we ask in faith through Christ according to your will. As we obtain the requests we have asked of you, we express our triumph by praising you. We are sure that you hear the prayers of your anointed Christ. For his sake you will hear us from your holy heaven with the saving strength of your right hand. As testimony to our assurance that you hear us when we pray in Christ's name, we conclude our prayer by a repeated Amen! Amen! *1 John* 5:14, 15; *John* 16:23; *Psa.* 106:47; 20:6; *2 Cor.* 1:20.

9

*Shorter Forms
of Prayer*

Shorter Forms of Prayer

A Prayer That Children Can Understand and Pray

O Lord, you are my God. I will seek you while I am young. I will praise you. I will exalt you because you are my father's God.

Who is a God like you? Who can do wonders like you? Who is glorious in holiness, awesome in praises like you?

Whom do I have in heaven apart from you? There is nothing on this earth that I desire more than you. When my flesh and my heart fail, you remain as the strength of my life and my most treasured possession forever. You made me for yourself to praise you.

But I am a sinner. I was sinful at birth. I was even sinful when my mother conceived me.

God, be merciful to me a sinner.

Deliver me from the wrath to come. Save me through Jesus, who died for me and rose again.

Lord, give me a new nature. Let Jesus Christ be formed in my soul. Let me live my life for Christ. Let death bring gain to me.

Lord, I was given to you in my baptism. Please receive me graciously and love me freely.

Lord Jesus, you have encouraged little children to come to you. You have said that the kingdom of God belongs to children and to people who are like children. I now come to you. Make me a faithful subject of your kingdom. Take me up in your arms. Put your hands on me and bless me.

Let me be redeemed by your grace from all iniquity. Especially deliver me from the vanity into which all children are led.

Lord, give me a wise and understanding heart. Let me know and do your will in everything. Help me so that I may not sin against you in anything. Deliver me from lips that lie.

Bless me from my childhood so that I may know the Holy Scriptures. Bless my parents and grandparents as they teach me. Graciously write your law in my heart. Let me remain faithful to the good things I have learned.

Be a father to me. Meet all my needs as my loving heavenly Father. Teach me. Guide me. Provide for me. Protect me. Bless me, O my Father.

Bless all my relatives. Bless my father, mother, brothers, sisters, cousins, aunts and uncles. Give me grace to do my duty to all of them.

Lord, prepare me for death. Give me grace and wisdom to consider how my life will end.

Thank you for all your mercies to me. Thank you for life, health, food, clothes, and my education. Thank you for creating and preserving me. Thank you for all the blessings of this life. Above all, thank you for your great and infinite love, for the gift of Jesus your Son, and for the hope of glory.

I thank you, O my God, for the amazing gift of your Son. I lift my voice in praise for JESUS CHRIST. I desire Jesus alone. There is no one else I need apart from him.

Now to God the Father, the Son, and the Holy Spirit, that great name into which I was baptized, be honour and glory, dominion and praise, forever and ever. Amen.

A Paraphrase of the Lord's Prayer for Children and Youth

Our Father in heaven, we come to you as children to a father who is able and ready to help us.

Let your name be sanctified. Order all things to your own glory. Let all people glorify you by honouring you for all the ways you have made yourself known.

Let your kingdom come. Let Satan's kingdom be destroyed. Let the kingdom of your grace be advanced. Let your chosen people be brought into it, and kept in it. Let the kingdom of your glory come quickly.

Let your will be done on earth as it is in heaven. By your grace make us able and willing to know your will in all its fullness. Enable us to obey and submit to your will in all things just as the angels do in heaven.

Give us our daily bread today. Let us receive just the right amount of the good and necessary things of this life. Bless us as we enjoy your blessings.

Forgive us our sins as we forgive those who sin against us. Freely pardon all our sins for Christ's sake. Enable us by your grace to forgive others from the heart for all the wrongs they do to us.

Do not lead us into temptation, but deliver us from evil. Either keep us from being tempted to sin, or support and deliver us when we are tempted.

The kingdom, the power, and the glory are yours forever. Lord, we take our encouragement in prayer only because of you. In our prayers we desire to praise you, ascribing kingdom, power, and glory to you. In testimony of our desires and our assurance that we are heard through Jesus Christ, we declare our Amen.

A Prayer Drawn from Matthew Henry's *Plain Catechism for Children*, First Published in 1703

Covenant LORD our God, you are an infinite and eternal Spirit. You are most wise, powerful, holy, just and good.

You are the great God who made the world. You are also my Creator. You preserve and maintain me. In you I live and move and have my being. Help me always to remember you as my Creator in the days of my youth, and never to forget you.

Give me grace to serve you. Enable me to always worship and honour you. Help me to trust you. Give me the grace to obey you and please you in all my ways.

I thank you for your holy Word which you have given me. It is the only perfect rule for my faith and my life. It can make me wise for salvation.

I confess that the condition in which I was born is sinful and miserable. I am naturally inclined to do evil. I find myself eager to do bad things and very slow to do good things. Foolishness is bound up in my heart. I am by nature a child under your wrath. I have been disobedient to the command of God, and have eaten forbidden fruit. If you had not raised up a Saviour for me, I would certainly be lost and doomed forever.

But I will praise you forever for Jesus Christ my Saviour. I glorify him as the eternal Son of God, the only Mediator between God and man. I marvel that he took on our nature and became man so that he might redeem and save lost sinners like me.

I bless you for his holy life. Give me the grace to follow his steps. I rejoice in the truth he taught and preached. Help me to respond in faith to the truth as it is found in Jesus. I am filled with wonder at the miraculous signs he did to confirm his doctrine. I humbly bow in awe as I consider the wondrous deliverance from the guilt of sin by his cursed death on the cross to pay for my debt of sin and to reconcile me to God. I am filled with happiness when I consider his miraculous rising again from the dead on the third day. I offer my adoration to Jesus, the one who ascended into heaven, where he now lives to make intercession for me. I step out in faith according to his commandment to go into all the world, since he has all power both in heaven and in earth. I live daily with the assured hope and expectation that he will soon come again in glory to judge the world at the last day.

I thank you that I am committed and marked forever as one of Christ's disciples, for I am baptized as a Christian. I give glory to the Father, the Son, and the Holy Spirit, the one God in whose name I was baptized.

Lord, be my God through Christ, and take me as one of your people. Be my best good and the highest goal of my life. Let Jesus Christ be my Prince and Saviour. Let the Holy Spirit be my Sanctifier, Teacher, Guide, and Comforter.

Enable me to deny all ungodliness and the sinful desires of the flesh. Give me the grace to be clear-headed and to live righteously and godly in this present world. Keep me always looking for the hope of Christ's return in glory.

Make me repentant toward God, and give me faith toward our Lord Jesus Christ. Give me the grace to live a life of faith and repentance.

Make me truly sorry for the sins I have committed against you in my thoughts, words, and actions. Give me grace to sin no more. Help me never to repeat the same sins over and over again.

Enable me to receive Jesus Christ as he is freely offered in the gospel. Constantly remind me to rely on him as my prophet, priest, and king. Let me totally surrender myself to him so I can be ruled, taught, and saved by him.

Lord, pardon all my sins and grant me the gift of the Holy Spirit as the beginning of my experience of eternal life. Give me grace to display the genuineness of my faith and repentance by a diligent obedience to all your commandments. Keep me from doing anything against my conscience.

Enable me to love you with all my heart. Let me also love my neighbour as myself.

Give me grace to always mention your name and your works in creation and redemption with reverence and seriousness. Enable me to read and hear your word with diligence and full attention. Help me to meditate on it, to believe it, and to frame my life according to it.

Teach me to receive all your mercies with thankfulness. Give me the grace to bear all afflictions with patience and submission to your holy will.

Never let my heart be lifted up in pride. Guard it from being disturbed by anger or any other sinful passion. Keep my body pure. Do not let it be defiled with over-indulgence, uncleanness, or any fleshly lusts. Restrain me from ever speaking sinful words.

Give me grace to honour and obey my parents and leaders. Thank you for their instructions and corrections. Place a special blessing on my parents and teachers. Help me be an encouragement to them in everything.

Pity, help, and give comfort to the poor and all those in affliction and distress.

Bless my friends. Forgive my enemies. Enable me to do my duty to all people.

For anything I have done that offends you, I humbly ask your pardon through the blood of Christ. Give me grace to do my duty better next time. Let me live in the fear of God so that I may be happy in this world as well as in the world to come.

Lord, prepare me to die and leave this world. Save me from everlasting misery and torment which will clearly be the portion of all the wicked and ungodly. Bring me safely to live with you and your Son Jesus Christ in the world of everlasting rest and joy.

Give me wisdom and grace to live a holy and godly life. Let my great concern and business be to serve you, and to save my own soul.

All these prayers I humbly beg in the name and for the sake of Jesus Christ, my only Saviour and Redeemer. To him, to you O Father, and to the eternal Spirit be honour, glory, and praise from now on and forever. Amen.

A Morning Prayer for a Family

Lord of the Covenant, it is our desire as a family to be bound in covenant with you. We desire to honour and adore you. You are infinitely bright, blessed and glorious. You are complete in yourself and have need of nothing else. You are the source, the fountain of all being, power, life, motion, and perfection.

You are good to all. Your tender mercies are over all your works. You are continually doing good things for us, though we are evil and unthankful.

We consider it a great privilege to address you as the Father of our family through Jesus Christ. How blessed we are to have freedom to approach you through him. Look down on us now and be merciful to us, as you always have been to those who love your name. Make our family worship the most important part of our daily business and the most delightful part of our daily enjoyments.

You are the God of every family that belongs to your chosen people. Be the God of our family. Whatever other families do, our whole household will serve the Lord. Let your blessing rest on our home from the beginning of the year to its end. If you will bless us, we will not need anyone else to bless us.

Thank you for the mercy you show us every night. Thank you for sustaining us. Enable us to lie down and sleep in safety every day. Then let us wake up refreshed and ready to serve you. Let no plague come near our home. Bring us each day to the light and comfort of one more day.

It is only because of your mercies that we are not consumed. Your compassions never fail. They are new every morning. Great is your faithfulness.

We have rested and are refreshed, while countless others were restlessly tossing throughout the night. You have kept our home safe and quiet, while many others had to lie down exposed to many dangers. We are unworthy of all the mercy, grace, and peace you have shown us.

We have sinned against you as a family. Our family has fallen far short of the glory of God. We are too often controlled by our corrupt, sinful natures that constantly show a determination to backslide from you. We are more inclined to do evil than to do good.

Vain thoughts take up lodging in us. They defile our minds and interfere with good thoughts. We willingly burden ourselves with the worries and cares of this world, even though you have encouraged us to cast all our cares on you.

We have failed to fulfil our obligations to the other members of our family. We provoke one another more to folly and passion than to love and good works. We have become lukewarm in our love to you. We are weak in our desires toward you. We are unsteady and uneven in our walk with you. We are not always prepared for your service.

Forgive all our sins for Christ's sake. Be at peace with us through Jesus Christ who died to reconcile us to you, and who ever lives to make intercession for us.

Many people say, 'Who will show us any good in this life?' Lord, let us never be satisfied with the good things this world can offer. Hear our heart's desire for you to enlighten us with a clear manifestation of your presence. Make us happier by our constant communion with you than people who get their pleasure from wealth and prosperity.

Let your peace rule in our hearts by faith. Let it guard our hearts and minds in Christ Jesus. May the consolations and comforts of God be our strength and our song even in the night.

We commit ourselves to your care and keeping this day. Watch over us for our good. Surround us with your favour as with a shield. Preserve us from all evil. Protect us in our going out and our coming in.

We commit our bodies and all our worldly affairs to your wise and gracious providence. We submit to the orderings of your eternal purposes. Let nothing harm us. Keep us healthy and safe. Bless our work. Prosper all our lawful undertakings. Give us pleasure and success in them. Let us eat the labour of our hands.

We commit our eternal souls to the care of your Spirit and your grace. Let grace work powerfully in us. Let it prove sufficient for us in all our troubles and trials. Let it strongly influence our determination and our desire to do good according to your good purpose for our lives.

Give us grace to do the work of this day in its day as the duty of the day requires. Help us do even common duties in a godly manner. Give us the grace to acknowledge you in all our ways. Let our eyes always look toward you. Direct our every step.

Restrain us from sinning. Help us exercise control over our own spirits. Keep us from breaking out in passion when we are provoked. Keep us from speaking foolishly with our lips. Give us grace to live together in peace and harmonious love. Place your ultimate blessing on us, which is life forever more. Make us conscientious in all our dealings. Let us always be watchful against sin, being fully aware that your eye is on us. Arm us against every temptation. Sustain us in our integrity. Keep us in the way of our duty. Let us always remember that the fear of the Lord is the beginning of wisdom. Move us to live in your fear every day, and all the day.

When the path we should follow is unclear, make the right way certain to us. When the correct decision is uncertain, give us the wisdom from above which is pure, peaceable, gentle and easy to be corrected, full of mercy and good fruits. Let our integrity preserve us, for by walking in uprightness we display our trust in you.

Sanctify to us all our losses, crosses, afflictions, and disappointments. Give us grace to submit to your will in all circumstances. Let us find it good to be afflicted, that we may participate more fully in your holiness.

Prepare us for the events of this day, for we cannot know what a day may bring forth. Make us stand complete in all aspects of your perfect will. Give us the grace to deny ourselves, take up our cross daily and follow Jesus Christ.

Lord, make us ready for death and the final judgment when we shall stand alone before your throne. Fit us for eternity in heaven. Give us the grace to live every day as if it were our last day on earth.

Lord, expand your kingdom throughout the world. Build up your church until it achieves its perfect beauty as the bride of Christ. Set up the throne of the exalted Redeemer on the ruins of the devil's kingdom. Let churches that have been once reformed by your grace be always reforming. Let everything that has gone wrong among your people be amended. Let those who suffer for righteousness' sake be supported and delivered.

Do good among all the nations of the world. Bless governors and all people in authority. Guide public affairs so that the nations may serve as nursing mothers to your church. Exercise authority over all peoples, nations, and tribes to your own glory. Let peace and truth prevail in our days. May the next generation enjoy the benefits of godly forefathers to the full.

Be gracious to our relatives, friends, neighbours, and acquaintances. Provide for them according to their necessities. Supply the needs of all your people according to the immeasurable wealth inherent in your glory through Christ Jesus. Take up your dwelling-place among all families that fear you and call on your name. Forgive our enemies and those that do not like us or even hate us. Give us a just, generous, and loving spirit toward all people and their possessions.

Care for the afflicted. Comfort them. Be an ever-present help in their time of special need. Heal the sick. Ease the pain of their suffering. Strengthen the powers of resistance for the tempted. Relieve the oppressed. Give joy to those that mourn in Zion.

Deal with us and our family according to the terms of your everlasting covenant, which is well ordered and certain in all its promises. For in its provisions we find full salvation and everything we desire.

We praise you for all the blessings of creation and redemption. We thank you for the blessings we receive in this life and for the blessings we hope to receive in the life to come. We thank you especially for Jesus Christ who is the fountain and foundation of all blessings. Thank you for giving us the incomprehensible gift of your Son, Jesus Christ.

We humbly ask you to forgive our sins and to accept our services for Christ's sake. Answer all our prayers according to the greatness of your wisdom and grace, to the honour of Christ who died for our sins and rose again.

An Evening Prayer for a Family

Most holy, blessed and glorious Covenant LORD, we belong to you and we are bound to serve you. You are our Maker and our Redeemer. We are yours, for you have made us and bought us with a price. We are not our own. We lift up our souls to seek your face. Where else can we go for happiness but to you, the one from whom we derive all our being.

Through the good hand of our God on us, we have come safely to the close of another day. At the end of the various activities of the day, we come together tonight as a family to recall your loving care, and to praise you, our Saviour and our God. For you are good and your mercy endures forever.

You are the great Benefactor of the whole creation. You give life and breath to all. You are the God that has fed and shepherded us through all our lives. We continue to live up to now as monuments of your sparing mercy and witnesses of your sovereign grace. We have received unbroken help from you, for you are an unchanging God and not like vacillating man. For this reason alone we are not destroyed.

One day testifies to the next, and one night affirms to another your goodness. You are always doing good. You have never disappointed anyone who seeks you and trusts in your grace. The dawning of the morning and the fading of the evening praise you.

Blessed be the Lord, who daily loads us with his benefits. You are the God of our salvation. We have received the mercies of the day from you according to this day's need. Yet we have fallen far short of doing the work of the day in its day as the duty of the day requires.

We bless you for the services performed on our behalf this day by your ministering angels who surround us. Thank you for the service that your more humble creatures have rendered to us. Thank you for the degree to which we have enjoyed bodily health and comfort. Thank you for the encouragement that has come from our relations, and for an adequate place to live. Thank you for not making the wilderness our home and the desert our dwelling-place. Thank you for allowing us to continue having the ability to understand your truth. Thank you for the calmness and peace of our consciences.

We praise you for peace in our country. Thank you for giving us a good land in which each family dwells safely under its own vine and fig-tree.

Above all, thank you for Jesus Christ and his mediation between a holy God and sinful man. Thank you for the covenant of grace you have made with us in him. Thank you for all the great and precious promises and privileges contained in that covenant. Thank you for our open access to the throne of grace. Let us come in his name and through his blood with humble boldness. Thank you for the hope of eternal life through him.

We confess we have sinned against you. Even today we have sinned and done foolish things. O God, you know our foolishness, and our sins are not hid from you. We waste our time. We neglect our duty. We chase after worthless things and forsake our own mercies. We offend with our tongues. Are we not living as though we had not been delivered from indecent desires? Do we not walk as mere men rather than as reborn and redeemed Christians? Who can understand his errors? Cleanse us from our secret faults.

Give us the grace to turn away from our sins. Make us fully aware of the evil in our sins and the danger they bring to us. Let the blood of Christ your Son cleanse us from all sin, so that this very night we may lie down at peace with you. Make our souls return to you and find our rest in you.

Give us grace to repent for the sins we commit each day so that when the day of our death comes, we may then have only the sins of that one day to confess before you, our God and our Judge. How much easier it is to confess our sins now than it will be when we stand in judgment before you.

Do good to us both in your merciful and in your afflicting providences. Give us grace to accept with joy all your divine appointments. Let your hand guide all the affairs of our life. Use every event and circumstance to bring us nearer to you. By all your sovereign and gracious providences make us more useful to you. We commit ourselves to you this night. Let us find our rest in the secret place of the Most High, and seek shelter under the shadow of the Almighty. Let the Lord be our dwelling-place, and let our lives be at home in him.

Put a protecting hedge around us, our home, and all we possess. Do not let any evil happen to us. Do not let any plague come near our home. O Lord, you never slumber or sleep. So be our keeper. Be a sun and a shield to us.

Refresh our bodies tonight with a peaceful and comfortable rest. Keep us from being disturbed by any distrustful or distressing thoughts and fears. Let our souls be refreshed with the light that comes from your smiling face. Let our experience of your love be better to us than life.

Give us grace to remember you as we lie on our beds. Let us meditate on you in the night seasons. Let us make the best possible use of the silence and solitude of our retreat from the daily cares of this life. Let us enjoy this special opportunity for communion with you to the fullest. When we are alone, let us not be alone, but with you. When we wake up in the morning, let us see that we are still with you.

Bring us to another day in safety, and prepare us for the duties and events that will come with it. By all the supports and comforts you provide for life, let our bodies and souls serve you well. Enable us to glorify you with body and soul, always remembering that we are not our own since we have been bought with the price of Christ's blood.

Since we are now one day nearer our end, enable us to carefully calculate the days remaining to us, so a heart filled with wisdom may direct our lives. As we remove our clothing at the end of the day and go to sleep in our beds, let us be reminded that very soon we will be putting off the body in a similar way and sleeping the sleep of death. Since we will soon be making our bed in the darkness of death, let us daily die to self in anticipation of that final death. Prepare us for the change that must occur, so that when death actually comes, it will hold no surprises for us. Let death's arrival not terrify us. Instead, let us calmly put off the body and commit our spirit to you, knowing very well the one we have trusted.

Lord, let our family be blessed in Christ, since all families of the earth may receive blessing in him. Let this family be blessed with all spiritual blessings in the realities of heaven that have come to earth by Christ Jesus. Let us also be blessed with the temporal blessings that you judge to be best for us. Give us the amount of health and prosperity that will promote our sanctification. Especially let our souls prosper and go from strength to strength, from glory to glory. Let all that belong to our family belong to Christ. As we live in one house together on earth, may we be together forever with the Lord in heaven.

Look with pity on this lost and dying world. Set up Christ's throne where Satan's seat of power is located. Send the gospel where it has never been heard, and make it successful where it has already come. Make the good news of Jesus Christ mighty through you to the pulling down of strongholds resistant to your truth.

Let the church of Christ flourish wherever it is found. Let your universal church be built on the rock of a true profession of faith concerning the Christ, the Son of the living God, so that the gates of hell cannot prevail against it. Do not allow the domineering rod of the wicked rest on the inheritance of your righteous people.

Let our native land continue under the blessing of your good providence. In its prevailing peace let us have peace. Let your glory dwell in our land. Let your glory cover us like a canopy over-arching a marriage chamber.

Rule in the hearts of our governors. Make all those who hold positions of public trust be faithful to the public interest. Let those in governmental positions who wield the sword be a terror to evil-doers, and a means of protection, encouragement and praise to those who do well. Support faithful ministers of your word in all their work. Give them skill to help souls prosper in doing the will of God both in this life and in that which is to come.

Be gracious to those that are near and dear to us. Let the rising generation offer more and better service to you in their day than we have in our own. Comfort those that are sorrowing or experiencing serious trials. Do not give them a load too great for them to bear. Give them daily strength so they can be more than conquerors through Christ who loves them.

Do for us far more than what we are able to ask or think for the glory of our Saviour Jesus Christ, who is the Lord our Righteousness. To him with the Father and the eternal Spirit, be glory and praise, now and forever. Amen.

A Family Prayer for the
Lord's Day Morning

Most gracious God and Father of our Lord Jesus Christ, it is good for us to draw near to you. The nearer we come to you the better it is for us. It will be best of all when we are nearest you in the kingdom of your glory.

We adore you as the great I Am, the Alpha and the Omega. Your existence and your happiness are inherent in yourself. We receive our being from you, and our happiness is altogether in you. Therefore it is our duty and essential for our wellbeing to seek you, to implore your favour, and to give you the glory due your name.

We bless you for the morning light, for showing the dawn its proper place and its right time. Let heaven's rising sun enlighten our darkened souls. Let the Sun of Righteousness rise with healing under his wings.

We bless you that every bit of light we see comes from you, the Father of lights. This is the day you have made both for man and for yourself. We will rejoice and be glad in it. We bless you that you have helped us understand your holy Sabbaths. We were taught early in life to put a difference between this day and other days of the week. We thank you that we live in a land where you are publicly and solemnly worshipped on this day.

We give thanks that the liberties and opportunities of the Sabbath still are ours. We thank you that we are not wishing in vain for one of the days of the Son of Man. The candlestick of our witness in the world has not been removed even though it could have been if you had acted in justice, for we have left our first love in so many ways.

We now gladly welcome this Sabbath. Hosanna to the son of David! Blessed is he that comes in the name of the Lord. May our hosannas ring out loudly in the highest heavens! Lord, let us be in the Spirit on this Lord's day. Let this day be the Sabbath of the Lord in our home and in our hearts. Make this day a Sabbath of rest from sin and a rest in you. Help us sanctify this Sabbath so it may be sanctified to us, and the means of our sanctification. As we rest today from our worldly employments, let the focus of our hearts turn away from the temporal things of this life to the things that will last for eternity. As we spend our time worshipping in your presence today, let us anticipate the joy of living before you in the world to come.

We confess we are totally unworthy of the privilege of personal communion with you. But we come in the name of the Lord Jesus Christ who is altogether worthy. We depend on the assistance of the Holy Spirit as he works in us. We trust him to strengthen us so we can overcome every obstacle, within and without, that hinders our close communion with you.

We keep this day holy to honour you, God the Father Almighty, Maker of heaven and earth. We sanctify this day as we remember the wondrous work of creation in which you made all things very good out of nothing, by the word of your power, in the space of six days. We acknowledge that we are your servants along with all other things you made. Everything continues to exist only because of your creative decree. You are worthy to receive blessing, honour, glory, and power, for you created all things and for your pleasure they are and were created. You are the one who first commanded light to shine out of darkness. On the first day of the first week you said, 'Let there be light', and there was light. On this first day of this week may you shine into our hearts to give us more and more of the light of the knowledge of your glory as it radiates in the face of Jesus Christ. Remake us today as your workmanship, created in Christ Jesus to do good works which give clear proof of our new creation in Christ.

We also sanctify this day to honour our Lord Jesus Christ, the eternal Son of God, our exalted Redeemer. We sanctify this day in remembrance of his resurrection from the dead on the first day of the week. We affirm that by his resurrection he was declared to be the Son of God with power. We bless you that having laid down his life to make atonement for sin, he rose again for our justification, that he might bring in everlasting righteousness. We praise you that the stone the builders refused and abused has become the chief cornerstone of your kingdom on earth. Only the Lord could accomplish this kind of thing, and it amazes us. We praise you that Christ has risen from the dead as the firstfruits of believers who have fallen asleep in death. Thank you for establishing him as the resurrection and the life. As we celebrate his resurrection with great joy on this day, let us experience in a new and fresh way the power of his resurrection. Let us rise with him from the death of sin to the life of righteousness, and from the dust of worldliness to a holy and godly life. As we have been planted with Christ in the likeness of his death, so let us come to life with him in the likeness of his resurrection. Just as Christ was raised from the dead by the glory of the Father, let us walk in glorious newness of life.

We also sanctify this day to the honour of the eternal Spirit of grace who is our Supporter and Comforter. We rejoice as we recall the descent of the Spirit on the day of Pentecost, which also was the first day of the week. We praise you that when Jesus left this earth at his ascension, he sent the promised Holy Spirit to apply the benefits of his completed work of redemption to people from all nations of the world. We honour the Spirit of Christ for preparing the world for his return in glory and for the restoration of all things. We thank you for the promise that the Holy Spirit will abide with us forever. Now may the Spirit that raised up Jesus from the dead rule in our hearts by faith. O Spirit of grace, breathe on these dry bones, these dead hearts of ours. Make them live. Be a Spirit of faith, love, holiness, and power in us.

O Lord, we praise you for your holy Word, which is a light to our feet and a lamp to our path. We thank you that it was written down for our learning, that we through patience and comfort of the Scriptures might have hope. We glorify you for preserving the Scriptures pure and complete for us. We are forever grateful that you have made them available to us in a language that we understand. Keep us from receiving this bountiful sign of your grace in vain. Thank you for letting our eyes see in the Scriptures a light that brings joy to our heart. Thank you that our ears hear the joyful sound of a Redeemer and a Saviour, of redemption and salvation through him. We glorify your name that life and immortality are brought to light by the gospel. We join the angels above in giving glory to you in the highest heavens that in Jesus Christ there is peace on earth among those with whom you are pleased.

We thank you for the great good news that you have given us eternal life, and this life is in your Son. Lord, we receive this gospel as truth worthy of total trust and unconditional acceptance. We entrust our immortal souls to this message of salvation in Jesus Christ. We rejoice that we are encouraged to come to you as our Father through your Son as our Mediator. Gracious Lord, let Jesus Christ your Son be wisdom, righteousness, sanctification, and redemption to us. Let your call to us be successful in bringing us into a living fellowship with Christ who is the head of all things. Let us be united to Christ by faith so that he may live in us and we may grow to maturity in him in all things. Let us have the joy of yielding fruit in our lives that gives glory to him. In whatever we do, both in our words and deeds, let us do everything in your name and to your glory. Let us have the Spirit of Christ as a solemn seal affirming that we belong to him. Let us experience life that is truly life, both now and throughout eternity by the indwelling, transforming Spirit. Let none of our family fall short of it. Put in us your Holy Spirit as the firstfruits of this eternal life abiding in us.

We praise you for the new covenant you have made with us in Jesus Christ. Thank you for the great mercy it displays to us. For when you saw that your original covenant made at creation had been broken so that fallen sinners could never be reconciled to you by the terms of that covenant, you were pleased to institute a covenant that provided blessing despite the demerit of sin. We thank you that we are under grace and not under the law. We rejoice that this covenant is established on better promises that find fulfilment in Christ our Mediator. Lord, we take hold of your gracious provision for covenant-breakers as the hope you have placed before us. Receive us graciously into the bonds of this covenant. Father, make us accepted in your Son according to the provisions of this gracious covenant. You have declared that the Lord Jesus is your beloved Son in whom you are altogether pleased. We humbly profess that he is our beloved Saviour. Lord, be altogether pleased with us in him.

On this your holy day let our hearts be filled with thoughts about Christ and his love to us. We stand in awe at the height, depth, length, and breadth of Christ's love which is beyond human understanding. How great is this love! Let your love constrain us to love him and live for him who died for us and rose again. Encourage us with the remembrance that while we pray at the footstool of the throne of grace, our Saviour sits at the right hand of the throne of glory interceding for us. Through his mediation let us find favour with you.

Let us be refreshed as we are renewed in covenant and communion with you.

For Christ's sake forgive all our known and unknown sins. Deliver us from our guilt through Christ. Accept us as righteous in your sight. Do not let us be condemned, which is what we deserve. Let our iniquity be taken away and our sin covered. Let us be clothed with the spotless robe of Christ's righteousness so that the shame of our nakedness before you may be covered. Let no cloud of guilt interfere with our relationship to you and our communion with you. Let our lusts be put to death. Keep our corruptions from hindering the ascent of our souls toward heaven.

On this sacred day, give us your special help in all our worship. Go with us to the solemn assembly of your people. For if your presence does not go up with us, what good will it do for us to go up without you? Give us grace to draw near to you with a singleness of heart and in full assurance of faith. Meet us with your blessing. Be present wherever two or three people gather together in your name. Show your saving grace through the prayers, the singing of psalms and hymns, the reading of Scripture, the confession of our faith, the testimony of the blessed, the preaching of your word, and the celebration of the sacraments. Help us overcome our many weaknesses and the sins that so easily distract us in our service of worship. Let your word come with life and power to our souls. Make it like the good seed sown in good soil. Let it take root and yield fruit to your glory. Let our prayers and praises be spiritual sacrifices acceptable in your sight through Christ Jesus. Display your gentle grace toward those that are providentially hindered from joining the worshipping assembly.

Let your presence be clearly manifested in all assemblies of faithful Christians. Be with all those who love the Lord Jesus Christ with sincerity. Let the great Redeemer ride on triumphantly in the chariot of the everlasting gospel as a conqueror sent forth to conquer. Let our every thought be brought into obedience to him. Let many come to believe the gospel. Let your saving arm be revealed to many. Let sinners be converted to you. Let your saints be built up in faith and holiness. Bring in the full number of your chosen people from both Jews and Gentiles. May your kingdom come soon in all its fullness.

Now may the Lord of peace give us peace always. May the God of hope fill us with joy and peace in believing, for the sake of Jesus Christ, who is our Saviour and Redeemer. Amen.

A Family Prayer for the
Lord's Day Evening

O eternal, forever blessed and glorious Lord God. You are God over all and rich in mercy to all that call on you. You are most wise and powerful, holy, just, and good. You are the King of kings and Lord of lords, our Lord and our God. You are completely blessed and happy without us. You have no need of our services. Our goodness contributes nothing to you. But we are miserable without you. We stand in constant need of your grace. We are forever ruined if your goodness does not reach out to bless us. Lord, we plead for your favour with our whole hearts. Let your blessings come to us in Jesus Christ, for all our happiness hinges on your good grace. Your favour is better than life.

We have forfeited every right to your goodness. We have made ourselves totally unworthy of the least of your blessings. But we humbly pray for your mercy in the name of Jesus Christ who loved us and gave himself for us. We confess our sin before you. By the corruption of our nature we have become repulsive to your holiness. We are completely unfit to be inheritors of your kingdom. Our transgressions have made us detestable to your justice and liable to your wrath and curse. By nature we are children of disobedience, deserving your righteous judgment. We blush and tremble whenever we approach you, the holy and righteous God. The defilement even of the things we have consecrated to you could be our ruin if you should deal with us according to what we deserve.

But there is mercy and full redemption with you. You have graciously provided the removal of sin's guilt through the merit of Christ's death for all those who repent and believe the gospel. You have promised that the power of sin will be broken by his Spirit and his grace. For he saves to the uttermost all those who come to you by him, since he lives forever to intercede for them.

Lord, we come to you as our Father through Jesus Christ the only Mediator between a holy God and a sinful humanity. Through him we earnestly desire to turn away from the world, the flesh, and the devil by repentance and faith. We turn to you as our ruler and judge. We repent for all the ways we have offended you. We are ashamed to think of our treacherous, ungrateful conduct toward you. Help us to have nothing more to do with sin. Break the power of sin in us. Remove its guilt. We look to the righteousness of Jesus Christ and the merit of his death as the only way to regain your favour. Graciously look on us in him and receive us for his sake. Heal our backslidings and love us freely. Do not let our iniquity be the cause of our ruin.

Having been justified by faith let us have peace with you through our Lord Jesus Christ. Let his death serve as a sacrifice to remove your wrath against us for our sin. In your perfect justice be just and the one who justifies those who have faith in him. Accept us as righteous through the sinless Christ whom you made to be sin for us, for we have no righteousness of our own.

May the God of peace sanctify us in all parts of our life. Carry on the good work of grace in our bodies and our souls. Renew us in the spirit of our minds. Make us what you want us to be in everything. Set up your throne in our hearts. Write your law in our minds. Plant your fear in our spirits. Fill us with all the graces of your Spirit that we may bear the fruit of righteousness to your glory and praise.

Put to death our pride and our passions. Clothe us with humility and the unfading beauty of a gentle and quiet spirit, which is of great worth in your sight. Put out of our minds all worthless thoughts. Let your grace be mighty to make us serious and sober-minded about the things of God. Let the flesh be crucified in us with all its affections and lusts. Give us grace to restrain the disordered desires of our bodies. Help us make them servants to the Holy Spirit who has made our bodies his temple. Enable us to control our bodies in a way that is holy and honourable.

Let love for the world be rooted out of us and love for Christ rooted in us. Deliver us from covetousness which is idolatry. Pour your love into our hearts through the Holy Spirit. Make us love you, the Lord our God, with all our heart, soul, mind, and might. Give us the grace to do all we do out of love for you.

Put to death all envy together with all hatred and wickedness. Deliver us from our lack of love. Rid us of every root of bitterness. Give us the grace to love one another fervently with a pure heart as followers of the Lord Jesus. Let us live by his new commandment that we love one another as he has loved us. Let brotherly love continue among us. Let our love always be without hypocrisy.

We humbly ask you to correct all our mistakes. If we have gone astray in anything, reveal our error to us. Let the Spirit of truth lead us into all truth as it is in Jesus. Help us to know the truth which leads to godliness. Give us that good understanding which belongs to those who do your commandments. Make our love abound more and more in knowledge and depth of insight.

Convince us of the vanity of this world and its inability to make us happy. Keep us from setting our affection on the things of this world. Preserve us from placing our expectations for good on temporal things. Make us fully convinced of the vileness of sin and its capacity to make us miserable. Give us grace to hate sin and the lust of our heart that leads us into it.

Convince us of the infinite value of our own souls. Help us to feel the weight of eternity and the awfulness of everlasting torment. Make us diligent and serious in our preparations for eternity. Let us work less for the food that spoils and more for the nourishment for our souls that endures forever. Give us grace to set our affections on things above, not on things on earth which are trifling and transitory.

Let the things of time be as nothing to us in comparison with the things of eternity. Let the life to come be constantly in our thoughts so we will be governed by the faith which makes substance of things not seen. Enable us to keep looking by faith at things that will always remain invisible to the human eye.

Give us grace to consider the world to come with a deep concern for pleasing you. Let us consider how even the passing things of this world may be made to have eternal significance. Give us grace to rejoice as if we did not, to weep as if we did not. Teach us to buy as if the things we acquire are not our own, and to use the things of this world without abusing them. For the world in its present form is passing away, and we are passing away with it.

Let your grace be sufficient to prepare us for the great change which will certainly come, and may come very suddenly and soon. Let us be ready for this change which will remove us from our state of trial to one of recompense and retribution. Make us suitable for joining the saints in their inheritance, so that when this life fails we may be received into everlasting habitations.

Prepare us for whatever we may encounter between now and the grave. We do not know what a day may bring forth. We have no idea how to prepare ourselves for the future. But you know all things. Prepare us by your grace for whatever you may appoint for us in terms of service and suffering. Arm us against every temptation that may assault us. Enable us to keep a clean conscience. Let us welcome whatever may be your holy will. At your return let us be found diligent in doing whatever may be our duty. Give us the grace to always glorify you in all circumstances. Enable us to keep up our hope and joy in Christ, and a strong belief in the prospect of eternal life.

Give us the grace to maintain close communion with you by the regular use of prayer and meditation on your word. Let our responses to your providential direction of our life draw us closer to you rather than driving us away from you. Help us to put you always right before our minds and hearts. Keep our eyes focused on you. Bless us so that we thrive by a life of dependence on you, relying on your providence, promise, and power. Give us the grace to trust you at all times and to pour out our hearts to you in prayer. Help us live in complete devotedness to you, with your honour and glory as our chief goal in life. Enable us to rejoice in you always, so that godly living becomes not only our duty but also our pleasure. Help us make you our heart's delight, so we may be sure to have our heart's desire. Let us please you and be pleased in you.

Preserve us in our integrity to our dying day. Let us never forsake you or turn away from following you. Enable us to always cling firmly to you the Lord our God, not counting life itself as more precious to us. Let us finish our life well. Strengthen us so that we can complete our course honourably and with fullness of joy.

Let your good providence order all the circumstances that will lead to our death and removal from this world to a better one. Let your ever-sufficient grace enable us to run the race of faith to the end so that we may experience a grand entrance into the everlasting kingdom of our Lord and Saviour Jesus Christ.

Make us wiser and better every day as we pass through this world. Wean us from our attachments to things that perish with the using. Let us grow in our realization that it is far better for us to depart and be with Christ. Give us the grace to be more holy the longer we live in this world so that we may be more fit for the world to come. May our last days be our best days, our last works our best works, and our last comforts our sweetest comforts.

Fulfil all your promises concerning your church in these last days. Let the whole earth be filled with your glory as the waters cover the sea. Let the mountain of the Lord's house be established on the top of the mountains and exalted above the hills. Move all nations to flow to the true house of the Lord. Let the fullness of the Gentiles be brought in so that the Jews may be moved to jealousy. In this glorious way let all the Israel of God be saved. Bring nations up and bring others down in a way that contributes to the expansion of Christ's kingdom and church. Let the kingdom of Christ be set up in all places on the ruins of the devil's kingdom.

Hasten the downfall of the man of sin. Let pure apostolic Christianity be revived and made to flourish among all nations. Let the power of true godliness prevail against all its opponents. Put down those who have a mere outward form of religion. Let the wars and the convulsion of nations end in peace and the enlargement of Christ's church and kingdom. Let the rise and fall of nations result in the advancement of the eternal kingdom of Christ among men.

Let your everlasting gospel be the glory in our midst. Let your providence be a wall of fire about us. Bless all ministers of your word and sacraments. Let them be burning and shining lights in the midst of a crooked and perverse generation. Make them faithful to Christ and anxious for the souls of men. Unite your ministers together in the truth. Remove jealousy and personal ambition far from them. Let them have true love for one another. Pour out on them a spirit of genuine love, proper tolerance, and personal humility. Bind them together as one man so that they may strive to promote only your glory and the salvation of the lost.

Bless the produce of the earth throughout the nations. Give abundant harvest to all the peoples of the world. Satisfy the poor with bread to sustain their lives. Establish justice in the commercial dealings among the nations. Expose the greed of those who exploit smaller, defenceless peoples. Restrain the rebellious. Bring them under submission to the governmental authorities you have set over them. Preserve the public peace, that the gospel may run and not be hindered.

Thank you for all the mercies of this holy day. For a day in your courts is better than a thousand days spent anywhere else. How lovely are your tabernacles,

O Lord of hosts! Bless the word we have heard today as the Scriptures have been read and preached to us. Hear our prayers, accept our praises, and forgive whatever your pure eye has seen that is wrong in us.

Protect us tonight. Help us to properly close the day with you. Let us lie down and sleep without disturbance. Be with us throughout the following week and guide us in all our ways. Forgive us that we brought so much of the week's business with us into the Sabbath. But now enable us to bring a great deal of the Sabbath with us into the week. Make us more ready for consecrating the next Sabbath to you if we should live to see it. Thank you for the taste of heaven we enjoyed this Sabbath day. Allow us to spend more of our time praising you, for this is the work that will occupy us throughout eternity.

Give us the grace to enter the everlasting Sabbath-rest of the Lord when time and days shall be no more. Let this day bring us one Sabbath-day's journey nearer heaven, and one Sabbath-day's work more prepared for it. We began this Lord's day with the joyful memory of Christ's resurrection. We conclude it with the joyful expectation of his return in glory, our own resurrection, and our triumph in the hope of seeing the fullness of your glory. Bless the Lord, O my soul! Let all that is within me bless your holy name, for you are good and your mercy endures forever.

Now to the King who is eternal, immortal, and invisible, the only wise God, our one God in three persons, Father, Son, and Holy Spirit, be honour and glory, dominion, and praise, from now on and forever. Amen.

A Prayer that Parents May Offer for Their Children

O Lord our God, you are the God of the spirits of all mankind. All souls are yours. The souls of parents and the souls of their children are yours, and your grace is sufficient for both. You were our father's God and we will exalt you. You are our children's God, and so we ask you to fulfil your promises to us and our children. We recognize that you are a God in covenant with believers and their seed.

Lord, your good providence has built us up into a family. We thank you for the blessing of the children you have graciously given us. Make them a real blessing to us so that we may never be tempted to wish we had been written down as childless.

We are saddened when we think of the iniquity in which our children are conceived and born. We grieve over the corrupt nature which they inherit from us. But we thank you that there is a fountain opened for their cleansing from the pollution that goes all the way back to their origins. We thank you that they were born in the bonds of the covenant, and committed to you in baptism by covenantal oath. Thank you that they are born in your house and received as members of your earthly family.

They are committed to you by their baptism. We humbly plead with you to save them. Regenerate them so they can make it their own act to be confirmed in covenant with you. Claim them as your own so they may be presented as your precious jewels in that great final day.

Give them a good disposition of spirit and a good capacity of mind. Make them obedient and willing to receive instruction. Incline them early in their childhood to a godly lifestyle. Let them grow in wisdom and knowledge, and in favour with God and man. Let the rod of your chastening as well as ours drive out the foolishness that is bound up in the hearts of our children. Save them from the vanity to which childhood and youth is subject.

We do not ask for the great things of this world for our children. But if it pleases you, give them good health and preserve them from severely harmful accidents. Feed them with food that is sufficient for them. Give them the special blessing of a life useful to your kingdom in this world.

Most importantly, pour out your Spirit on them. Let this greatest of blessings rest on our offspring so they may serve you in their generation. Let them find their chief pleasure in that best part of life which is living in closest fellowship with you. Let this blessing never be taken away from them.

Give us wisdom, meekness, tenderness, and grace to bring them up in your fear and in the nurture and admonition of the Lord. Help us to raise them up as obedient and respectful children. Teach us how to teach them the things of God suited to their level of understanding. Give us wisdom to know how to reprove, admonish, encourage, and correct them in a right manner. Enable us to always set before them good examples of a life that is virtuous and deserving of praise from you. Give us success in promoting a lifestyle for them that pleases you. Help us train them up in the right way in which they should go, so that if they live to be old they will never depart from it.

Keep them from the snare of evil company. Protect them from all the temptations to which they will be exposed. Enable them to recognize at an early age how important it is for their own good as well as their obligation to you to live a God-pleasing life.

Let Christ be formed in the souls of our children while they are still young. Let seeds of grace be sown in their hearts at a tender age. Let us have the satisfaction of seeing them walking in the truth and setting their faces toward heaven. Give them the grace to hear counsel and receive instruction that they may be filled with the wisdom that is from above.

Prosper their education. Be the teacher of our children so their lives may be characterized by your peace. Give them the grace to know you as the only true God and Jesus Christ as the only Saviour you have sent into this world. Let them begin to enjoy the gift of eternal life while they are still living on this earth.

Help our children get wisdom and understanding early in life. Let them never forget the lessons they learn in their youth. Give them the grace to continue living in light of the things they have been taught. Let them never forget what they have learned about the truth as it is in Jesus.

It is our heart's desire and prayer that our children may be praising you on earth after we have gone to praise you in heaven. O Lord, give us that highest privilege of being together forever with our children, serving you in heaven above as we have done during this life on earth. If it should please you to remove any of them from us while they are young, let us have grace to submissively commit them to you. Let us live in hope at their death. Let none of our children fall short of possessing eternal life. Let none of them be found at the left hand of Christ on the Day of Judgment.

If you remove us from them while they are young, be a Father to them. Provide for them and teach them, for with you the fatherless finds mercy.

You know the many concerns we have for our children. We cast all these cares on you. We commit ourselves and our children to you. Do not let the light of your truth be extinguished in our family when we die. Do not allow the treasure of the gospel to be buried in our graves. Instead, let those that come after us offer better service in their day than we have in ours. Let them bring honour and praise to your name.

In all these prayers for our children we seek your glory. Father, let your name be sanctified in our family. Let your kingdom come in our family. Let your will be done by us and our children as it is done by the angels in heaven. We ask all these things for the sake of Jesus Christ, our blessed Saviour and Redeemer whose seed shall endure forever, and whose throne shall last as long as heaven. Now to the Father, Son, and Holy Spirit, that great and sacred name into which we and our children were baptized, be honour and glory, dominion and praise, now and for ever. Amen.

A Prayer for an Individual to Use before Receiving the Sacrament of the Lord's Supper

Most holy, blessed, and gracious Lord God, with all humility and reverence I present myself before you. I seek your face and beg your favour. Let me experience your good work in me as an evidence of your good will toward me.

I acknowledge myself to be totally unworthy of this blessing. I am unfit to be invited to your table. You have graciously permitted me to hear from you in your word and to speak to you in prayer. Now I am also invited to fellowship with you at your holy table. I am summoned to celebrate the memorial of my Saviour's death, and to participate by faith in the countless benefits that flow from his sacrifice. I do not deserve to eat the crumbs that fall from this table, and yet I am invited to feast on the children's bread.

Thank you for the institution of this gracious feast-day. Thank you for this celebration of love which the Lord Jesus left for his church. Thank you that this ordinance has been preserved across millennia up to the present day and age. Thank you that it is regularly administered in this land. Thank you that I am personally invited by Christ to this table. Thank you that I now have before me an opportunity to share at your bountiful table of grace. Lord, let me never receive this abundant provision of your grace in an unworthy manner.

You have called me to the marriage-supper of the Lamb. Give me the proper and necessary wedding garment. Remove the putrid garments of my sin by the life-blood of the Lamb of God that was shed to take away the sin of the world. Clothe me in the perfection of Christ's righteous life. Prepare me for the proper receiving of the remembrance of his sacred sacrifice.

Give my soul a right disposition. Move me by your Spirit to have all the consecrated attitudes that are suitable for a proper participation in this ordinance. The preparation of the heart and the answer of the tongue are both from you. Lord, prepare my unprepared heart for this special moment of intimate fellowship with you.

I confess that I have sinned against you. I have done foolish things. Foolishness is bound up in my heart. I have sinned and fallen far short of glorifying you as I should. The imagination of my heart concocts evil thoughts continually. The bias of my corrupt nature is strongly inclined toward the gratification of sin's desires. I am swift to commit sin and inclined to do evil. My spirit is very reluctant to be moved by the things of God. I have a natural aversion to the concerns of your kingdom. I have wasted my time and trifled with my opportunities. I have followed after worthless idols and forsaken my true source of blessing. God be merciful to me the sinner. How little have I done since I came into the world of the great work that I was sent to do.

You have taken me into covenant with yourself. You have set me apart and sealed me as your own. I have obligated myself to you by many promises. But I have broken my vows repeatedly and been unreliable like a warped bow. I have not kept my covenant with you. The temper of my mind and the tenor of my conversation have not supported my profession of loyalty to you. My way of life has been contrary to your expectations and my own personal commitments. I tend to backslide from you, the one and only living God. If I were under the law, I would be doomed to destruction without hope.

I praise you that I am under a covenant of grace, which provides a way for pardon through repentance from sin and trust in the provision of your mercy in Christ. This covenant invites even backsliding children to return, and promises that their backslidings shall be healed. Lord, I take hold of this covenant. Seal it to me as I come to your table. Let me find my heart truly humbled for its sin. Lead me to sorrow in a godly way. Enable me to look on him, the one

I have pierced as I sit at your table. Let me mourn and be in bitterness for him so that I may receive a broken Christ with a broken heart. Let the blood of Christ, which speaks better things than that of Abel, sprinkle my conscience so that it may be purified and at peace. As I come to your table let me be assured that you are reconciled to me. Give me the grace to believe that my iniquities are pardoned and that I shall not come into condemnation. While I am at your table let me hear you say to me, 'Be encouraged, my son, your sins are forgiven.'

God forbid that I should come in an unworthy manner to this moment of supreme grace and blessing. Lord, lead me into a more intimate fellowship with your son Jesus Christ and him crucified and glorified. Let me know the power of his resurrection and the fellowship of his suffering. Let me be identified with both, that I may comprehend the significance of the Lord's body in its death and resurrection. As I participate in the Lord's table let me be among those who clearly proclaim the benefits of the Lord's death.

Lord, I desire to have a closer walk with Jesus Christ by a true and living faith. By my lips and my life I long to confess him more fully as my Lord and my God. I surrender my life to him as my prophet, priest, and king. Let me be taught, cleansed, and ruled by him. O Christ, you alone are all I need, for you are my Saviour, my Lord and my Friend. Lord, increase my faith and perfect what is lacking in it. In receiving the bread and wine at your table, enable me to receive Christ Jesus the Lord by a living and lively faith. Let the great gospel of Christ's dying to save sinners as represented in the breaking of bread and the pouring out of wine be real food and drink to my soul. Let this sacred ordinance be both nourishing and refreshing to me. Let it be my strength and my song. Let it be the source of my holiness and my comfort. Let this celebration of the Lord's supper make deep and lasting impressions on my soul that will have a powerful influence on me for the rest of my life. Let it affect me deeply so that the life I now live in the flesh I will live by faith in the Son of God who loved me and gave himself for me.

Lord, help me focus my thoughts on your sacrifice for me. Let my heart be centred on you alone that I may approach you and concentrate on you without distraction. Draw all my desires toward you. Make me hunger and thirst after righteousness, and then satisfy my hunger as I receive the Lord's body by faith. Let me draw near to you with a true heart and in full assurance of faith.

Draw me close to you, O Lord. Send out your light and your truth. Let them lead me and guide me. Pour your Spirit on me. Put your Spirit in me, and let him work in me the desire to do that which is good before you. Do not leave me to myself. Come, blessed Spirit of grace and enlighten my mind with the knowledge of Christ. Bow my will to the will of Christ. Fill my heart with the love of Christ. Give me strength of resolve to live and to die for him.

Work in me a principle of holy love toward all men. Give me the grace to forgive my enemies. Help me keep up a close fellowship in faith, hope, and love with all that in every place call on the name of Jesus Christ our Lord. Lord, bless all who are united to Christ by faith. Particularly bless this congregation of Christ with which I now join in the solemn celebration of this supper. Gracious Lord, pardon everyone that directs his heart to seek you, the God of their fathers. Hear my prayer, O Lord, and heal your people.

Lord, meet me with a father's blessing at your table. Magnify the grace of your own institution with the fullness of your presence. Fulfil in me all the good pleasure of your will. Lord Jesus, be my blessed Saviour and Redeemer. To him, with the Father and the eternal Spirit, be honour, glory and everlasting praise. Amen.

A Prayer for an Individual To Use after Receiving the Lord's Supper

O Lord my God, my Father in Jesus Christ, how can I ever express my gratitude to you for the way you have humbled yourself to show grace to me. What is man that you have had so many careful thoughts about him? Who am I that you have shown such concern for me? What is my family that you have brought me to this point of participation in your grand plan of redemption for fallen humanity? I can honestly say that a day in your glorious courts and an hour at your bountiful table is far better than a thousand days or ten thousand hours anywhere else. How good it has been for me to draw near to you. I stand amazed at the privilege you have given me to be so close to you in your own house. I revel in the refreshment that makes your people so joyful in your house of prayer.

But I blush and am ashamed that the great things you have offered me at your table have not affected me more. What a trifling heart I have! Even when I sincerely want to do my best in your presence, evil is still present with me. Lord, be merciful to me and pardon the iniquity that pollutes my most holy services. Do not let my many defects of mind and heart be held against me. Be merciful and do not let them keep me from the great profit I should receive through your holy ordinance of the Lord's Supper.

I have been remembering the death of Christ. Now let sin be put to death in me by the power of his death. Let the world be crucified to me and I to the world. Wherever I go, let me carry along with me the dying of the Lord Jesus in my body, so that the life also of Jesus may be manifested in my dying flesh.

I have now been receiving the many benefits that flow from Christ's death. Let me never forfeit those blessings. As I have received Christ Jesus the Lord by faith, give me the faith to walk in him. Help me recognize that I am not my own, that I have been bought with the price of Christ's blood. Let me glorify God with my body and my spirit, which are his.

This day I have been renewing my covenant with you. I have been committing myself afresh to be yours. Now give me grace to perform my solemn covenantal vows. Keep this bond of the covenant always in my heart, and establish my way before you. Preserve me by your grace that I may never again return to my foolish, sinful ways. After you have spoken peace through the blood of your Son, may I never undo what I have been doing on this sacred day by loose and careless living. Now that my heart has been expanded to comprehend the incomprehensible gift of your love, let me walk every moment of the day in the ways of your commandments with cheerfulness and consistency.

I commit this precious soul of mine to you. It is the work of your own hands and the purchase of your Son's blood. Sanctify it by your Spirit and grace. Let my will be brought into conformity to your will in everything. Lord, set up your throne within me and write your law on the fleshly tablets of my heart. Pour out your love in me, and bring my every thought into obedience to you. Let all my thoughts be shaped by the enlightening power of your law and the constraining power of your love. Keep what I commit to you through the power of your own name. Guard my life. I have entrusted it to you until that Day in which I will appear before your judgment throne. Preserve me as blameless until the time of your glorious coming that I may be presented before you without fault and with unimaginable joy.

I submit all my outward affairs to your wise and gracious providence. Lord, save my soul and then do all other things to me as you please. Be gracious and make all your divine appointments work together for my spiritual and eternal good.

Let everything in your creation be pure to me. Let me see your covenant love appearing in commonplace mercies. Teach me how to live in contentment both in need and in abundance. Teach me how to enjoy prosperity and to bear adversity as a Christian. Let your grace be sufficient for me and mighty in me at all times. Work in me both the desire and the will to do the good thing according to your own good purpose.

Enable me to always do my duty in everything and stand as a completed person in it. Let my heart be stretched to new dimensions of worship and service by my love to Jesus Christ. Let the height and depth, the length and breadth of the love of Christ have a profound effect on me as I come to appreciate that love which goes far beyond all human comprehension.

As an evidence of my love to you, let my mouth be filled with your praises. Worthy is the Lamb that was slain to receive blessing, honour, glory, and power. He was slain, and has redeemed your chosen remnant by his blood. He has made them into a kingdom of priests to serve him. Bless the Lord, O my soul, and let all my inmost being bless his holy name. Bless the Lord who has forgiven all my sins, healed all my diseases, redeemed my life from destruction, and crowned me with his covenant love and tender mercies. You have begun a good work in me and will carry it on until it is completed at the day of Christ. I will praise the Lord as long as I live.

When I am no longer living on this earth, I hope to be living in heaven. There I will be praising the Lord even better. Let me be carried up in your everlasting arms. Lead me from strength to strength until I appear before you in the heavenly Mount Zion, for Jesus' sake, who died for me and rose again. I desire to be found living and dying in him. Now to God the Father, Son, and Spirit be ascribed kingdom, power, and glory from now on and forever. Amen.

A prayer to God before a meal

O Lord our God, in you we live and move and have our being. From you we receive all the support and sustenance we need for life. You spread our table, fill our cup, and comfort us with the gifts of your generosity from day to day. We are totally dependent on you. Forgive our sins. Sanctify the whole of your creation that you declared to be good, and let it be useful to us. Give us grace to receive all your gifts with gratitude and thankfulness. Let us never eat and drink to ourselves but always to your glory, for the sake of Jesus Christ, our blessed Lord and Saviour. Amen.

Another

Gracious God, you are the Protector and Preserver of the whole creation. You have nourished us throughout our lives up to the present day with sufficient food, though we are evil and unthankful. Forgive all our sins, for by them we have forfeited all your mercies. Restore our right standing with you in Christ Jesus. Enable us to taste covenant love in commonplace mercies. Give us the grace to use these mercies and all the comforts of your creation to the glory of Christ our great Benefactor and Redeemer. Amen.

A prayer to God after a meal

Blessed be the Lord who daily loads us with his benefits. Praise be to the one who gives us all things richly to enjoy, though we serve him so poorly. Thank you for the refreshments you have allowed us to enjoy. Thank you for your love to our souls as seen in the gift of your Son Jesus Christ, which makes all your blessings even more enjoyable to us. Forgive our sins. Show your ongoing mercy as you keep doing good to us. Provide for the poor that are destitute of daily food. Make us able to do all your perfect will. Be our God, our guide and our portion forever, through Jesus Christ our Lord and Saviour. Amen.

ANOTHER

Father, Lord of heaven and earth, we thank you. We thank you for all the gifts of your grace and providence. We thank you for the blessings of this life and the life to come. We thank you for the privilege of enjoying the bounties of all your good creation throughout our life on this earth. Perfect all the affairs of our life. Nourish our souls with the bread of life that we may enjoy life eternal. Let us be among those that will eat bread in your consummate kingdom, for the sake of Christ Jesus our Lord and Saviour. Amen.

A Short Summary of Prayer Topics

Once a person has become familiar with the substance of scriptural prayers in this book, it may be helpful to order one's prayers by means of an outline or summary of the various topics to be remembered in prayer. The following materials provide a 'Short Summary' and then an 'Expanded Summary' following the topics covered in the book. Using these outlines may encourage the mind and heart to recall the biblical expressions related to the various topics. At the same time, these summarizing outlines may serve to develop a greater freedom in giving expression to the heart as the face of God is sought in prayer, both publicly and privately.

1: PRAISE

Approach God with a heart full of praise for the glories of his person and work.

Acknowledge God's existence to be beyond dispute.

Admit that you can never fully grasp the greatness of God.

Bring before your mind some of the glorious aspects of this great God.

Give glory to God as the Creator of all things, the Ruler and Benefactor of the world.

Give distinctive honour to each of the three Persons in the Godhead.

Gratefully acknowledge the privilege of approaching God in prayer.

2: CONFESSION

Confess your sins before a holy God, and humbly repent for them all.

Confess the many ways you have rebelled against him and violated his laws.

Acknowledge the corruption of your origins.

Grieve over your controlling inclination toward thinking and doing evil, and your inherent alienation from everything good.

Make full confession of your failure to do your duty.

Repent for your many specific transgressions in thought, word and deed.

Ask God to show you the great evil in sin.

Be aware of the things that make sin more abhorrent in the sight of God.

Earnestly pray for the full and free forgiveness of all your sins.

Base your plea for the pardon of your sin on God's self-revelation about his nature as the true and living God.

May God be fully reconciled to you so that you can receive his favour, his blessing, and his gracious acceptance.

3: PETITION
Pray earnestly for the many things you constantly need from God's gracious hand.

Plead the promises of God as the supporting foundation of all your petitions.

Ask the Lord to give you grace to resist every evil thought, word and deed.

Pray that the work of grace will be perfected in you. Pray for grace to equip you for every good thought, word and work.

Pray for the particular grace that you need in all the different areas of your life.

Pray that in all your duties God will direct you, enliven you, strengthen and assist you.

Ask the Lord to enable you to grow in grace every day.

Pray for grace to persevere to the end.

4: THANKSGIVING

Give thanks to God for the mercies he has shown you, and for the many blessings he daily brings into your life.

Praise God that you have so many reasons to thank him, and for the encouragements he has given you to offer this sacrifice of praise.

Thank God for the goodness inherent in his nature.

Thank God for the many concrete manifestations of his goodness to this fallen world.

Consider the goodness of the Lord shown to yourself in particular.

Give thanks for God's purpose and plan of redemption.

Give thanks for the manifestation of God's grace under the old covenant.

Give thanks for the accomplishment of redemption by the Son of God.

Give thanks for the establishment of the church in the world.

Thank the Lord for the personal application of the saving work of Christ in your life.

5: INTERCESSION

Intercede for others in your prayers to God.

Pray that grace will become active among people and places where it has not yet begun its work.

Pray to the Lord of the harvest for the worldwide spread of the gospel.

Pray for Christ's church and kingdom.

Pray for the nations of the world.

Offer special prayers for your own land and nation.

Offer specific prayers for the various ages and conditions of men.

6: PRAYERS FOR PARTICULAR OCCASIONS
Offer prayers for particular occasions related to both public and private life.

Pray for the regular course of the day.

Pray for your life in Christ's church.

Pray for God's blessing on all aspects of life in the community.

Intercede for people with bodily weaknesses.

Offer special prayers for people with spiritual problems.

Pray for people facing special challenges.

An Expanded Summary of Prayer Topics

1: PRAISE

Approach God with a heart full of praise for the glories of his person and work.

Acknowledge God's existence to be beyond dispute.

Admit that you can never fully grasp the greatness of God.

Bring before your mind some of the glorious aspects of this great God.

1. He is an eternal God who has no beginning of days, end of life, or change caused by the passing of time.

2. He is present in all places and at all times with all his glory.

3. He knows all persons and things perfectly, and sees clearly their most hidden secrets.

4. His wisdom is unsearchable, and its ultimate purposes past human comprehension.

5. His sovereignty is incontestable, for he is the absolute Lord of all.

6. His power is irresistible, and his exercise of it cannot be limited by anyone in heaven or on earth.

7. He is a God of unspotted holiness and perfect uprightness.

8. He is just in the administration of his government, for he has never done wrong to any of his creatures, and never will.

9. His truth is unchangeable, and the treasures of his goodness inexhaustible.

10. Praise God for what you have heard about the glory he manifests in heaven above.

11. After having said everything you can about the glorious perfections of the Lord, admit that you fall infinitely short of adequately proclaiming his greatness.

Give glory to God as the Creator of all things, the Ruler and Benefactor of the world.

Give distinctive honour to each of the three Persons in the Godhead.

Gratefully acknowledge the privilege of approaching God in prayer.

1. Affirm this God to be your God, and acknowledge his ownership of you and his dominion over you.

2. Accept with deepest gratitude the enormous privilege you have of being not only allowed but even encouraged to draw near to God in prayer.

3. Express your own unworthiness to approach God and speak to him.

4. Make known to God the longing of your heart toward him, for he alone is the source of true happiness. Recognize him to be the only thing worth possessing in this life, and the fountain of every other blessing.

5. Make clear profession of your believing hope and confidence in God, and in his all-sufficiency, his power, providence, and promise.

6. Ask the Lord to accept you despite the pitifulness of your prayers.

7. Openly profess your entire reliance on the Lord Jesus Christ alone for acceptance with God, and come in his name.

8. Plead with the Lord for the powerful assistance of his Spirit in your prayers.

9. Make the glory of God your highest goal in all your prayers.

2: CONFESSION

Confess your sins before a holy God, and
humbly repent for them all.

Confess the many ways you have rebelled against
him and violated his laws.

Acknowledge the corruption of your origins.

Grieve over your controlling inclination toward
thinking and doing evil, and your inherent alienation
from everything good.

1. Note the blindness of your mind toward the things
   of God, and its inability to receive rays of divine
   enlightenment.

2. Lament the stubbornness of your will, and its
   constant resistance to every suggestion that it
   should live in submission to God's law.

3. Ask God's forgiveness for your absorption with
   things that deserve little or no consideration, and
   your failure to concentrate on subjects that nourish
   the soul.

4. Be ashamed for the lust of your flesh, and the
   disorder of your desires.

5. Express your deepest heartfelt sorrow over the
   corruption of your whole person, which has
   fostered inordinate passions while alienating
   your mind from the life of the Spirit.

Make full confession of your failure to do your duty.

Repent for your many specific transgressions in thought, word and deed.

1. Humble yourself by confessing the pride of your life.
2. Be ashamed for the times you have broken out in passion and rash anger.
3. Repent for your covetousness and love of the world.
4. Repudiate your sensuality and flesh-pleasing.
5. Renounce your self-security and disregard for the changes that inevitably come in the course of this life.
6. Express genuine sorrow for your fretfulness and impatience, your murmuring under affliction, your inordinate dejection, and your distrust of God and his providence.
7. Repent for the lack of love you have displayed toward your brothers and sisters. Confess with sorrow the times you have not lived in peace with your relatives, neighbours and friends. Seek God's pardon for the times you have treated them unjustly.
8. Confess that your tongue leads you into sin.
9. Confess your slothfulness and spiritual decay.

Ask God to show you the great evil in sin.

1. Consider the sinfulness of sin.
2. Recognize the foolishness of sin.

3. Admit the unprofitableness of sin.

4. Beware of the deceitfulness of sin.

5. Recognize the offence sin has committed against a Holy God.

6. Become fully aware of the damage sin has done to your own soul.

Be aware of the things that make sin more abhorrent in the sight of God.

1. The clearer your understanding of what is good and what is evil in God's eyes, the greater your sin.

2. The greater profession you have made of devotion to Christ, the greater your sin.

3. The more mercies you have received from God, the greater your sin.

4. The fuller the warning you have received from the Word of God as well as from your own conscience about the danger of sin, the greater the sin when you have gone on in it.

5. The greater the chastenings you have received for your sin, the greater the sin if you go on in it.

6. The more vows and promises you have made of better obedience, the greater your sin.

7. The more aware you are that you are violating God's law, the more liable you are to his just punishments.

Earnestly pray for the full and free forgiveness of all your sins.

1. Give God the glory for his patience and long-suffering toward you, and his willingness to be reconciled to you.

2. Claim for yourself the great encouragement God has given sinners to humble themselves before him, and confess your sins with sorrow and shame.

3. Humbly express your sorrow and sense of shame for your sin. Seek an abundant supply of God's grace, so that you can live a life more honouring to him from this day forward.

Base your plea for the pardon of your sin on God's self-revelation about his nature as the true and living God.

1. Remind yourself of the Lord's infinite goodness, his readiness to forgive, and his delight in displaying his mercy.

2. Be greatly encouraged as you consider the merit and righteousness of the Lord Jesus Christ. Rely completely on the virtues of his life and death as the basis of your right-standing before God despite your sinfulness.

3. Plead before the Lord the promises he himself has made to pardon all those who truly repent and believe his gospel.

4. Rejoice in the blessedness of those whose sins are forgiven.

May God be fully reconciled to you so that you can receive his favour, his blessing, and his gracious acceptance.

1. May God be at peace with you, so that his anger is totally turned away from you.

2. May you be sealed in covenant with God, so that you will have a permanently binding relationship to him.

3. May you continue to have God's favour as the object of his special love.

4. May you always have God's blessing on your life.

5. May the presence of God always be with you.

6. May you have a comforting sense of your reconciliation to God, and your acceptance by him.

    i. May he graciously allow you to have some clear evidence that all your sins are pardoned and you have been adopted as his son.

    ii. May God bless you with a well-grounded peace of conscience. May he give you a peace of mind arising from your justification, and a sense of the good work he has done in you.

3: PETITION

Pray earnestly for the many things you constantly need from God's gracious hand.

Plead the promises of God as the supporting foundation of all your petitions.

Ask the Lord to give you grace to resist every evil thought, word and deed.

Pray that the work of grace will be perfected in you. Pray for grace to equip you for every good thought, word and work.

Pray for the particular grace that you need in all the different areas of your life.

1. Let your grace make us intelligent in the things of God.

2. Let your grace lead us into all truth.

3. Help our memories so your truth will be immediately accessible to us.

4. Educate our consciences, show us our duty, and make us wise and judicious Christians.

5. Sanctify our nature, and implant in our inmost being all the principles and graces necessary for living a God-glorifying life.
    i. Pray for faith.
    ii. Pray for the fear of God.

iii. Pray that love for God may be rooted in you and love for the world rooted out of you.

iv. Pray that your conscience may be always tender, and that you may live a life of repentance.

v. Pray that God will work compassion and brotherly love in you.

vi. Pray for the grace of self-denial.

vii. Pray for humility and meekness.

viii. Pray for the graces of contentment, patience, and a selfless indifference to all the things of sense and time.

ix. Pray for the grace of a hope focused on God and Christ that anticipates eternal life.

x. Pray for grace to preserve you from sin, and from all approaches you may be tempted to make toward it.

xi. Pray for grace that will enable you to govern your tongue, and to use it well.

Pray that in all your duties God will direct you, enliven you, strengthen and assist you.

1. May God make you wise so you can fulfil all your duties.

2. May you be honest and straightforward in your duty.

3. May you be diligent in your duty.

4. May you be courageous in your duty, knowing that though you may be temporarily losers for Christ, you will not be losers by him in the end.

5. May you be pleasant and cheerful in your duty.

6. May you fulfil every duty required by every situation of life, every event of providence, and every relation in which you stand.

7. May you be made altogether complete in your duty.

Ask the Lord to enable you to grow in grace every day.

1. May the Lord give abundant grace when you undergo the crosses and afflictions of this world.

2. May God preserve you from the calamities that always threaten your life and your well-being.

3. May the Lord supply you with the provisions, supports and comforts you need each day, as you receive them with a humble spirit of submission to God.

Pray for grace to persevere to the end.

1. May the Lord prepare you for whatever lies before you between this day and the grave.

2. May God preserve you in the hour of your death and sustain you through your dying moments.

3. May the Lord prepare you for heaven so that in due time you may be a full possessor of eternal life.

4: THANKSGIVING

*Give thanks to God for the mercies he has shown you, and
for the many blessings he daily brings into your life.*

Praise God that you have so many reasons to thank
him, and for the encouragements he has given you
to offer this sacrifice of praise.

Thank God for the goodness inherent in his nature.

Thank God for the many concrete manifestations
of his goodness to this fallen world.

Give thanks for God's purpose and plan of redemption. Praise him for the goodness of his redemptive
grace.

1. Give thanks for God's grand design for man's
   redemption when he was seen as lost and
   devastated by sin.

2. Stand in awe when you consider the eternal
   purposes and plans of God concerning the
   redemption of his people.

3. Give glory to God for the appointing of a
   perfect Redeemer for his chosen people.

Give thanks for the manifestation of God's grace
under the old covenant.

1. Thank the Lord for the ancient indications of his
   gracious design toward a fallen humanity.

2. Give thanks for the many glorious instances of
   God's favour to the church under the old covenant.

Give thanks for the accomplishment of redemption by the Son of God.

1. Give thanks for the Father's commitment with the Son to redeem lost sinners.

2. Never cease to wonder at the mysterious and miraculous incarnation of the Son of God.

3. May God's name be magnified for the holy life Jesus lived, for his illuminating teaching, and the glorious miracles he worked to confirm the truths he taught.

4. Rejoice at the great encouragement Jesus gave to poor sinners to come to him while he was on earth.

5. Express your deepest awe at the full satisfaction he made to the justice of God for man's sin by the blood of his cross. Rejoice at the triumphs of the cross and all the benefits that flow to you by the dying of the Lord Jesus.

6. Honour Christ for his resurrection from the dead on the third day.

7. Worship him for his ascension into heaven, where he continues to sit as sovereign at God's right hand.

8. Express your everlasting gratitude to God for the intercession which Christ continually makes on your behalf by virtue of the satisfaction made by his sacrifice for your sins.

9. Give glory to Christ our Redeemer for his exalted position at God's right hand where he rules over heaven and earth.

10. Thank the Lord for the hope he has given you that he will return in glory to judge the world.

11. Give special thanks for God's grace in sending the Holy Spirit to sustain you beyond the days of Christ's bodily presence on earth.

Give thanks for the establishment of the church in the world.

1. All glory to God for the covenant of grace made with us in Jesus Christ.

2. Thank the Lord for recording his eternal Word in the written form of Scripture, and for preserving his Word in its purity and entirety up to the present day.

3. Accept with gratitude the directions God has set down for the well-being of his church.

4. Give glory to God for establishing Christianity throughout the world, and for planting a church true to the gospel despite all the opposition of the powers of darkness.

5. Give God the glory for preserving Christianity in this fallen world up to the present day.

6. Express your personal appreciation to God for the good examples set by those who have gone to heaven before you.

7. Thank God for the communion of the saints which we enjoy because of our common faith, hope and love.

Thank the Lord for the personal application of the saving work of Christ in your life.

1. Praise God that he has not abandoned you in your sin, and has provided your conscience as a constant restraint.

2. Praise God for the saving change worked in you by the Holy Spirit.

3. Express your unending gratitude for the forgiveness of your sins and the peace of your conscience.

4. Give God the glory for the powerful influence of divine grace in sanctifying and preserving you, in preventing you from falling into sin, and in strengthening you to do your duty.

5. Refresh yourself through your close fellowship with God and your sense of his favourable attitude toward you.

6. Thank the Lord for his gracious answers to your prayers.

Consider the goodness of the Lord shown to you through all the varying seasons of your life.

1. Give thanks that he has made you capable of knowing, loving, serving and enjoying him; for he has not made you like the beasts that perish forever.

2. Give thanks that he preserves you day after day and year after year.

3. Gratefully remember the divine interventions that have delivered you from sickness and many other threats to your well-being.

4. Thank God for the supports and comforts that have made your pilgrimage through life easier and more pleasant.

5. Offer thanks to God for success in your callings, encouragement in your relations, and convenience in your places of residence.

6. Honour your sovereign Lord for the share he has given you of the public plenty and peace.

7. Thank the Lord for the support he gives you when you are under affliction. Praise him for the benefit you receive even from your trials.

8. Give honour to God for the fulfilment of all his promises to you.

9. Be inspired to look eagerly toward the prospect of eternal life, when time shall be no more.

5: INTERCESSION

Intercede for others in your prayers to God.

Pray that grace will become active among people and places where it has not yet begun its work.

Pray to the Lord of the harvest for the worldwide spread of the gospel.

1. Intercede for the whole world of mankind in its lostness from God.

2. Earnestly pray for the spread of the saving gospel of Christ among all nations and the expansion of his church by the constant conversion of many.

3. Make a special plea for God's ancient covenant people the Jews, that they may see Jesus as their promised Messiah.

4. Intercede for the ancient churches of Asia and Africa, as well as the Reformation churches of Europe, that have suffered large setbacks.

5. Pray for the spread of the gospel to every corner of this vast world. Plead for God's mercy to extend to each and every continent, including North America, South America, Australia, and Antarctica.

6. Pray for the conviction and conversion of atheists, hardened sinners, profane scoffers, and those that disgrace Christ by their immoral lives even while professing faith.

Pray for Christ's church and kingdom.

1. Pray to the Lord for the well-being of his church throughout the world in all aspects of its life.

2. Ask the Lord to pour out his Spirit on the church in a fresh and powerful way. Entreat him to unleash the power of true godliness. Plead for the revival of apostolic Christianity, and the correcting of everything that has gone wrong in the church.

3. Plead with the Lord to break the power of all the enemies of his righteous kingdom, and defeat all their Satan-inspired schemes.

4. Ask the Lord to send relief to churches suffering under oppression. Entreat him to provide support, comfort, and deliverance for everyone who is being persecuted for righteousness' sake.

5. Pray with great earnestness for the healing of the unhappy divisions within the church.

6. Pray for all the ministers of God's Word and sacraments.

Pray for the nations of the world.

Offer special prayers for your own land and nation.

1. Thank God for his mercies to your land.

2. Humble yourself before God for national sins that could easily provoke his wrath.

3. Pray earnestly for God's mercy toward your nation.

   i. Humbly ask God for the manifestation of his favour toward your nation, since every blessing depends on his grace.

   ii. Pray that the gospel will always continue among your nation, and the means of grace remain available to all your people. Ask the Lord to allow a door to remain open in your nation for the spread of the saving gospel of Christ.

iii. Pray for the outward peace and tranquility of your nation, and the continuation of its liberty. Ask for God's abundant blessing on the fruitfulness of your land.

iv. Offer your petitions for God's blessing on all efforts to reform your nation's lifestyle and to suppress all its vices.

v. Pray for the protection of your people as they enter the conflict against evil and untruth as it manifests itself within your own nation, among your national neighbours, and throughout distant countries.

vi. Pray for all those who work as public servants throughout your land.

vii. Pray specifically for magistrates, judges, and supreme court justices of the land.

Offer specific prayers for the various ages and conditions of men.

1. Remember the special needs of those that are young and just now setting out in the world.

2. Pray for those that are old, in view of their special testings.

3. Do not neglect to pray for the rich and prosperous in this world, for they need prayer as much as anyone else. In fact, considering how hard it is for the rich to enter the kingdom of God, they may need our prayers more than other people.

4. Never fail to pray for the poor and those who are afflicted with many needs in this world. For they are always present among us, and we must not miss any opportunity to minister to them in Christ's name.

5. Pray for your enemies and those that hate you.

6. Never forget to pray for your friends and those that love you.

6: PRAYERS FOR PARTICULAR OCCASIONS

Offer prayers for particular occasions related to both public and private life.

Pray for the regular course of the day.

1. Begin your morning with prayers to God your Saviour.

2. Conclude your day with prayers to God your Preserver.

3. Before a meal, ask God's blessing.

4. After you have eaten, give thanks to God.

5. Before departing on a journey, pray for God's protection.

6. When you return safely from a journey, give thanks to the Lord.

Pray for your life in Christ's church.

1. On the evening before the Lord's Day, prepare yourself through prayer.

2. On the morning of the Lord's day, consecrate yourself to God.

3. As you begin your public worship on the Lord's day, remember that you are being led by the one God, the Great Shepherd of the sheep who presides over all the masters of Christian assemblies.

4. At the baptism of adults, rejoice with the angels in heaven.

5. At the baptism of children, claim God's covenant promises.

6. Before celebrating the Lord's Supper, prepare yourself for the special manifestation of God's grace.

7. During the celebration of the Lord's Supper, make the most of this moment of special grace.

8 After celebrating the Lord's Supper, renew your vows to God.

9. At a service of ordination to the gospel ministry, offer special prayers for the pure proclamation of the Word.

Pray for God's blessing on all aspects of life in the community.

1. On the occasion of a marriage, ask the Lord Jesus to be personally present.

2. On the occasion of a funeral, ask the Lord to enable you to reflect soberly about your life.

3. When rain is lacking, come before the Lord with special confessions and petitions.

4. When there is too much rain, ask the Lord to be gracious.

5. When a plague of infectious disease strikes your land, cry out for the Lord's mercy.

6 In the event of large calamities, earnestly seek the Lord's face.

Intercede for people with bodily weaknesses.

1. Pray for the sick.
   When an illness continues for a long time.
   If recovery seems fairly certain.
   If they appear to be at the point of death.

2. Pray for sick children.

3. Pray for women that are about to give birth.

4. When people have recovered from sickness or have been safely delivered at the time of giving birth, give thanks to the Lord along with them.

Offer special prayers for people with spiritual problems.

1. Pray for those who are under the conviction of sin and are seeking Christ.

2. Pray for those that live with doubts and fears about their spiritual state, and tend to be melancholy in mind.

3. Pray with parents whose children are a great concern to them or have become a grief to them.

4. Pray for those who have lost their senses or their memory.

Pray for people facing special challenges.

1. Pray for people in prison.

2. Pray for criminals condemned to death who have only a little longer to live.

3. Pray for those that sail the seas or fly the skies.

4. Pray for people who have had a death in the family, especially when the head of the family has been lost.

7: CONCLUDING OUR PRAYERS

Conclude your time of prayer by asking that all your prayers will give glory to God the Father, the Son, and the Holy Spirit.

1. Sum up your requests in a few comprehensive petitions.

2. Humbly beg the Lord to accept your poor weak prayers for Christ's sake.

3. Ask forgiveness for anything that has been wrong with your prayers.

4. Commit yourself to divine grace in all other services that lie before you today, and throughout the rest of your life.

5. Conclude all your prayers with doxologies that ascribe honour and glory to the Father, the Son and the Holy Spirit. Then seal up all your praises and prayers with a heartfelt 'AMEN!'

6. Finalize your prayers by using the form Christ taught his disciples.

Subject Index

❧